News Clippings from Caliente, Elgin, Hiko, Alamo, Pahranagat Valley, Delamar & Lund,Nevada

1866 - 1924

Compiled from the Las Vegas Age (Nevada), Davis County Clipper (Utah), Deseret News (Utah), Eastern Utah Advocate, Emery County Progress (Utah), Ephraim Enterprise (Utah), Eureka Reporter (Utah), Gunnison Gazette (Utah), InterMountain Catholic (Utah), Intermountain Republican (Utah), Iron County Record (Utah), Lehi Banner (Utah), Manti Messenger (Utah), Richfield Reaper (Utah), Salt Lake Democrat (Utah), Salt Lake Herald (Utah), Salt Lake Mining Review (Utah), Salt Lake Telegraph (Utah), Washington County News (Utah),   & with contributions from other regional papers.

Often while working on family history (genealogy) I wonder about more than is listed on the pedigree sheets and am so grateful for their sacrifices and love for the generations to follow.

Some of the names include: Adair, Ashworth, Bailey, Bain, Banovich, Bartlett, Barton, Baudreau, Blanchard, Blunt, Boyd, Burns, Colton, Conoway, Corden, Culverwell, Dale, Delamore, Denton, Dranga, Duffin, Dugan, Durango, Erickson, Ernest, Fawcett, Fetterman, Fieldson, Foster, Geer, Graham, Hamilton, Hanson, Hemstreet, Ivins, Johnson, Keith, King, Kinney, Lee, Lillis, Liston, Locke, Lowell, Loy, Manners, McCracken, McGaughey, McIntosh, McManus, McNamee, Miller, Milsap, Mitchell, Morris, Murray, Nelson, Norris, Olson, Oxborrow, Pace, Patterson, Preston, Rives, Schmidt, Sibert, Shier, Shirley, Slattery, Smith, Stewart, Sturgis, Sweeney, Taylor, Tennish, Tobin,Trimbell, Underhill, VanHousen, Vaught, Wadsworth, Wakening, Walker, Wilson, Wood

Some of the articles are easier to read than others, please consider that they are nearly 100 years old.

Copyright 2014

ISBN-13: 978-1505528121

ISBN-10: 1505528127

PAHRANAGAT VALLEY. — We have been shown a letter written from Pahranagat Valley, December 22d, to a resident of this city, from which we have been permitted to make extracts. The writer says: "It has been storming ever since I went to the mines, and I have not had a very good chance to prospect. I visited some of the prominent claims, and I must say that I found them much finer than I expected. From what I have seen of the country, I consider it one of the best I have seen for prospecting. It is the very country that the Austin people have tried so long to find. The valley is the finest I have seen on the east side of the Sierra Nevadas, and it is about 110 miles from the Colorado river. I have located 2,700 feet on the best coal bed you ever saw, which must prove very valuable. Timber is not very large or abundant near the mines, but I understand there is large timber some twenty or thirty miles from the mines — Water is also scarce, but is plentiful in the mines only ten miles distant. Tea, sugar and coffee are very high, and we have no tools to work with. I am in the right place at last."—*Reese River Reveille.*

Deseret News (Utah)
February 16, 1870

EAGLEVILLE, Iron Co., Jan., 25, 1870.

Editor Deseret News:—Dear Sir.—On the 28th of August last, Mr. N. H. Carlow came into our settlement as Assessor of Lincoln county, Nevada. He required a list of our taxable property for assessment in that county. He stated, as a reason for his demand, that a United States commission for establishing the boundary line between Utah and Nevada would be through here in a few days, and that reports had reached him that there was but little doubt of our being in Nevada. Furthermore, 'that the time allowed by the law of Nevada, for the assessment of taxes had nearly expired, and perhaps it might save him considerable trouble and expense to make the assessment then.

Said Carlow, did not claim that the assessment was legal, unless the adjustment of the boundary line should establish the fact that we were citizens of Nevada,

The citizens of Eagle and Spring Valley did not see the necessity of this premature assessment in the light Mr. Carlow did. They placed in his hands a written protest against his proceedings, of which a copy was retained. This protest stated in substance that we were still citizens of Utah Territory;

and should continue to consider ourselves as such, until the boundary line between Utah and Nevada was established by proper authority, when, if we were set off to Nevada, as law abiding citizens, we should pay our taxes to that State, and, further, that at present we did not recognize the right of the State of Nevada or any portion of it to assume jurisdiction over us. This protest Mr. Carlow agreed to file, with his returns, to the proper authorities of Lincoln county.

Some time previous to the appearance of Mr. Carlow, we had been assessed, as usual, by the assessor of Iron county, with the expectation, on his part of taking no farther action in the matter until the boundary line was established.

The supposed commission for defining the boundary line between Utah and Nevada, proved to be Lt. Wheeler's exploring party, and we supposed the subject would be allowed to rest until we were properly notified as to our future condition.

In October following, notices requiring the payment of taxes, dated Hiko, Oct. 18th, 1869, and signed, Peter.Goodfellow, county treasurer, and addressed to the tax payers of Lincoln county, were sent to our settlements to be posted.

On the 20th inst., a Mr. Ritter, claiming to be sheriff of Lincoln Co, appeared in our settlements, and served writs on the tax payers of Eagle and Spring valleys wherein they are required to appear, in the Justice's court, township of Hiko, Lincoln Co., on the 28th of Feb. 1870, to answer complaint of the State of Nevada, wherein it sues for the recovery of delinquent taxes for 1869, with ten per cent interest thereon for delinquency. Mr. Ritter acknowledged that he failed to comprehend the legality of this proceeding, but stated that he was only carrying out the instructions of those under whose orders he was required to act.

He was fully advised that it would not be wisdom to attempt to enforce the collection of such taxes, until we became citizens of Nevada, when there would be no necessity of doing so, as we were a law abiding people.

This is a short and simple statement of the facts in these novel proceedings. They speak for themselves.

Respectfully,
Your brother in the Gospel.
JAMES A. LITTLE.

Salt Lake Herald (Utah)
June 6, 1873

Meagre details of a late cutting affray in Pahranagat valley have been received here. It appears two men named Ferguson and Bennett had a dispute about water rights, when Ferguson attacked Bennett with a knife, severely, if not fatally wounding him.

BULLIONVILLE, Nev.,
December 16th.

An Indian boy, about sixteen years of age, accompanied by some twenty-five other Indians, came to Bishop Barron, of Panacca, yesterday, and volunteered a statement of the murder of two citizens and the severe wounding of a third, some eight or ten days ago, near Hiko, Lincoln Co. The Indian boy was an eye-witness to the whole affair. He will be taken to Pioche to-morrow, together with the interpreter and captain of the tribe, by Bishop Barron, to make his statement before the proper authorities. The Indians who committed the murders have scattered, some have gone towards Belmont, others took the mountains. Other more atrocious murders have been committed since. A French family—man, wife and three children—and another man, it is positively asserted, have been murdered; they left Panamint four days ago, and it is said they have all been murdered. We have no witness to the deed as yet.

The Utah girls are not so green as many put them up to be, as one of them, who was visiting in Pahranagat Valley, last week, taught the girls in that locality a new method in the production of rosy cheeks without the aid of vermillion paint. After each dance the Utah damsel would rush into the toilet-room, scratch her cheeks with her finger-nails, then re-enter the dance-room with a pair of as rosy cheeks as ever graced beautiful maiden.

Salt Lake Herald (Utah)
May 25, 1887

DEATH ON THE DESERT.

Another Unfortunate Perishes on the Sandy Waste.

Another unfortunate, unaccustomed to the perils of the desert, has perished on the sandy waste. Recently a party of four men, one old lady and daughter and child, left Muddy Valley for Coyote Springs, a distance of thirty-five miles from the Muddy, and on the road to Pahranagat Valley. An exchange has the following account of the tragedy: Mistaking the road, they took a wood road, missed the spring, and were for two days out in a burning sun without water. Confused and bewildered they wandered, until Arnhold came back within two miles of the Muddy River, and then turned around and went back a few miles and, evidently exhausted, lay down and died. In the meantime another of the party reached the Muddy and obtained aid. William Sprouse went out and found that another of the men had reached Coyote Springs and was packing water eight miles to his companions. As the old lady of the party was missing Sprouse went in search of her and, with difficulty, found her quite a distance away, just as he was about to abandon the search for her. After having supplied the party with water enough to save their lives, Sprouse assisted them to move their teams up to Coyote Springs and returned to the Muddy, reporting that all would recover. On Sunday, May 21st, the only victim, Dr. Arnold, was buried by James Harris and William Sproule. He had with him a complete dental outfit, a silver watch and $13 in money. The party was traveling from Arizona to California and as soon as they recover, they will move on. At present they are camped at Coyote Springs. It is only by the merest accident that the entire party did not perish, as the man who found the spring was lame and it was with the greatest difficulty that he managed to pack water enough to sustain life until aid reached them.

LOST ON THE DESERT.

Vincenzo Scappatura Found After Five Days' Starvation.

"Lost on the Desert," as the announcement of the fate of an individual brings with it a nameless sensation of dread. In this western region many have lost their way and perished, and their bleaching bones have been subsequently discovered by the hardy explorer. In one place in Nevada, on the Desert—which takes up a considerable portion of Western Utah and Nevada—the numbers that have met with such a fate are so great that the place is called Death Valley. A few travelers have been rescued in time to give to the world an idea of the terrible sufferings that have to be endured under the scorching sun and amid the burning sands, where no draught of water, nor cool breeze, nor even passing cloud comes to relieve the awful agony that must be borne. To this dreadful end it was feared that Vincenzo Scappatura, of this city, had been consigned. He has been engaged with the Utah Central surveying party in going over the proposed route to Southern California. He is of a peculiar disposition, and given to spells of despondency. He was with the party under the direction of Joseph A. West, and appeared to get an idea that the other members of the party were not desirous of his association. Mr. West endeavored to disabuse his mind, but failed in doing so. Accordingly, on the 25th of July last, Mr. West sent Mr. Scappatura home in company with two men who were in the employ of Allen G. Campbell, and who were heading for Milford.

The two men arrived there last Saturday, but Scappatura was not with them. Superintendent John Sharp did not learn of this fact until yesterday; when he sent a telegram to one of the men, asking that particulars be forwarded to him immediately. As a result he received the following:

"*Superintendent Sharp:*—Mr. Scappatura left Yunt's Ranche, in Southern Nye County, Nev., with George Ross and myself on July 25th, for Milford. Immediately after breakfast at Quartz Springs, on the fourth day out, Scappatura shouldered his canteen of water and started out for Summit Springs, twenty-five miles distant, where we expected to camp that night. After driving an hour or two we saw him two or three miles ahead, but on arriving at the springs, about 5 o'clock in the evening, we found he had not been there. I went back to the road that crosses the Summit Springs road for Groom, and satisfied myself he had not gone that way. On returning to camp, we found the teams would not drink Summit Springs water, and having dipped Quartz Springs dry that morning, were compelled to come on to Crystal Springs for water, and at once informed one of Mr. Snow's surveying party and Mr. Gear of the missing man; also the men in charge of Eisman's ranch, who promised to look after the missing man at once. Owing to delayed mail matter, which had caused me to be late in reaching Milford, I felt myself bound to come on."

It was understood that Messrs. Snow and Gear would use every endeavor to find the missing man, and the ranchmen would probably do the same. However, there was considerable anxiety as to his fate. He had been over the country several times, and there was a road well enough beaten to be easily followed, and leading to where relief could be obtained. But he was of an excitable nature, and it was feared that the excessive heat might dethrone his reason, and that he would wander about and perish. Superintendent Sharp, therefore, sent a dispatch to Pioche, and this afternoon received tidings that Scappatura had been found. The answer reads:

PIOCHE, Nev., Aug. 11, 1888.

John. Sharp:

News from Hiko is that Scappatura had started ahead of the team in the morning. He rested under a tree while the wagon passed unobserved. He went back to Quartz Spring, and stayed in the vicinity five days. He was found digging a rabbit out of a hole on the side hill. He was taken to Hiko, and is there now, a little flighty, it is supposed either from a touch of sunstroke or five days' starvation.

S. T. GODBE.

Hiko is a mail station, about 115 miles from Milford, 50 from Pioche, and nine miles from Crystal Springs, where Mr. Standley and Mr. Rose camped the night after their comrade was lost. There is but a weekly mail from the place, and while Mr. Scappatura's friends will be greatly relieved by the news that he is among friends, they are still somewhat concerned regarding his condition.

Salt Lake Herald (Utah)
April 30, 1895

DE LAMAR MILL CLOSES

This Was the Report Received Here Yesterday.

LACK OF WATER THE CAUSE

CAPTAIN DE LAMAR WILL ADOPT SOME SPEEDY REMEDY.

He Never Allows Grass to Grow Under His Feet—May Pump From Meadow Valley Wash—Extensive Operations in the Marysvale County—Sevier Mill is in Operation and Two More Plants Will Be Started Within the Next Few Days—General Mining News.

From DeLamar, Nevada, right in the heart of the famous Ferguson gold district, word was yesterday received to the effect that all operations at the new mill put in by Captain John R. DeLamar for the purpose of treating the gold ores taken from his properties, have been discontinued and it is not known just when they will be resumed. It is now, as ever, the question of water supply and the indications are that the captain will, within a comparatively short time, order his men to make some extensive changes in order to secure the requisite amount of water for the use of the mill and mines in their successful operation. There is some talk even now of the company going as far as the Meadow Valley wash and there establishing a pumping station for the purpose of forcing the water back to the properties. Just what will be the course pursued in this matter is, of course, a matter of secrecy. But of one thing the people may rest assured, that the captain will not, for long allow his properties to remain idle, but will, if necessary, go to practically unlimited expense before he gives up the water question.

The mill of the DeLamar company had been in operation about a month and a half and the capacity was being constantly enlarged. Its work is perfect and during the time of operation shipments of gold bullion aggregating over $50,000 were made, the last coming up about ten days ago. There is another consignment due. For some time past there has been a gradual decrease in the flow of the springs, from which the mills and mines of the company secured the water necessary in their operations, until now, it is stated, the flow is far less than the needs of the company demand. There is a spring in close proximity to the properties, which is owned by Nesbitt Bros., but the latter have their ideas up and say they will not sell for less than $50,000. This proposition has been rejected by Captain DeLamar, who is considering several other offers. He never allows the grass to grow under his feet, but, on the contrary, saws mightily at the wood. He has too much at stake to allow the water proposition to long delay him in the carrying out of his plans for the future.

Salt Lake Herald (Utah)
October 12, 1895

Another De Lamar Shipment.

The remaining tanks and tank valves for the enlargement of the DeLamar mill at DeLamar, Nevada, have been shipped south, the whole lot making a ful lcarload. It is anticipated that within the next ten days the new mill and the water system will be in operation.

Salt Lake Herald (Utah)
July 5, 1896

Delamar, Lincoln County, Nevada, June 23, 1896.

Mr. Charles S. Burton:

Dear Sir—I write to ask a favor of you. The young people of Delamar, Nevada, a new mining camp, are desirous of forming an amateur dramatic company, and have asked me to select a play for them, and, being short of scenery, I have selected one that requires but one parlor scene through the entire piece, viz., "A Bird in the Hand Is Worth two in the Bush." If you could accommodate me with a copy from the theatre library, or could obtain one for me in the city, I should esteem it a great favor; if I knew the address of any book dealer that kept plays in stock I would not put you to the trouble. But knowing the old theatre library was very complete in the early '70's when I was a member of the old stock company, I have taken the liberty to write to you. I enclose 25 cents in postage stamps for same.

With kind regards, and best wishes for the success of the old temple of the drama, I remain, yours truly,
ALFRED THORNE.

* * *

Salt Lake Herald (Utah)
July 8, 1896

Frank Wilson, of the April Fool mine, at DeLamar, Nevada, who came in a few days ago with a bar of bullion from the mine, left for home yesterday. Mr. Wilson informs The Herald that his new mill is giving excellent satisfaction, and that now, instead of shipping ore to this market, he is sending in the "pure stuff," which is a great saving in expenses. He is now treating about twenty tons of ore daily and the mine is looking well. He will make another shipment of gold bars next month.

Deseret Evening News (Utah)
August 24, 1896

The Wolf Brothers Wednesday even-

ng brought in from their Alamo lease some truck that will go 20 per cent copper.

Salt Lake Herald (Utah)
September 11, 1896

A contract has been let on the Jumbo mine for a large amount of work.—Lode, DeLamar, Nevada.

On Tuesday last at the DeLamar mill 365 tons of ore were crushed in twenty-four hours. This is the highest run that has been made since the mill started.—Lode, DeLamar, Nevada.

Salt Lake Herald (Utah)
January 6, 1897

Another gentleman with a long head on his shoulders ventures the prediction that John Hays Cook will soon follow in the footsteps of Professor Butters and that together they will journey to the great DeLamar gold mine at DeLamar, Nevada, and that the result of their trip will be the purchase of this property and the Golden Gate, and that the same syndicate will control and operate these two properties.

Deseret Evening News (Utah)
November 27, 1897

Miss Hattie Hellifalch of Brooklyn, N. Y., arrived in Caliente, Cal., a day or two ago to marry Frank Potts, a gold-mining contractor of Havilah. Miss Hellifalch never saw Mr. Potts until the day of her arrival and all their courtship was carried on by correspondence. Miss Hellifalch is a beautiful young woman of 24 years, rather brunette. She claims she took the adventurous journey all the way across the continent to better her condition in life. Even though she had never seen her lover she was confident she would be happy with him when married, and it promises to be so.

Salt Lake Mining Review (Utah)
June 15, 1899

J. P. Sterling, of Kansas City, representing the Prinz & Rau Manufacturing company, of Milwaukee, Wis., who was in Utah a short time ago in the interest of his people, took a flying trip to DeLamar, Nevada, before returning home, the result of his visit there being that Captain J. R. DeLamar has ordered the installation at his DeLamar mill one of the Prinz & Rau perfection dust collectors. These collectors have been used to excellent advantage in other localities. They are great value savers besides which they add to the general health of employees and make operations more pleasant. Mr. Sterling will doubtless return to Salt Lake at an early day with the intention of establishing a branch office for the company in Utah.

DeLamar, Nevada, has not been left out of the cold of late in the way of big mining deals. Not long ago the April Fool, the second largest producer in this great gold

camp, was sold on an option to Hon. W. A. Clark of Butte; a deal was made involving the Magnolia mine, the first gold discovery made in Ferguson district, and now it is learned that Hon. A. W. McCune, of this city, has secured a bond on the control of Mono and April Fool No. 2 group, a property of undeniable merit. The extension of the Utah & Pacific towards the camp of DeLamar is having a beneficial effect upon this locality, and while this has always been a heavy producer of the Wall street metal, the probabilities are that in the future it will discount all previous records. both as to ore production and heavy mining transactions.

Salt Lake Mining Review (Utah)
July 31, 1899

THE APRIL FOOL DEAL.

The deal involving the sale of the April Fool mine at DeLamar, Nevada, was consumated in this city on Thursday of last week when A. H. Wethey, for himself and his Butte associates, made the final payment of $75,000 on the property to Frank Wilson, one of the original discoverers and principal owner of this magnificent gold producer, a payment of $25,000 having been made at the time of the giving of the bond and option.

Upon the conveyance of the property and the signing of the papers the purchasers held a meeting and declared a dividend of six cents a share on the 100,000 shares embraced in the April Fool incorporation, the same being payable tomorrow, August 1st, in addition to which a special meeting of the stockholders was called for August 21st for the express purpose of so amending the articles of incorporation of the company as to increase the capitalization from 100,000 shares of a par value of $5 each to 500,000 shares of $1 each, and at the same meeting the official directory of the association was revised as follows: William Thompson, of Butte, president; C. K. McCornick, of Salt Lake, vice-president; A. H. Wethey, of Butte, secretary and treasurer; and these, with W. S. Godbe, of Salt Lake, and J. B. Leggat, of Butte, fill out the directory, J. M. Healey being retained as manager and Frank M. Sizer being appointed consulting engineer of the mine.

This is a happy termination of a heavy deal and the new purchasers are to be congratulated over their valuable acquisition.

The Perfection Dust Collector.

Captain J. P. Sterling of Kansas City, Mo., representing Prinz & Rau of Milwaukee, manufacturers of the Perfection Dust Collector, has been in Salt Lake for several days' past.

This is not Mr. Sterling's first visit to Utah, as he was here during April of the present year, one of the results of his visit at that time being the introduction of a dust collector in the DeLamar mill at DeLamar, Nevada, and THE REVIEW is informed by Mr. Sterling, and by officials of the DeLamar company, as well, that the machine gave such excellent satisfaction that since then three more machines have been ordered and put in place, so that now the plant is virtually free from the death-dealing dust which has been so detrimental to successful operation, much to the gratification of everyone concerned, the benefits being manifold, as not only is human life protected by the innovation, but a saving has been made in the recovery of the fine dust, which is valued in the neighborhood of $45 per ton in gold, each machine reclaiming about a ton a day, while the machinery of the mill has been given a longer lease on wear and usefulness, the dust being very detrimental to the wearing parts.

Encouraged by the success experienced at the DeLamar works Mr. Sterling will now devote considerable time in the effort of placing this machine in other mills in this intermountain country, and he is sanguine that in this line he will soon be able to build up a healthy and growing business for his company.

MINE ACCIDENTS AND CASUALTIES

Not long ago a miner named Joseph Mirk, in the employ of the DeLamar company at DeLamar, Nevada, drilled into a missed hole and caused an explosion which cost him his life. His remains were interred under the auspices of the Lincoln Miners Union.

Hon. W. J. Dooley, of DeLamar, Nevada, has been appointed a delegate from his state to the International Mining Congress at Milwaukee.

Frank Swindler, superintendent of the great DeLamar gold mines at DeLamar, Nevada, was in the city last week and was warmly greeted by a host of friends. Mr. Swindler brings with him good reports from this magnificent wealth producer, and states that at the present time there is not a better or safer mill in the west, as far as dust is concerned, than the one which embellishes this Nevada property.

A. W. Gear, of Hiko, Nevada, was in the city last week on mining business. Mr. Gear is one of the pioneers of Lincoln county, and has valuable mining interests in that section, included in his holdings being the cream of Monkey Wrench hill, to develop which he is now running a tunnel for the purpose of tapping a strong ledge of quartz at a considerable depth.

Salt Lake Mining Review (Utah)
May 15, 1900

The Mining and Scientific Press, of San Francisco, in its issue of April 28th, contained finely illustrated write-ups of the Horn Silver mine and hoisting works at Frisco, and of the metallurgical plant of Charles Butters & Co., Ltd., of this city. The Press is an excellent mining paper and has a host of friends in this intermountain region. The cuts which embellish the article on DeLamar, Nevada, published in this issue of The Mining Review, were kindly furnished us through the courtesy of Mr. Halloran, publisher of the Press.

Salt Lake Mining Review (Utah)
June 30, 1900

T. H. Oxnam, formerly superintendent of the DeLamar mines at DeLamar, Nevada, left San Francisco on the 17th for London, where he will organize a syndicate for the purpose of buying and selling mines. The parties interested in the project are ready and awaiting his arrival, when the syndicate will be perfected with Mr. Oxnam as manager. His ripe experience and extensive acquaintance with the mining situation in this country should enable him to secure valuable properties. It is highly probable that upon his return to this country he will give employment to one or two capable mining engineers who will work under his direction. The headquarters of the syndicate will be at San Francisco and Los Angeles.

Report has it that Frank P. Swindler has resigned his superintendency of the DeLamar mine at DeLamar, Nevada, and that he will open an office in this city. DeLamar's loss will be our gain and many Salt Lakers will extend the glad hand to Mr. Swindler.

Frank M. Wilson, a poor man eight years ago, but who made a fortune out of the April Fool mine at DeLamar, Nevada, has still further added to his extensive holdings of Salt Lake realty in the purchase of the property on Main street now occupied by the New York Grocery, for which he paid $21,480. Although Mr. Wilson is now one of the "mining kings" of the west, he takes his good fortune modestly and is as diffident and retiring as a girl of sixteen.

Word comes from DeLamar, Nevada, that A. W. Geer has made a rich strike of gold ore on a claim near the April Fool mine.

Salt Lake Mining Review (Utah)
January 30, 1901

W. H. Paddock, who recently had charge of the Columbia mill near Sumpter, Oregon, is now a resident of this city. Mr. Paddock is a gold mill man of extensive experience, having been with the DeLamar company at DeLamar, Nevada, the Searchlight mill in California, while he has seen service in Arizona and New Mexico. For a short time he will be open for an engagement in his line.

Salt Lake Mining Review (Utah)
February 15, 1901

John Biggins, one of the millmen at the DeLamar plant at DeLamar, Nevada, was in the city several days ago visiting his old-time friends and acquaintances.

CLASH ON THE GRADE.

Further Details of the Exciting Incident at Calientes on Sunday.

Hugh McBride, an Oregon Short Line bridge builder who has returned from Calientes, has some additional light to throw on the clash between the Short Line tracklaying forces and the men who were guarding the Clark grade which happened on Sunday afternoon. According to the bridge carpenter the Clark forces were caught napping, as they did not expect the Short Line gangs to reach the boundary line at the time they did. When Engineer Ashton jumped over the fence and called on his men to tear down the barrier three Clark men, he said, appeared on the scenes armed with rifles and threatened to shoot if the Short Line men did not keep off the property. The bluff was called and a shot was fired from a blank cartridge. At this juncture the invading force with one accord promised that if anyone got shot that the entire Clark guard would be strung up at short order without the chance of an appeal from Judge Lynch's court. As the Short Line men on the ground numbered over one hundred and there were three San Pedro men, the latter very discreetly allowed the invaders to enter upon their territory, after a very strong protest to the proceeding had been entered.

Today up to a late hour this afternoon the situation down at Calientes is said to be quiet. The Short Line forces under Engineer, Ashton are now actively engaged in putting in a Y. Attorney Whittemore of the San Pedro this morning stated that all was quiet at the front and no further trouble was anticipated right at present. Just what steps he was going to take in the matter of the alleged trespass of Sunday, he was not prepared to state, but at the same time he intimated that there would be some surprises in store.

The real trouble it is anticipated will occur when the Short Line gangs arrive at Meadow Valley wash and attempt to lay their tracks over the grade and through the cuts that have been constructed by the San Pedro contractors, who are actively at work below the scene of last Sunday's clash.

As was stated by Attorney Parley L. Williams in last night's "News," the Short Line proposes to go right through the Meadow Valley wash over a portion of the work of the Clark enterprise. The San Pedro officials say that they will do no such thing and there the matter rests. The next physical clash promises to develop some exciting incidents.

George E. Fetterman, one of the leading merchants of DeLamar, Nevada, was in the city last week, and while here concluded the purchase of the Magnolia gold mine at that place. The Magnolia was the first gold discovery to be made in Ferguson district, the find being purely accidental. The property has been extensively developed and vast reserves of high grade milling gold ore are blocked out in its workings. For years the property has been owned by T. R. Jones of this city and J. Eisemann of DeLamar, who preferred to let the mineral wealth of the property remain in the mine rather than ship with railroad facilities more than 150 miles distant. Now however, with the Short Line much nearer and headed towards this prolific camp, the mine will be extensively operated, it being the intention of Mr. Fetterman to begin operations at once. It goes without saying that in the Magnolia Mr. Fetterman has secured a bonanza. Mr. Fetterman states that the DeLamar mine at that place is all O. K., and that the reported strike in virgin ground in its workings is true.

R. A. Young dropped into the Cullen this morning from Caliente, the growing town formerly known as Clover Junction. He reports conditions there as more than prosperous, and says that the town is growing at a marvellous rate.

Salt Lake Mining Review (Utah)
September 30, 1901

The Magnolia Mining & Milling company of DeLamar, Nevada, has been re-organized with a new board as follows: George C. Fetterman, president; E. C. Coffin, vice president; J. F. Allen, secretary; A. W. Mountney, treasurer, and Joe Oberndorfer. The Magnolia was the first gold discovery made at DeLamar, and is a well-developed mine with large bodies of pay gold ore blocked out in its workings.

Salt Lake Mining Review (Utah)
October 30, 1901

The April Fool gold mine at DeLamar, Nevada, has again changed hands, and several Salt Lakers have become interested in this bonanza mine, included in the list being Simon Bamberger, J.D. Wood and W.S. Godbe. The deal is said to have been consummated on a basis of $100,000 for the whole property. Since the transaction has been completed the board has been reorganized with W. S. Godbe as president; Simon Bamberger, treasurer; L. Wertheimer, secretary, and these, with R. Lieber and J. Benton Leggat, of Butte, comprise the directory. S. F. Mountney, of this city, has been designated as assistant secretary. The company will doubtless remodel the April Fool mill at no distant day.

Salt Lake Mining Review (Utah)
December 30, 1901

The April Fool Mining company, of De-Lamar, Nevada, held its annual meeting recently and elected a new board as follows: W. S. Godbe, president; J. D. Wood, vice president; Simon Bamberger, treasurer; L. D. Wertheimer, secretary, and R. Sieber. The general office of the company is now located in this city. Ernest Godbe is making experiments for the purpose of evolving a process for the more economical treatment of April Fool ores.

Emery County Progress (Utah)
January 11, 1902

The Railroad Still Coming

The Gould system has several extensions under contemplation. The probabilities are that the first important piece of work of this kind will be the building of the Castle valley and Salina canyon road. A route was surveyed years ago for a narrow gauge road to leave the main line near Price running through Castle valley and coming out through Salina canyon to the Sanpete valley branch at Salina. This route passes through a region rich in coal and other resources. A force of surveyors has been in the field for some time relocating this line with the necessary variations for a broad gauge road.

It is expected that the building of the Castle valley road will be simultaneous with the extension of the Sanpete valley branch past the vicinity of Cedar City to a connection with the San Pedro and Oregon Short Line at Caliente. The object of this is to afford a route by which the coal and coke of Carbon and Emery counties can be hauled to the iron region in case the expected large iron works are put in in that region while the manufactured product would find an outlet both ways.

It is learned that the sale of the DeLamar mines, at DeLamar, Nevada, has been consummated, upon the report of James W. Neill, E. M., to the Bamberger syndicate. The initial payment of $150,000 has been made, and the balance of the million, the purchase price, will be made within a very short time. It is stated that W. H. Linney will be continued in charge of the mine and mill. The consolidation of the April Fool and the Magnolia mines with the DeLamar property is in contemplation and will doubtless be made. The company will be known as the Bamberger-DeLamar Mines company, an eastern office for which has already been established at 25 Broad street, New York City. A proposition is on foot to increase the capacity of the DeLamar mill.

W. H. Linney, who has charge of the De Lamar mine and mill at DeLamar, Nevada, was in the city last week, bringing with him four bars of gold from the company's reduction works.

GEOLOGY OF DELAMAR, NEVADA.

.....J. W. Neill, in Mining and Scientific Press....

The De Lamar mines are located in the Meadow Valley range, about thirty miles by wagon road from Calientes. The rock formation is quartzite, uptilted and dipping to the north and east on an incline of 30 degrees. The quartzite is cut by three porphyry dikes which strike approximately east and west, and by another porphyry dike which strikes approximately north

J. W. NEILL, C. E.

and south with the strike of the quartzite beds and dips at an angle of 68 degrees to the west. The ore bodies make at the intersections of the two major east and west porphyry dikes, and the north and south porphyry dikes. This latter has been the seat of profound fissuring and this movement has fractured the quartzite of the sourrounding country on both sides, producing two parallel fissures, which are similar in strike and dip to the black porphyry fissure itself. The east and west porphyry dikes are approximately 300 feet apart at the nearest point, and at this point the black porphyry, which is the main north and south fracture, cuts through both porphyries. In relative age the east and west porphyries are probably the younger. The quartzite is most profoundly shattered in the neighborhood of the corners of these three porphyries, and in this locality the mineral solutions which have followed the fissuring have entered the communited quartzite and have been most active. The result has been the production of numerous brecciated ore zones which filled up the corners where the north and south dike has crossed the east and west dikes. Thus, today, these well known ore shoots have been developed in six of these eight corners, and the other two corners give promise of producing equal results in the future. The diagrammatic sketch, herewith shows the relations of the several por-

with, shows the relations of the several porphyries and fissures just descirbed. It is not drawn to scale. The known ore shoots are indicated in their respective corners, and the empty corners are indicated by "?" In two of these corners, recent exploration has proved the existence of good ore bodies.

It is pertinent to state here that the material of the porphyry dikes, no matter how much decomposed, or how close to the ore bodies, does not carry pay values. These ore bodies have evidently been mineralized through the openings at the corners where the dikes make their crossings, and the quartzite which has been broken into more or less small pieces has been recemented by the mineral solutions into a compact mass of silica, thus forming bodies of extreme hardness. These ore bodies have had great areas, in places over 100 feet square, and are developed from the surface to the 700-foot level, and are now being developed below this level. In addition to these shoots of ore in the quartzite, there are several known shoots developed on the main black porphyry dike and partaking of the nature of regular fissure vein ore shoots, differing only in that the quartzite adjoining the porphyry has been mineralized to a greater or less extent sometimes on the hanging and sometimes on the foot wall side of the dike, but without any well developed walls to the ore deposit itself. Further than this at least two of the parallel platings or fissures have developed ore bodies, and one of these promises to be of very great magnitude and importance. This is the new "Hog-Pen shoot" which lies to the south of and 700 or 800 feet away from the other and older ore bodies. It is from twelve to eighteen feet in thickness and several hundred feet in length on the strike of the fissure, and is of peculiar interest and importance aside from its commercial value, which is great, as evidencing the fact that he ore bodies will make in the fissure in the quartzite away from the black porphyry itself.

The April Fool mine has been developed on another series of fractures which are parallel to the main black porphyry fissure, and they resemble to a marked degree the ores produced in the recently discovered

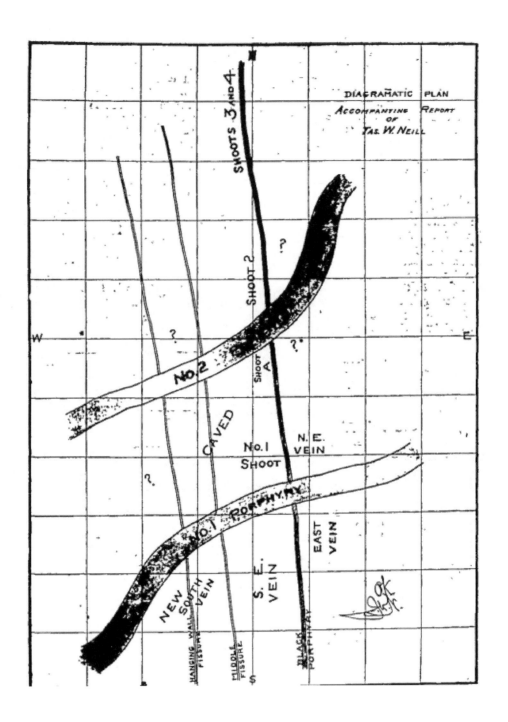

DIAGRAMATIC PLAN
ACCOMPANYING REPORT
OF
JAS. W. NEILL

Hog-Pen shoot of the De Lamar. The ores of the quartzite bodies are peculiar, in that they show no evidence to justify their commercial character. It is a silicified and often glassy mass of quartzite which, under the microscope, shows that it is very largely a readjusted, or at least a recemented quartzite. The gold contents in these ore bodies is contained in exceedingly minute form, practically never visible to the naked eye or in the pan, but has yielded readily to the treatment by cyanide. In the upper levels, particularly in the stopes of the black porphyry fissure, considerable native tellurium has been found, and, strange to say, this mineral is almost barren in gold, which is contrary to local belief, but this mineral has been associated with some of the richest ore bodies in the mine, and is an indicator of the origin of the gold from tellurides. In some places in these stopes tellurides of gold have been found and it is probable that the gold throughout the mine has been and is more or less in this form. In the new Hog Pen shoot the ore differs from the old parts of the mine in that it is more stained with iron and yields considerable gold to amalgamation, which the old mine did not do. The ores of the April Fool fissure system are stained with iron oxide, and, moreover, carry considerable silver values, thus differing from the De Lamar mine. In this mine in several places the undecomposed iron pyrites has been found in small patches where it has been protected by a clay gangue. Otherwise the ore is oxidized to the depth of 1100 feet, and at this depth the values are still of commercial grade.

Differing from both the De Lamar and April Fool mines, the ores of the Magnolia group occur in a porphyry dike at the contact with quartzite. These ores differ in character from the other two mines, in that they are heavily stained with manganese, and show a heavy percentage of free gold, and contain silver values which usually average in the neighborhood of an ounce in silver to a dollar in gold. Development on this property has followed this formation to a depth of 300 feet, and the promises of the future are bright. From the surface of all these properties very rich ores were taken out and much of it shipped by wagon to Milford and thence to the smelters at Salt Lake. These ores abounded in free gold, and to this fact the development of the camp is largely due. The treatment of the lower grades called for the piping of water and building of mills. The efficiency of the method employed, viz., cyaniding, is vouched for by the fact that fully 90 per cent of the meal values were extracted. The camp has produced a gross valuation in the neighborhood of $13,000,000, and of this fully one-half has been in dividends, which is certainly a very large proportion. The present consolidation of interests under one company and one management, with the enlargement of mill facilities and cheapening the handling through the introduction of electric power, will result in a renewed activity and renew a large production. The plans now perfected will result in an output from this supposed-to-be-worked-out camp in the neighborhood of $125,000 to $150,000 per month.

THISTLE MINES IN CAMP OF DE LAMAR

Some Great Ore Bodies Said to Be Blocked Out.

SUP'T REESE'S STATEMENT.

The Veins He States, Are From 30 to 40 Feet Wide—Outlook for Camp Never Brighter.

An arrival from the camp of Delamar, Nevada, yesterday was Mr. A. J. Reese, superintendent of the Thistle mine near that place. He came to the city for the purpose of purchasing some supplies for this valuable property which is on the highroad to prominence. Several Springville people are interested in the mine and they have every reason to feel well pleased with the manner in which developments have progressed in the past.

The shaft, Mr. Reese states, is now nearing the 200 level, from which point another drift will be run to block out ore preparatory to future removal. There is already a great amount of ore shaped up so that it can be relied upon to respond satisfactorily when the proper time comes. Much of it is a high grade shipping product, while no small portion of it will come in all right when the company have a mill ready for treatment on the ground. It is not the intention of the company to take steps of this kind just now, but it is the policy to push development work and open up new bodies of ore for three or four months to come, at the end of which time Mr. Reese believes that arrangements will be completed for the marketing of the product of the mine. The veins found in the property are said to be large and the principal one measures from 30 to 40 feet in width in places.

Speaking of the camp in general, the visitor declares that it was never in a more prosperous condition and predicts much activity in that section during the present year. The improvement in mining conditions, together with the building of the Los Angeles railroad is certain to bring about many important changes in the district in another year.

Mr. Reese will leave for camp again tomorrow.

OREGON SHORT LINE RAILROAD

Time Table

In Effect Feb. 1, 1903.

ARRIVE.

From Ogden, Portland, Butte, San Francisco and Omaha	8:30 a.m
From Ogden and intermediate points	9:10 a.m
From Callentes, Milford, Nephi, Provo, and intermediate points.	9:35 a.m
From Ogden, Cache Valley, Chicago, St. Louis, Omaha, Denver and Intermediate points	12:01 p.m
From Ogden, Chicago, St. Louis, Kansas City, Omaha, Denver and San Francisco	4:05 p.m
*From Garfield Beach, Tooele and Terminus	5:00 p.m
From Tintic, Mercur, Nephi, Provo, and Manti	5:35 p.m
From Ogden, Cache Valley, Butte, Portland, San Francisco	8:10 p.m

DEPART.

For Ogden, Omaha, Chicago, Denver, Kansas City and St. Louis	7:00 a.m
For Tintic, Mercur, Provo, Nephi and Manti	7:30 a.m
*For Garfield Beach, Tooele and Terminus	7:45 a.m
For Ogden, Butte, Helena, Portland, San Francisco and intermediate points	8:45 a.m
For Ogden, Omaha, Chicago, Denver, Kansas City, St. Louis and San Francisco	12:50 p.m
For Ogden, Cache Valley, Denver, Kansas City, Omaha, St. Louis and Chicago	5:45 p.m
For Provo, Nephi, Milford, Callentes and intermediate points	6:05 p.m
For Ogden, Cache Valley, Butte, Helena, Portland, San Francisco and intermediate points	12:50 a.m

T. M. SCHUMACHER, Act. Traf. Mgr.
D. E. BURLEY, G. P. & T. A.
D. S. SPENCER, A. G. P. & T. A.
City Ticket Office, 201 Main Street.
Telephone 250.
*Daily except Sunday.

Senator Simon Bamberger will leave for DeLamar, Nevada, tonight with a party of friends to see the new mill at the big Bamberger-DeLamar mines placed in commission.

Manti Messenger (Utah)
April 25, 1903

Word came Tuesday from Lund, Nevada to the effect that Alex Reid had died on Easter Sunday of miner's consumption He leaves a wife and four small children. Mr Reid had been in very poor health for years and of late had been unable to attend to his work. W. K. Reid of this city has kept up Alex Reid's dues in the lodge he was a member of, and the family will be entitled to money due on the life policy.

Salt Lake Mining Review (Utah)
April 30, 1903

The Bamberger-DeLamar Gold Mines company, operating at DeLamar, Nevada, has put the finishing touches on its 1,200 horsepower electric plant, and the new works will be started up about May 1st. This plant was furnished by the General Electric company, and gives a motive power fully ample for the treatment of 700 tons of ore daily.

Deseret News (Utah)
May 8, 1903

Resolutions of Condolence

Hall of Tintic Lodge No 711 B P O Elks Eureka May 7th 1903

WHEREAS, On April 30th 1903 our respected brother, G W Wright formerly of Mercur Utah died at DeLamar Nevada by Tintic Lodge No 711 B P O Elks be it

RESOLVED That in the death of our brother G W Wright this lodge has lost a faithful member and society an upright and honored young man whose life was in the morning sun and full of promise and we hereby tender our sincere sympathy to the bereaved family of our deceased brother in their hour of sorrow and be it further

RESOLVED That as a mark of respect to our deceased brother the charter of this lodge be draped for a period of thirty days and a copy of these resolutions be placed upon our records and also forwarded to the family of our deceased brother

Committee { EDWARD PIKE
GUS J HENRIOD
J W EMBLETON

(Mercur Miner please copy)

Salt Lake Mining Review (Utah)
May 15, 1903

Harry Colbath, for several years with the Con. Mercur company as assayer and metallurgist, has accepted a position with the Bamberger-DeLamar Gold Mines company at DeLamar, Nevada. Upon his leaving Mercur his associates presented him with a fine gold watch and chain and an Elks' charm.

LUND, NEVADA.

Peace Meeting — Much New Land Broken—Favorable Crop Outlook.

Special Correspondence.

Lund, Nevada, May 18.—A very successful peace meeting was held here on the evening of May 18 under the auspices of th Relief society and Y. L. M. I. A., and a very interesting program was rendered, consisting of appropriate speeches, songs, reading, recitations and instrumental music.

Spring has opened favorably for farmers and stockmen. Most of the crops are in. Considerable new land has been broken up and fenced th spring.

The two departments of the district school closed last week, after a run of twenty-eight weeks.

Bishop Thomas Judd from St. George is with us again, on business pertaining to land matters.

Will Treweek, who is rapidly attaining prominence in his chosen profession of mining and mine examination, has returned from a visit to Delamar, Nevada, where he made an inspection of the great Bamberger-Delamar gold mine and equipment.

H. V. Croll, local manager for the Allis-Chalmers company, was at DeLamar, Nevada, recently, being present and assisting in the starting up and testing of the crushing portion of the big plant in course of construction for the Bamberger-DeLamar company.

Deseret News (Utah)
August 17, 1903

ARRIVES FROM DELAMAR.

Sidney Bamberger Says Big Mill Will Soon be Treating 500 Tons Daily.

Among the arrivals from the south this forenoon was Sidney Bamberger, who has been making a study of the big Bamberger-Delamar mines at Delamar, Nevada. He reported everything going going along smoothly and the mill will soon be adjusted so that it will be handling the ore from the mines at the rate of 500 tons per day. The plant has been running under 400 tons, but as is the case with all other new plants it takes some little time to get everything in first class running order.

Mr. Bamberger says the San Pedro railway is preparing to commence pushing the extension towards Los Angeles. During the past few days some big outfits to be employed in building the grades has arrived at Caliente.

San Pedro Los Angeles and Salt Lake R. R.

—IN CONNECTION—

San Pete Valley Ry.

Trains leave Ephraim daily except Sunday, at 9.37 a. m. Arrive Ephraim at 3.15 p. m., connecting at Nephi with San Pedro trains for Calientes, Frisco, Milford, Payson, Provo, Mercur, Eureka, Salt Lake and intermediate points.

Southbound trains leave Salt Lake daily at 7.30 a. m. and 6.05 p. m.

At Salt Lake City direct connection is made with the O. S. L. R. R., the only line to northern Idaho, Montana, Oregon and Washington, which is also in connection with the Union Pacific, the shortest quickest and best route to all points East.

E. W. GILLET, G. F. & P. A., S. P. L. A. & S. L. R. R., Salt Lake City Utah.

H. S. KERR, G. F. & P. A., S. P. V. Ry. Manti, Utah.

P. RASMUSSEN, Agt., Ephraim, Utah.

A large number of their friends partook of the hospitality of Mr. and Mrs. W. F. Reid at their home Jan. 1st. An elaborate and well prepared dinner was served at 6 p. m., after which the evening was spent in games, recitations and selections from the graphaphone. Mrs. Reid was assisted by Mrs. Mary Lowry, Miss Lydia Jensen and the Misses Iris and Helen Lowry. Those present were: Mr. and Mrs. W. T. Reid, Mr. and Mrs. J. Lowry, Sr., Mr. and Mrs. J. Lowry, Jr., Mr. and Mrs. Orson Lowry, Mr. and Mrs. S. L. Vorhees, Dr. and Mrs. C. H. Bird, Dr. and Mrs. C. W. Bird, Mr. and Mrs. Geo. Peacock, Mr. and Mrs. W. K. Reid, Mr. and Mrs. J. M. Burns. Mrs. May Reid of Lund, Nevada, Mr. and Mrs. Edward Reid, Mr. and Mrs. J. Tatton, Mrs. W. B. Lowry, Mrs. Maria Lowry, Mr. Geo. Scott, Miss Luella Lowry.

The Mining Review is pleased to hear that our old friend, Frank P. Swindler, at one time superintendent of the DeLamar gold mines at DeLamar, Nevada, has been induced by Manager Simon Bamberger to go back to his old position. Mr. Swindler was in Salt Lake a few days ago, but left for the mine as soon as he had completed arrangements with the company.

Mining Near Caliente.

Special Correspondence.

Caliente, Nev., May 19.—Work on the Grand View group of gold-copper claims, 20 miles south of Caliente, is being carried on steadily by owners of the group and some fine samples of ore have reached camp, taken from large ledges which have been stripped on several of the claims.

Local miners and prospectors here are anxiously awaiting the result of Hon. C. O. Whittemore's examination of mines in which the recent strike was made near Panaca, in which he is part owner, as it is understood that in the event he receives favorable news as to values and extent of ore bodies Caliente will have a mill where custom ore can be treated at reasonable prices and this means much to this camp where dozens of low grade ledges have been opened up which carry values from $3 to $6 in free gold, which, while it will not pay to ship, would be first class milling propositions were a mill to be installed in this camp.

The weather here is magnificent, the cool breezes constantly relieving the heat, which does not average over 90 degrees in the middle of the day and cools down to 50 degrees through the night.

L. M. Harwood, one of the leading business men of DeLamar, Nevada, and who has valuable mining possessions in this great gold camp, took advantage of the Conference rates to transact a little business in Zion, meeting quite a number of old-time friends while here. Mr. Harwood will soon make a visit to Nevada's two most popular camps, Tonopah and Goldfield.

MINING NEAR CALIENTE.

Several Properties Being Worked With Prospects of Success.

Special Correspondence.

Caliente, Nev., May 28.—Wilson Mc-Carty and Jos. Hendley of Denver, Colo., passed through camp today enroute to Colville, southeast of the San Pedro line, where they have large mining interests in gold-copper properties, and which they will develop at once, installing modern machinery for treatment of their ore.

The Fetterman tunnel is now in 190 feet, and within the next 20 feet the owners expect to crosscut a large ledge of free gold.

There are a large number of prospectors at work in the hills around here, and they are bringing into camp some very fine specimens of high grade silver, lead and copper ore, which they are locating within a radius of 10 to 15 miles from camp.

CALIENTE GOLD MINE.

Officers Chosen at Annual Meeting Held Last Monday.

The Caliente Gold Mining Co. held its annual meeting yesterday morning and the following officers were elected for the ensuing year: Geo. C. Fetterman, president; A. H. Gentry, vice president; A. R. Parsons, secretary and treasurer. These with C. Holmes comprise the board of directors.

Arthur Parsons was the unanimous choice for the office of superintendent and it was decided to continue the work on the tunnel for the present. The tunnel is still some distance from the intersection of the ledge for which it was started. The work will be continued along the same lines for some time.
—Delamar Lode.

Fred Foster came in today from Arden and will continue eastward to his home in the World's Fair city. He will return here in the fall to continue work on his claim close to this camp.

A sale for $1,500 is reported as being made this week by Messrs. Maynard and others owners of a promising prospect about two miles from Caliente, to Salt Lake parties.

Frank Parker and his partner, Mr. Alexander, started work on their rich free gold claims three miles from Caliente today.

Davis County Clipper (Utah)
June 17, 1904

J. A. Vallentine, a prospector, was found dead in a cabin twelve miles from Caliente. It is believed he was murdered, although some declare it was a case of suicide.

Deseret News (Utah)
June 17, 1904

CALIENTE GOLD MINE.

Officers Chosen at Annual Meeting Held Last Monday.

The Caliente Gold Mining Co. held its annual meeting yesterday morning and the following officers were elected for the ensuing year: Geo. C. Fetterman, president; A. H. Gentry, vice president; A. R. Parsons, secretary and treasurer. These with C. Holmes comprise the board of directors.

Arthur Parsons was the unanimous choice for the office of superintendent and it was decided to continue the work on the tunnel for the present. The tunnel is still some distance from the intersection of the ledge for which it was started. The work will be continued along the same lines for some time. —Delamar Lode.

Deseret News (Utah)
July 4, 1904

FROM CALIENTE.

News Correspondent Sends Budget of Information From There.

Special Correspondence.

Caliente, Nev., July 3.—Fourth of July is being celebrated in Caliente with great enthusiasm and plenty of fireworks, the edict of the county commissioners notwithstanding, and the festivities close with a big ball in the evening on an immense platform built by the railroad company. A one-fare rate has been put on between the front and camp to allow those desiring to participate in the celebration to attend.

General Foreman Conway is putting in the finest new line of track ever laid in the western country for stability, safety and speed.

Charles Culverwell has laid a water pipe line from the San Pedro tanks to his hotel.

G. R. Reinard, conductor at the front, went to Salt Lake for the holidays.

A gang of 80 Austrians and Mexicans landed in camp today for work at the front, as it is difficult to get white men to stay in the warm climate, although thus far there has been no unbearable weather anywhere along the line.

Chief Clerk C. W. Draper was today called by wire to Ogden, where his wife is seriously ill.

Division Engineer A. L. Jones arrived today from Salt Lake.

The W. U. T. Co. wires are strung to Elgin, 30 miles southwest of Caliente and a big supply of poles went west to them today which will carry the line to Galt, 50 miles below Caliente. They expect to complete the line to the front inside of the next 30 days.

Track laying will be renewed by the San Pedro line on July 15, the big cut

west of Moapa having been completed
by the Utah Construction Co., and it is
now certain that the line will be completed to Los Vegas ranch by Aug. 15.

Caliente Mining Notes.

Special Correspondence.

Caliente, Nev., July 3.—A large number of mining men and prospectors
have been going down the line to Moapa and Los Vegas, and thence to the
upper Colorado river country, and districts lying north from these points,
where free gold and gold copper
strikes have been numerous during the
past month.

The Fetterman tunnel, close to camp,
is now in 205 feet, and is within about
20 feet of the rich ledge which they in-
tend cross cutting at a depth of 80
feet.

A seven and one-half foot ledge of
gold-copper ore was struck this week
in one of the Grand View claims, 20
miles west of Caliente.

Deseret News (Utah)
July 14, 1904

KILLED AT CALIENTE.

Brakeman Sullivan Crushed to Death—
News on San Pedro.

Special Correspondence.

Caliente, Nev., July 12.—John Sullivan was almost instantly killed and G.
McConaghy injured by piles falling
from the train while running about 20
miles an hour, 88 miles west from Caliente on the San Pedro line. Both
were brakemen. Relatives in Salt
Lake wired for the remains of deceased to be shipped there and the
body was sent to Salt Lake today. Mc-
Conaghy will recover. The coroner's
jury returned a verdict of accidental
death due to cause above stated.

Manager and vice president of the
Utah Construction Co. Wattis, came in
from the front today and went on to
Salt Lake. He states that his company's graders are rushing the line
through and hope to keep in advance
of the railroad company track layers
until the line reaches Los Vegas ranch,
which will undoubtedly be by Aug. 14.

It is reported here that Senator Clark,
president of the San Pedro road, is expected through here by special this
week.

A special came in yesterday from
Salt Lake and departed in the evening
for 'Frisco with General Manager
Wells, Superintendent Henderson and
their staff on board. They would not
state the object of their visit and returned as soon as the engine was coal-
ed.

MINING NEAR CALIENTE.

Clark Brothers Have Found a Gold Property Not Far from Moapa.

Special Correspondence.

Caliente, Nev., July 22.—Clark Bros., merchants here and at Moapa, have struck a very rich free gold mine between the upper Virgin and Moapa rivers, and some of their ore, of which they claim to have 2½ feet, will go around a thousand dollars per ton. They are developing their properties.

Charles French, a Denver, Colo., mining man, in company with Bert Jordan and Pete Manard, two prospectors passed through camp today en route to Moapa, whence they will go north about 23 miles to a group of gold-copper claims which the prospectors located last January and on which they have done over 500 feet of development work, opening up a six-foot vein of ore going $8 gold and 22 to 43 per cent copper.

The copper values are found in a black oxide and show every evidence of increasing strength and permanency with development. If these claims give a satisfactory result to Mr. French he and his Spokane associates will take a short time option on them.

Henry Judd, a prospector who has been locating and developing claims sought from Moapa since March 1, passed through Caliente today with over $500 worth of coarse and wire gold, taken from a vein on the Blue Bell, one of his claims. He has erected an arasta and his partner, Mike Brady, is grinding out the yellow metal while Judd is getting assays made of their find.

L. M. Harwood, of De Lamar, Nevada, has been making a visit to the new camp of Goldfield of late.

Frank P. Swindler, of DeLamar, Nevada, superintendent of the Bamberger-De-Lamar mines and mills, arrived in Salt Lake the first of the week, accompanied by his wife, who is in poor health.

Deseret News (Utah)
August 12, 1904

CALIENTE GOLD MINE.

A Night Shift Put On in the Long Tunnel.

Special Correspondence.

Caliente, Nev., Aug. 11.—The Caliente Gold Mining company, whose properties adjoin the townsite here, has put on a day and night shift on the tunnel of the Blue Bird, which is in 155 feet, and within the next 15 feet it is expected the free gold ledge will be struck, which shows a width of 22 feet at grass roots, and an assay value of $38 per ton.

Salt Lake Mining Review (Utah)
August 15, 1904

Thirty thousand in gold bars, from a two weeks' run of the Bamberger-DeLamar, Nevada, mill, passed through on the 1st, en route to an eastern refinery.

Deseret News (Utah)
August 15, 1904

LUND, NEVADA.

TERRIFIC ELECTRICAL STORM

Heavy Rainfall—Good Crops of Grain And Hay.

Special Correspondence.

Lund, White Pine Co., Nevada, Aug. 11.—A very severe electrical storm passed over this place yesterday evening between the hours of 7 and 10 o'clock. The lightning was something terrific. The flashes were so frequent and of such long duration that the horizon was almost constantly lighted. This was accompanied by heavy rainfall and but occasional thundering. The rain did some damage to the ripened grain in beating it to the ground. Harvesting is now on. Much of the grain is ripe and some is already in the shock. The grain crop is good. The second crop of lucern is almost ready for cutting. The hay yield is heavier than in past seasons.

We have had some very warm weather the past few weeks with occasional refreshing showers to gladden the earth. Garden stuff looks well. The health of the people is good.

A cloudburst washed out the track at Minto ten miles east of Caliente Nevada The westbound train was delayed four hours There was no damage to train or passengers Six miles below Caliente two work trains collided and six laborers were injured

CALIENTE, NEVADA.

FEVER EPIDEMIC.

Telegraph Line Completed 100 Miles West—Surprise Party.

Caliente, Nev., Sept. 9.—Hans Olson, a leading merchant here, returned from a business trip to Pioche today.

A largely attended surprise party was given last night to Mrs. James Nesbitt, wife of the county clerk, at the residence of her sister, Mrs. Hans Olson.

Willie, son of Hon. Chas. Culrevell, has recovered from a dangerous attack of typhoid fever.

There is a large amount of fever among the San Pedro laborers down the line near Nevapa.

The W. U. Telegraph Co. wires are now strung to a point 100 miles west of Caliente and six telephones also installed between Caliente and Nevapa.

State Senator Denton has returned from Winnemucca, where he went to meet Senator Newlands and other state politicians.

Deseret News (Utah)
September 17, 1904

Goes to Bamberger-Delaman.

Reginald Heath has been appointed to the position of foreman of the Bamberger-Delamar mines at Delamar, Nevada, in the place of James F. Hendricson, resigned.

Deseret News (Utah)
September 20, 1904

ACTIVITY NEAR MOAPA.

A Number of Prospectors Have Made Good Strikes Near There.

Special Correspondence.

Caliente, Nev., Sept. 18.—John Husely and Miles Brown, owners of the Little Jim group, southeast of Moapa, have just cross-cut a 7-foot vein of free gold ore going $23.70 per ton, in a 90-foot tunnel run to cross-cut the ledge at a depth of 70 feet.

John Finley, owner of the Black Diamond Copper mine, north of Good Springs, has received assays of 18 and 22 per cent copper per ton from ore taken from a 13 foot ledge.

J. T. Miles of Colorado came through camp today enroute to Los Vegas, where he will prospect southerly to the Colorado river.

Mike Dolan and H. Finks have cross-cut a 4-foot ledge of gold-silver ore going $8 gold and 210 ounces silver on their Mizpah claim at a depth of 119 feet, 24 miles north of Los Vegas.

J. M. Dicker and Ralph Wells have struck a 14-inch vein of $182 free gold ore on their Virgin River claims. They are running a 300-foot tunnel to open a 12-foot ledge of $42 ore, and struck the big values at 147 feet from beginning of tunnel.

Joe Bullard brought in two sacks of rich copper (black oxide) ore from their Good Springs claim.

Deseret News (Utah)
September 21, 1904

CALIENTE, NEVADA.

SUICIDE OF OLD MAN.

Hank Connors, Despondent Over Financial Distress, Takes His Own Life.

Special Correspondence.

Caliente, Nevada, Sept. 17.—Hank Connors, aged 67 years, an old resident of Caliente, committed suicide by taking two ounces of laudanum, last night. Cause, despondency and lack of finances, and refusal of his sons to contribute to their father's support.

Two new residences and a saloon building, a new stone jail and additions to several stores is the building record for Caliente this week.

Everything in Lincoln county politically looks like a Democratic majority, although the Republican "barrel" is on the ground all along the line of the San Pedro road and is being tapped with wonderful regularity. State Senator J. A. Denton of Caliente was again nominated for state senatorial honors by the Democratic county delegation at Caliente on the 15th.

Miss Rita Turnwalk, who has been nursing Mrs. W. R. Frost of Salt Lake, now recuperating here, returned to her home in Salt Lake today.

Caliente Mining Notes.

Special Correspondence.

Caliente, Nev., Sept. 20.—The Caliente Gold Mining Co.'s new tunnel is in 28 feet on a 12 foot ledge of $28.50 gold ore adjoining the townsite at Caliente.

Hans Olson, R. W. Frost and Will Lee of Caliente have located the Butte claim adjoining the townsite of Caliente as a mill site for their San Pedro, Japan and Venus claims and began location work on same yesterday, running an open cut on a four foot ledge.

J. M. Harris, owner of the Las Vegas claim, 28 miles northwest of Caliente, received $12 gold assays today from a two-foot ledge.

Eureka Reporter (Utah)
September 30, 1904

Miss Turner of DeLamar Nevada left for her home last Saturday after a visit with Mr and Mrs Frank Newton Mrs Newton accompanied her as far as Salt Lake

---

Eureka Reporter (Utah)
October 14, 1904

The Salt Lake Route now has track laid 116 miles below Caliente and within six miles of Vegas Some California peaks can be seen from the terminus

While Caliente is still the terminus of the operated road of the Salt Lake route the traffic to the front now about 117 miles below there is very heavy and shows an increase daily

Emery County Progress (Utah)
October 15, 1904

While Caliente is still the terminus
of the operated road of the Salt Lale
route the traffic to the front now
about 117 miles below there is very
heavy and shows an increase daily

Davis County Clipper (Utah)
October 21, 1904

The Salt Lake route has reached the
Vegas ranch, 116 miles from Caliente.
The Vegas ranch is but forty-seven
miles from the California line.

Deseret News (Utah)
October 22, 1904

AFTER IDAHO CONVICT.

Got Away With Handcuffs on, but Probably Got Rid of Them.

C. S. Ferrin, warden of the Idaho state penitentiary, is a visitor in Salt Lake today. He is out in search of an escaped convict named Harry Dougherty, who broke away from his keepers at the Idaho prison while at work in the stone quarry, and was afterwards apprehended in Las Vegas. Warden Ferrin says that Dougherty is a clever man at jail breaking, and it is due to his skill in that line that his capture has not been effected. When caught at Las Vegas he was taken to Callentes, and placed in jail to await the coming of Warden Ferrin. The warden left at once upon receipt of the news of his capture, but had to go by a round about way to Carson to get the proper requisition papers. When he arrived at Callentes, the man had made his escape from the jail in a most novel manner. With a pair of handcuffs on his hands he had succeeded in loosening a ball from a slop bucket which stood in the cell. With this weapon he had gouged out the cement and lime from a stone in the prison wall, and had finally removed enough stone and cement to crawl out, and make his escape.

The warden said this morning, when asked if he had any trace of the man yet: "Yes, we have, and I expect to locate him very shortly. When he escaped from the Caliente jail, he had on a pair of handcuffs, but I suppose he had no trouble in getting rid of them, as the country down there is full of pretty bad characters. Officers are now hunting for him on the trails leading into Goldfield, as it is supposed that he headed in that direction across country. He is about 25 years old, stoop shouldered, weighs about 160 pounds, has a sallow complexion, grey eyes, dark hair, and has a slight dimple on his chin. While at Caliente I met a railroad detective from Ogden, who said that the man was wanted there for a burglary committed before the offense for which he was arrested in Idaho. A daring robbery occurred near Caliente since he escaped, and he probably is guilty of that crime, too. There is a standing reward of $50 offered by the state for the apprehension of escaped convicts, and I should have endeavored to have a larger reward offered in this case had the governor of Idaho not been absent when I left."

Warden Ferrin is in touch by wire with the officers searching for Dougherty, and hopes to receive favorable reports from them in the near future.

Emery County Progress (Utah)
November 12, 1904

Persistent complaints come from Caliente of the great number of laborers stranded there who it is alleged have been sent by an employment agency with offices in Salt Lake City and Ogden with the assurance that there would be work for them at the front

Ephraim Enterprise (Utah)
November 17, 1904

The tracklayers of the Salt Lake
Route have reached a point 148.5 miles
below Caliente. This is the end of the
line to be constructed from this end.

Emery County News (Utah)
December 17, 1904

The Salt Lake Route is making im
portant improvements in the town of
Caliente and has now nearly com
pleted the erection of a big coal chute
and twelve two-story frame dwellings
for the use of their mechanics who are
to be employed in the new seventen
stall roundhouse

Deseret News (Utah)
December 26, 1904

COURT NOTES.

In the damage suit of John Faedie
against the San Pedro, Los Angeles &
Salt Lake Railroad company, Judge
Morse has rendered judgment by consent in favor of plaintiff for $150. The
action was brought to recover $1,000
damages for injuries received by plaintiff while working for defendant near
Caliente, Nev.

LUND, NEVADA.

CASPER F. BRYNER DEAD.

Prominent Young Citizen and Church Worker Succumbs to Paralysis.

Special Correspondence.

Lund, Whitepine Co., Nev., Jan. 9.—On the 5th of January Casper F. Bryner, one of our most respected citizens, died very suddenly of paralysis, at his home in Lund, Whitepine county, Nev. He was about 35 years of age, and came here from Price, Emery county, Utah, to assist in the colonization of the White river settlements. He leaves a wife and five small childre nto mourn his demise. His labors here have been somewhat varied, and generally successful. He purchased land and engaged in farming, his inclination favoring this occupation, but he engaged in other labors as well, working some at the carpenter's trade, and also at one time for a short period venturing in the mercantile business and conducting the affairs of the Lund Co-op. very successfully.

He was an untiring church worker, and at the time of his death was first assistant superintendent of the Sunday school and one of the stake aids in the Religion class work. He has also acted as a ward teacher and held the position of first counselor in the Y. M. M. I. A. of our ward, which position he filled creditably. During his residence here he has acted as agent for the Deseret News and worked to increase the circulation in the ward.

The whole community is cast into gloom over his sad and sudden death and extend sympathy to his grief-stricken wife and family.

William Andres and William Jones two prospectors report the discovery of another strange cave in the south western portion of Nevada The cave has been explored to a depth of 300 feet and shows evidence of a prehistoric race The cavern is located on the line of the new San Pedro road near Caliente

Deseret News (Utah)
February 10, 1905

LUND, NEVADA.

Market for Farm Produce — Sickness Prevalent.

Special Correspondence.

Lund, Nev., Feb. 2.—Quite a number of the men of our settlement are working at present hauling produce to the mining camps at Tonopah, Goldfield, and Reveille.

There is some sickness here at present, and the weather has been quite stormy for the past two weeks. E. A. Cripps' little girl is quite ill, and at this writing is very low.

Deseret News (Utah)
February 13, 1905

Manager Sidney Bamberger of the Fortuna mine at Bingham will visit that property during the week and will be accompanied by Frank P. Swindler, superintendent of the Bamberger-DeLamar mine at DeLamar, Nevada.

Deseret News (Utah)
February 24, 1905

PROSPECTORS NUMEROUS.

Herman W. Horne Finds Swarms of Them in Southern Nevada.

Herman W. Horne, the well known civil and mining engineer, returned from southern Nevada this morning, where he was employed to survey the property of the Arrow Mining company, near Caliente.

Mr. Horne was favorably impressed with the Arrow company's ground and says the whole country down that way is alive with prospectors. He met several Salt Lakers out on the desert west of Caliente, where they outfitted, and were going across the country towards Tonopah and Goldfield.

Considerable interest is being manifested in the districts contiguous to Caliente, and people generally express the belief that the old camp of Pioche is on the eve of a revival. There are several large deals pending and the Venture company of London is said to figure in some of them. The same concern is also interested in the Fay and Deer Lodge districts, where it recently secured options on property.

Salt Lake Mining Review (Utah)
February 28, 1905

L. M. Harwood, a prominent business man of DeLamar, Nevada, but who is now sojourning at Columbia, near Goldfield, Nevada, was in Salt Lake a few days ago. Mr. Harwood predicts great things for the Goldfield region this summer.

Morrison, Merrill & Co., of Salt Lake, wholesale lumber dealers, has an order from the Bamberger-DeLamar Mining company, of DeLamar, Nevada, for half a carload of Malthoid roofing. Morrison, Merrill & Co. have handled three carloads of this paint since accepting the agency for the same from the Paraffine Paint company less than two months ago.

Deseret News (Utah)
March 11, 1905

Caliente Wants It.

Caliente has blossomed out with a commercial club, and at a meeting of the same Wednesday night, it was the unanimous decision that Caliente was the only station on the San Pedro road from which to start the Goldfield freight route. A committee of five consisting of Messrs. Fetterman, Denton, Shier, Culverwell and Clark were appointed to assist Mr. Marsh in every way possible with the installation of Caliente as the initial point.

CALIENTE TO KAWICH.

Character of Country and Its Mineral Possibilities Described.

Th Caliente Express of recent date gives a good description of the country between Caliente and Kawich, where some good mining camps are being opened up.

Coming east from the Kawich range across a narrow tract of what might fitly be termed desert, one unfamiliar with the western wilds is overawed with the wonders of the sandy waste.

The Reveille range was the scene of great activity in the early seventies, when its numerous camps were active producers and shippers, via the lumbering ox teams of Argonaut days, when it paid the early prospector to haul 300 miles over mountain passes and through deserts the richest ore found in this range. This district has since the opening of the Salt Lake Route been reopened and its mountains are teeming with life and renewed energy. Coming east toward Caliente the prospector reaches the famous Timpiute range south of which lie the Trachyte mountains, both rich in gold, silver and other precious metals, and claims have been staked out in both these rich districts and are now receiving the attention of a horde of prospectors who are reporting daily strikes of fabulously rich ore. Following the trail eastward it crosses the Silver Canyon mountains, in the depths of which high grade gold and silver ore has been opened up within the past 90 days and which promises to yield immense returns to the indefatigable knight of the pick and shovel. A little north of this district lie the Irish mountains which are just now receiving the attention of representatives of a Boston syndicate who, while conservative as becomes the natives of Beanland, have been unable to conceal the fact that they are meeting with unexpected returns from their labors. Journeying easterly from the Silver Canyon range, the road enters the rich Pahranagat Valley, whose lands are as fertile, its springs as cool, its verdure as green and its garden products as palatable as may be found in any part of the western country. Bordering the valley on the east is the Hiko range, long known to the prospector as a richly mineralized country, whose values make shipping profitable even with a long haul to the railroad. Down the trail to the east lies the Meadow Valley range and in the depths of this range lies the well-known prosperous mining camp of Delamar, which has produced millions and whose output at this date averages nearly $100,000 in bullion per month. This camp has been famous for years for its rich ores, and not many years ago the world was startled by authentic reports or ore values from the April Fool the Mangolia and the Delamar mines, and now she is singing anew the songs of the siren, save that now the song is true and with each day comes the report of increasing richness of ore, size of ledges and extent of deposit.

Then down the trail 25 miles comes the growing town of Caliente, rich in mineral throughout the encircling ranges amid which she nestles like an emerald within a golden circle. Following the line of travel northward from Caliente, through the Meadow Valley Wash the road enters Panaca Valley, in the midst of which lie the old time high grade camps of Panaca and Bullionville, the latter the scene of one of Mark Twain's semi-tragic stories of early days. Up the stage road to the northward some 15 miles lies the present county seat and reawakened camp of Pioche, whose history has been written in letters of gold, for in the days when silver had the ring of gold, Pioche lead the western world in value and extent of production in the white metal. Recently new discoveries have been made, old mines re-opened, new blood, brawn and capital installed into the famous old camp and now with the assurance of big pay values in her mines, and direct connection with Salt Lake mills, via the branch line soon to be established between that camp and Caliente, Pioche bids fair to lead eastern Nevada in point of ore product, high in values and boundless in extent. That stirring scenes were enacted in the boom days of Pioche is clearly proven by a visit to the old, dust-swept graveyard close to the town, where a long row of rudely pencilled headboards tell the tale of adventurers who crossed the Great Divide with their boots on, when Pioche boasted 5,00 souls and silver was king.

The recent successful exploitation of new districts surrounding Pioche, Panaca, Caliente and other Lincoln county camps, points clearly to the fact that the wealth of Lincoln county mines has not as yet been scratched and the promise of its future greatness is painted in the colors of the rainbow, a perpetual promise of a future surpassing its past records even in its best days.

Lincoln county is almost a virgin field for the sturdy prospector, and miles of rich mineral land are as yet undisturbed by the pick or drill, giving to the prospecting, investment and speculative world such an opportunity for research as exists nowhere in the limits of Uncle Sam's broad domain.

Las Vegas Age
April 7, 1905

Buy a Half - Acre Home

Lots 100 by 145 feet for sale in the

WESTERN ADDITION TO CALIENTE, NEVADA

Adjoining townsite of Caliente Fresh Spring Water, Rich Soil, Delightful Climate. Close to line of Salt Lake Route. Prices from $125 upward.

Write WILL J. LEE, Agent, Caliente, Nevada
for further information

CALIENTE, NEVADA.

COLLAPSE OF STONE BUILDING

Chinese Laundrymen Escape Unhurt—
Trains on Schedule Time.

Special Correspondence.

Caliente, Nevada., April 12.—The newly erected stone laundry building on H. W. Underhill's lot met with a disaster last week during a heavy rain storm. The masonry evidently was weak jointed and unable to stand the strain put upon it by the heavy roof, weakened as well by the rain on inferior mortar, fell and great was the fall of it, the walls squashed down to the level of the ground and the roof dropped through carrying the timbers with it. The Chinamen occupying the building escaped with their lives, more scared than hurt.

The big coal chute in Caliente yards is at last completed and is now supplying engines with their quota of coal.

A Mexican named Martini with two Indian witnesses were taken over to Delamar by Deputy Sheriff Monahan this week for trial before United States Commissioner McNamee for selling liquor to Indians.

Peter Breen, a young man who has been working for the railroad for the past year, was taken severely ill with pneumonia this week, and as there is no hospital here was taken in charge by the county, being an indigent, and placed in the jail building under the care of John Shier for treatment.

The new meat market building of Chas. Culverwell, Jr., on Clover street is nearly completed and when finished will be the finest building in Caliente.

Through trains to Las Vegas are now running on schedule time through Caliente to the material benefit of the town both as to convenience for southern travelers and to postoffice patrons.

C L Marsh and Hon H P Myton have formed a partnership for the purpose of handling and forwarding freight between Caliente on the Salt Lake Route and the Bullfrog and Goldfield districts, Nevada. Two hundred horses and mules will be utilized on the line, which, it is understood, is now open for business. The making of Caliente as one of the terminals of this line will mean much for this rapidly growing and prosperous little city, and the proposed extension of a branch line of the San Pedro from this point to Pioche will also give it added importance.—Salt Lake Mining Review.

Las Vegas Age
April 28, 1905

CALIENTE

[Special Correspondence]

Caliente, Nev., April 22.—The frame work of the new depot at Caliente is completed and the fixtures will be in place the coming week. Trains running through to Las Vegas now stop at the hotel of James A. Denton for breakfast going west and for dinner going east. The big new coal chute is in operation and the large steel water tank will be delivering water this week. Twelve new cottages for the use of employes will be built at once in addition to the twelve now occupied on the railroad grounds. Everyone not in the employ of the railroad company has been notified to get off of the railroad grounds and moving has been the order of the day this week. The right of way through the townsite will be widened below Culverwell's land to the south end of the wash and new supply and section buildings will be erected on the land thus acquired.

W. H. Frost, the Salt Lake mining man, went to Kawich Springs today to look over some mining properties in that district.

Henry Burbank, of Provo, who has been in the Kawich country for the past month, passed through Caliente today with samples of free gold ore taken from four claims which he has located, the ore going from $150 to $7800 per ton. He states that he has stripped a three-foot ledge for over 1200 feet and the ore is frozen to the foot wall, widening as it goes down and showing good evidence of permanency. He will go on to Ogden to consult with his backers in regard to making an immediate shipment.

The Jobbers committee of Salt Lake and Ogden who are going to look over the proposed freighting road between Caliente and Kawich, passed through town today enroute west. They expressed themselves as very sanguine of successful trade conditions in the new districts west of here and will make every effort to gain and control the trade of Goldfield, Lida and Kawich via the new line.

Representatives of New York capitalists are in town looking over several groups of claims near Caliente with an idea of investment. They are looking for large low-grade properties and that is just what they will find in the vicinity of Caliente, no high-grade values having been found in this locality, although with depth they give fair promise of increased values.

Salt Lake Mining Review (Utah)
April 30, 1905

George Crismon, one of the officers of the noted Utah mine, of Fish Springs, has secured a valuable mining property near Hiko in Lincoln county, Nevada.

CALIENTE NEWS

[Special Correspondence]

Death of Dr. C. A. Blanchard

Caliente, Nevada, May 13, 1905.--Dr. C. A. Blanchard, a well-known dentist, aged about 40 years, died here last evening of congestion of the lungs after an illness of three weeks. He was attended by one of his oldest friends, Dr. J. W. Smith, but he was unable to save the patient as the trouble was augmented by years of heart trouble. Deceased left a letter directed to Bishop Lee requesting that he be buried at Panaca by the Mormon church, of which he was an elder. Deceased leaves a wife and little, girl resident at Woodstock, Oregon, and a brother and sister at West Plains, Mo.

Deceased was well and favorably known in Lincoln county, where he has pursued his profession for years.

Col. H. P. Maxson, president; P. S. Triplett, secretary of the Nevada board of land commissioners, have been in Caliente for several days in company with Dr. Kennedy, professor of botany of the Nevada State University, looking up the conditions along the Salt Lake route for the location of a site for a branch agricultural farm. They decided to go to Moapa and look over land there for this purpose, having decided that the early frosts at Caliente would dispose of this as a site for the purpose and believe that the vicinity of Moapa will be most favorable for their purpose, although they do not think the site will be definitely settled upon during this trip.

Miss Annie Sparks, for the past three months visiting with Mrs. W. J. Lee, of Caliente, left this week for her home at Santa Rosa, Cal., via the Salt Lake route and Los Angeles.

H. W. Underhill sold a 50-foot lot on Clover street to J. McManus, a Los Angeles merchant, for $800 cash. Mr. McManus has also taken an option on a 5-acre tract of townsite property embracing the new hot springs here from Chas. Culverwell, senior, for $5000.

Rev. Albert Bartley, Methodist minister, held his first services here last Sunday and the meetings were well attended. He intends remaining here and building the first church ever located in Lincoln county.

A group of free-gold mines were located this week twelve miles south of Caliente and two miles from the railroad, showing a mountain of $12 ore.

The new stone hotel building erected by James A. Denton was opened for business this week with a ball and banquet.

W. J. Lee has been appointed agent for Lincoln county for the Pacific Coast Steel and Wire company.

A carload of ice, first of the season, was shipped from here to Las Vegas this week and brought from $2 to $2.50 per hundred.

George Fetterman, of the Caliente Mercantile company is sending out six-horse teams regularly daily with supplies to the Kawich country from Caliente.

Sidewalks and awnings are being added to business properties all along Clover street and the railroad company is erecting twelve fine residence cottages for their employes.

Peter Delmue sold his meat market and lot this week to Hans Olson for $900 cash.

Samples of free gold ore from the Burnside group, west of Caliente, were brought in today by Morris and Nelson showing assay values of $145 per ton.

The railroad people started running a fence the length of Spring street taking up one half of the road, but were stopped in their work by C. O. Whittemore, general attorney for the road, who passed through town with the Commercial club excursion, owing to a protest made by property owners against the establishment of a fence through the important street.

It is reported that Frank Palmer, president of the Louisiana Purchase Mining and Milling company, of Caliente, has given an option on twenty-three oil claims wich he is interested in at St. George, Utah, to the Standard Oil company for a large amount.

Las Vegas Age
May 27, 1905

Sure Thing

The first car of merchandise from California billed to Caliente arrived on one of the freight trains last Saturday. The Los Angeles wholesalers are an enterprising lot of business men, and unless the Salt Lake dealers wake up the entire trade of Southern Nevada will soon be in the hands of the Californians.—Caliente Express.

For reliable local news—THE AGE; $3 the year, three months, $1.

Deseret News (Utah)
June 6, 1905

GOLD ORE NEAR CALIENTE.

Strike Made Near Nevada Town Creates A Little Excitement.

Special Correspondence,

Caliente, Nev., June 5.—About two weeks ago, a couple of prospectors, who had been looking over the hills near Caliente for the past two months, discovered an immense ledge of gold bearing rock. Returns received from local assayers, as well as from others in Salt Lake and Denver, shows values of $11.20, an average taken from over 25 samples. The lowest returns obtained were $4.80 in gold, and the highest $14.10. A tunnel has been started; it is now in 10 feet. The ledge is over 40 feet wide and can be traced for 3,400 feet; at this point it dips and rises again about half a mile away.

Considerable excitement exists in Caliente, and a large number of claims have been staked off. Colorado parties who have seen the property have offered $50,000 for the ground, but it has been refused.

Intermountain Catholic (Utah)
June 10, 1905

Obituary.

Connervey.

John C. Connervey of Caliente was drowned at Twin Falls, Ida., Sunday. Mr. Connervey met his death by falling into the water while crossing the bridge at night. The night was unusually dark and, although Mr. Connervey's cries for help were heard and immediately responded to, the rescuers were unable to render him any assistance. The body was recovered the following morning. The remains are now at the undertaking parlors of O'Donnell. Funeral announcements will be made later. Mr. Connervey was in the employ of the Oregon Short Line as bridge foreman.

Mrs. Loftus came up from Caliente to attend the funeral of John C. Connorvey, who fell from a bridge at Twin Falls last Sunday and was drowned in the river beneath.

Salt Lake Mining Review (Utah)
June 15, 1905

Frank Swindler, of DeLamar, Nevada, superintendent for the Bamberger-DeLamar Mining company, has been in Salt Lake of late on mining business.

Emery County News (Utah)
June 24, 1905

Prospectors are not leaving there on account of the heat and lack of water. Where there is plenty of grass water and timber although al of these items are scarce in Nevada prospecting is all right. I didn't go north of Caliente and Las Vegas because of reports I got from returning miners and prospectors from whom I learn that water is selling at Bullfrog and Rhyolyte for $2 per barrel, hay is selling from $110 to $120 per ton, and other necessaries are proportionately high. Beatty is best fixed for water of any of the real mining camps. The freight rate on ore from Bullfrog to Las Vegas is $60 a ton hence there will be little mining at that and some of the other camps until a railroad pushes in and cuts down the freight charges.

Deseret News (Utah)
July 5, 1905

LUND, NEVADA.

GOOD OIL PROSPECTS.

Experts from Bakersfield Make Locations—Death from Spinal Meningitis.

Special Correspondence.

Lund, Nev., June 29.—Rulon L., son of
Geo. E. and Emily A. Burgess, died
June 24 of spinal meningitis. The fu-
neral was held June 27, the speakers
were Elder Robert Reid and Bishop O.
H. Snow.

A short time ago some prospectors
came here from Tonopah, and after
they had been here a few days it was
learned that they were oil experts from
Bakersfield, Cal. They claim there are
good prospects here for oil fields, and
that it will only be a matter of time
until there will be an oil boom here.
They located a number of sections of
land.

Salt Lake Mining Review (Utah)
July 15, 1905

Frank Wilson, the discoverer of the great
DeLamar mines at DeLamar, Nevada, and
the April Fool, of the same camp, has returned to Salt Lake from an extended visit
to southern Nevada camps.

Las Vegas Age
July 29, 1905

CALIENTE CULLINGS

Pioche Railroad, New Shops and Round House

[Special Correspondence]

The much talked of branch line from Caliente to Pioche is promised within the next sixty days and work will probably begin on restoring the former grade between the two towns.

New machinery, drill presses, lathes, etc., have been received by the railroad here and installed in the machine shops for use in repairing engines and cars at this point.

The 17-stall round house at Caliente is rapidly nearing completion and will be in commission within the coming month.

Benj. Sanders, district attorney, spent a few days in town this week looking over the school bond question and awarding contract for erection of the new building.

Location work has been completed on the group of gold claims known as the Gold Bug group 12 miles west of Caliente and the claims recorded this week.

W. J. Lee has taken the agency for Lincoln county for the Pacific Coast wire fence company of San Francisco and is furnishing fencing at about one-half usual price, laid down anywhere along the line of the Salt Lake road.

Mr. and Mrs. Sibert who recently purchased the properties of the Caliente Gold Mining Company have gone to Los Angeles for a short visit. They expect to return inside of two weeks and put a gang at work on the claims.

The morning passenger trains from Salt Lake to Los Angeles have been running in two sections for the past two weeks to accomodate the immense passenger traffic.

The Doppes King Mining Co's properties eleven miles east of Caliente have been attached and advertised for sale by F. A. Palmer, vice-president of the company.

Salt Lake Mining Review (Utah)
July 30, 1905

THE BAMBERGER-DELAMAR.

Word comes from DeLamar, Nevada, that most important disclosures have been made of late in the property of the Bamberger-DeLamar Gold Mining company of that place, and that the discoveries made have added greatly to the value and life of this magnificent mine, which has produced its millions in the past, and which promises, in the future, to more than duplicate its past record.

The recent strike in this mine, The Mining Review is informed, was made on the 700-foot level at a point believed to be the juncture of the DeLamar and April Fool veins, or ledges. The ore body, it is stated, is seventy feet in width, and will average $13 in gold to the ton, which is a profitable product to handle, and especially so when it is stated that the company's big reduction works can make money in the treatment of $4 ore. But this is not all, even though this is good enough, for it is rumored that three feet of the vein averages $350 to the ton in the yellow metal while one foot of it goes $1,070. If The Mining Review's informant is correct, and his information came from a trustworthy source, the Bamberger-DeLamar mine is bigger and greater than it ever was before.

In still another way the company is forging to the front on the top wave of success, as if one big strike were not enough in one month, for it appears that the company has another bonanza proposition in a different portion of the district. The news of this new acquisition is given out by the Lode, of DeLamar, which says: During the past week ore assaying $10,000 to the ton has been brought to town. The discovery was made between DeLamar and Rock Springs, a pump station of the Bamberger-DeLamar Gold Mining company. The company has made several locations. A general stampede to the new Eldorado is now taking place. DeLamar is destined to be the leading gold camp of Nevada. By our next issue we hope to be able to give our readers a more detailed account of this marvelous strike.

Las Vegas Age
August 12, 1905

The famous hot springs at Caliente seem to be failing. The flow is now smaller than ever known.

A brick round house of 17 stalls is nearly ready for use, part of which will be used for repair shops.

The prospects surrounding Caliente have not been developed. The owners hope for the establishment of a smelter, but the railroad will profit more by carrying ore to Salt Lake.

Ex-Senator Denton and son run good stages from the Denton Hotel at Caliente to Pioche and De Lamar connecting with trains.

The distance from Caliente to Pioche, the county seat, is thirty miles by stage, and round trip costs $7.00.

The Denton Hotel at Caliente is a substantial stone structure, a credit to the town and the Ex-Senator alike.

Caliente is well supplied with water, which might be made to yield pressure for fire purposes.   TRAVELER.

TAX RATE

Tax rates in Lincoln county for 1905 are: County, 2.05; Pioche, $3.25; De-Lamar, $3.10 and Caliente, $3.40, on each $100 valuation. Taxes are due November 6, 1905, and become delinquent December 4, 1905, when 10 per cent will be added.

Board of equalization meets third Monday in September to first Monday in October.

Deseret News (Utah)
October 4, 1905

MINERS EXCURSION RATES.

Ho! For the Mining Center of the West via "The Salt Lake Route."

Commencing October 1st, daily excursions will be run from Salt Lake to Nevada's great mineral belt at following rates.

Caliente and return $15.50
Moapa and return 24.80
Las Vegas and return 26.86
Good Springs and return ... 31.25
Nippeno and return 33.30
Final Limit 30 days from date of sale.

City Ticket Office, 17 W. 2nd South.
J. L. MOORE,
Dist. Pass. Agt.

COUNTY COMMISSIONERS

The board then convened as county commissioners, with all members present. Minutes of last meeting read and approved.

Two bills of Caliente school house, allowed on the 18th, were declared illegal and reallowed in proper form signed by the chairman.

Reports of officers for the quarter and month of September were read and approved.

Transfers of money were made as follows: From general fund to jury fund, $1500.00; general county to current expense fund, $1,000.00; general county to salary fund, $700.00; general county to indigent fund, $100.00.

All bills as per register of claims allowed.

Hugh Percy and C. C. Corkhill, representing Las Vegas Age, appeared and requested the fulfillment of the printing contracts awarded The Age August 8th, maintaining that the rescinding of said contracts at the September meeting was unwarranted. After considerable discussion the board ordered that the legal advertising contract stand as made, but that the job printing contract be submitted to competitive bids. Bond for $500 for faithful performance of advertising contract was approved.

A notice was served of the withdrawal of over one-half of the bondsmen of H. J. Goodrich, Clerk and Treasurer. H. J. Goodrich then, by proper notice to the board, relinquished balance of bondsmen that had not withdrawn from further liability on the bond. Eugene Goodrich was then appointed to serve as acting Clerk and Treasurer until such time as a regular appointment will be made according to law by Board of Commissioners, or until such time as H. J. Goodrich furnish a new bond.

The board, on order of the court, drew 100 names for members of trial jury.

Bids were opened for furnishing thirty-five cords of wood. Three bids were received and a contract let to J. H. Peaslee at $5.75 per cord.

In the matter of special tax levy for Caliente public school bonds, it was ordered that an extra levy of $1.05 be made to meet interest, etc., said levy making a total special school tax of $1.45 on each $100.00 valuation in Caliente school district. Said tax is for 1905.

Petition asking for the appointment of H. H. Church as justice of the peace for Logan and Moapa received and Clerk ordered to notify petitioners that J. Houghton has not resigned and no vacancy yet declared.

In the matter of justice of the peace of Caliente, J. A. Denton's resignation was received, and all official acts legalized during his term of office.

A special school tax levy for Bunkerville was made at the rate of 45c on each $100.00, effective in 1905.

M'CARTHY IS SET AT LIBERTY.

Man Charged With the Murder Of Joseph Mulholland Found Not Guilty by a Jury.

SHOOTING WAS JUSTIFIABLE.

Had Been Pursued by Deputy Constable and Threatened With Death if He Did Not Leave Town.

(Special to the "News.")

Caliente, Nev., Oct. 25.—William McCarthy, charged with the killing of Joseph Mulholland at Las Vegas Sept. 1, came to trial at Ploche before Hon. Judge Brown and the following named jurors: O. B. Landon, Ed. F. Fruedenthal, Arthur Gentry, W. O. Huston, H. P. Heminger, Dave Jenkins, Carl Fernandi, Charles Atkinson, W. C. Bowman, F. E. Edwards, George Connolly and C. E. Lytle. The state was represented by Prosecuting Atty. Sanders and the defense had M. M. Warner of the firm of Warner & Davis of Salt Lake and Atty. Horsey of Ploche.

STORY OF THE KILLING.

At the time of the shooting newspaper reports had it that the killing was unprovoked and a cold blooded murder, but the evidence detailed by witnesses both for the state and the defense disclosed an entirely different state of facts. Mulholland, the deceased, was a deputy constable at Las Vegas and as such served as night watchman. On the night of the killing he had been drinking heavily and on account of his drunken condition he so far forgot himself as to assault McCarthy with a revolver, frequently pointing it at him and threatening to kill McCarthy, and without cause or justification locked him up in the town jail, which was not a fit place for a human being to be put into. Later he liberated McCarthy with an injunction to leave town and never speak of the occurrence and saying to McCarthy that if he did not leave town that night he would kill him in the morning.

TRIED TO AVOID TROUBLE.

The evidence showed plainly that McCarthy tried to avoid trouble and begged Mulholland not to follow him, but to let him alone. The evidence further showed that Mulholland had told others that he was going to kill McCarthy before morning. About six in the morning Mulholland followed McCarthy into Arthur Fry's saloon and made an effort to draw his gun, when McCarthy being prepared and watching for the assault, fired three shots into Mulholland, any one of which would have proved fatal.

CASE HOTLY CONTESTED.

The case was hotly contested on both sides. It was submitted to the jury at 6 p. m. Tuesday and the jury promptly returned a verdict of not guilty. To the people who have read the reports of this case heretofore published, the verdict will be a surprise, but to those who attended the trial and heard the evidence the verdict was only as they predicted it would be.

Deseret News (Utah)
November 10, 1905

An additional force of men will be set at work on the Scottish Chief mine, five miles north of Caliente, Nev.

Las Vegas Age
November 11, 1905

CALIENTE

The Salt Lake Railroad is the backbone of Caliente. The community has developed to the proportions warranted by the railroad payroll and appears to be satisfied to remain within this limit.

About 250 men have been employed by the railroad during the past year. Construction work is about completed. The permanent payroll will probably not exceed 100.

Caliente is situated in a small valley almost completely surrounded by hills. There is but a limited area adapted to townsite purposes, yet no lots have sold for $100 per front foot.

The railroad company has erected a couple of dozen cottages for the use of its employes. The buildings are aligned in a monotonous row, the same as army barracks. The precise line of uniform closets in the rear loom up conspicuously from the main business street.

Denton Heights is the latest addition to the community. Several small dwellings have recently been erected there.

Col. Jim Brown and his weekly comic paper keep the natives from lapsing into a state of complete ennui.

The stage lines to the county seat connect only with trains from and for the east. Citizens of the county who have occasion to visit Pioche must lay over in Caliente about 18 hours going and coming, or else hire a special conveyance.

It is snowing a little here today, Nov. 5th. Snow seldom stays long on the ground in the valley, but in the mountains and even in the low hills it often remains all winter. Early snow is most likely to remain.

Caliente now has the finest school house in Lincoln county. It is built of native stone with walls 21 inches thick. The building is one story in height, containing two good-sized rooms, with a seating capacity of about sixty pupils. The cost to the community was about

$7,000, which was raised by a special tax levy.

MARRIAGE OF DE LAMAR.

Commenting upon the recent marriage of Captain J. R. DeLamar to Madame Nordica, the Lode, of DeLamar, Nevada, says:

Captain DeLamar, after whom was named the famous Bamberger-DeLamar mine, and in fact our town, is about to lead to the altar Madame Nordica, the world-famed opera singer. Although Madame Nordica's "stage name" is foreign, she is a native of America, having been born at Farmington, Me., about forty-six years ago. The captain is past fifty, and together with his little daughter by his first wife, has already occupied the first two floors of his Murray Hill home, which, when completed, will cost more than $1,000,000. The captain and Madame Nordica should end their days with a happy career, as they have both had a checkered matrimonial experience, and are both worthy of a happy old age. The madame has been married twice before and the captain once. Many happy days for Mr. and Mrs. DeLamar is the wish of the Lode.

LUND, NEVADA.

Farewell Social Tendered to Elder William A. Terry.

Special Correspondence.

Lund, Nev. Nov. 13.—Last Friday evening the members of the Lund ward tendered a farewell party to Elder Wm. A. Terry, who will leave Lund Nov. 16, on a mission to the central states. A fine program was rendered, consisting of singing, speeches, recitations, dancing and refreshments.

Bishop O. H. Snow and Counselor A. R. Whitehead of the Lund ward will leave Lund today for Salt Lake City.

BIG COMPANY FOR CALIENTE.

Colorado and Missouri Capitalists Will Operate Many Mining Claims.

FORTY-STAMP GOLD MILL.

Large Body of Ore Already Opened up In Mines, With Values About $20 Per Ton.

Word comes up from Caliente of the formation of a big mining company company composed of noted capitalists of Colorado and Missouri. The company is named the Josephine Mining company and its promoters will start mining on an extensive scale.

In speaking of the company the Caliente Express has the following to say:

"Among the names of the officers are found some of the leading men in both Missouri and Colorado. The president is a large mine operator in the North American British possession, while Mr. Hall of Carthage, Mo., is recognized as one of the successful financiers and capitalists of which his state boasts the most. The other gentlemen are all well known and highly respected in their several states, being all of trained business experience together with possessing the qualifications for handling an enterprise of such worth, with the properties presenting the possibilities of a future that they do. This enterprise is certainly inviting."

"There are a great many locations in the Josephine Consolidated Gold Mining company, the most promising, and the following are those upon which the most development work is being done for the present: The Little Johnnie, the Tilton, Randolph and the Gold Coin. Some good ore is being taken from the Little Johnnie as development progresses, and this ore is made ready for shipment as they take it out of the mine. The ore body is of considerable width, varying all the way from 5 feet to as high as 50, and the ore varies from $20 to $35 to the ton, and these returns are gained by careful sampling and returns on assays done both here in Caliente and at the City of the Saints. It not only carries that value in the most precious metals, but in addition the ore goes 45 per cent in lead, the gold values being $8.50, being a pretty good thing for Caliente and only the commencement of a mining future for the place."

A 40-stamp mill is one of the possibilities of the near future in connection with the development of the company's mines. The company is operating in what is known as the Chief Mountain district, about five miles from Caliente. The ground has been honey-combed with locations all the way from town and far on the other side of where operations are being confined.

RICH CALIENTE ORE.

Quartz Runs $160 to the Ton in the Three Pines Mine.

Word comes up from Caliente that Hewetson and Landers of the Three Pines group of claims near that place have uncovered a two-foot vein of gold ore which runs $463.20 to the ton. The quartz is filled with hematite of iron to which is attached nuggets of the yellow metal. The two are on the way to New York with several sacks of samples to exhibit to their New York backers. A 10-stamp mill will be installed at the mine during the winter.

BASEBALL

Las Vegas May Play Caliente Christmas Day

There will be a practice game of baseball next Sunday at the public square between the Eagles' nine and a picked nine outside that order.

Local baseball enthusiasts are endeavoring to arrange a game with Caliente to be played in Las Vegas Christmas day. Practice games will be played frequently and the best players will be chosen to go against the visitors from the north, if they can be persuaded to come.

It is said that Fred. L. Fallas will be one of the star performers provided enough umpires can be found to keep him pacified.

COLD MILLION FOR NEVADA-UTAH.

Col. John Weir is Said to Have Raised This Sum for Pioche Operations.

READY TO BUILD RAILROAD.

Money for Construction of Feeder for Salt Lake Route is Available— Col. Weir Coming West.

A local mining man claims to be in possession of information from a private source that the Nevada-Utah Mines & Smelters corporation has a million dollars in cold cash to carry ward its campaign at Pioche and that Col. John Weir will shortly arrive on the scene within a few weeks, when orders will be given to open the year's campaign with more vigor than ever.

It is claimed that the construction of the proposed branch line of the Salt Lake route from Callente and Pioche will commence at an early day.

It is said the Nevada-Utah corporation is ready to put up the cash, if it has not already done so, for the cost of building the new line, which is to be returned in the shape of credits on freight hauled out of the camp for that mining company. When the work starts, it is the intention to push it forward as rapidly as possible, so that it will be ready for operation early in the coming summer.

The grade between Callente and Pioche was done a number of years ago and with repair can soon be made ready for the laying of rails.

Las Vegas Age
January 13, 1906

COMMISSIONERS' MEETINGS

The Caliente Express says that the monthly meetings of the Board of County Commissioners are not authorized by law. Section 2016 of the Statutes of Nevada says:

"The meetings of the Board of County Commissioners shall be held at the county seats of their respective counties on the first Mondays in January, April, July and October of each year, and shall continue from time to time until all the business before them is disposed of."

The statute also provides for special meetings whenever a majority of the board shall so order.

Salt Lake Herald
January 21, 1906

TWO NEW MINING COMPANIES.

Both Made Up of Salt Lake Talent to Operate in Nevada.

Articles of incorporation of the Hiko-Nevada Mining company of Salt Lake were filed in the office of the county clerk yesterday. The company has a capital stock of $500,000, in $1 shares, and owns the Irene, Irene No. 2, Utah Boy, Maxfield, Maxfield No. 1, Stanley, Stanley No. 1, Stanley No. 2, Dilworth and Dilworth No. 1 claims in Pahranagat Lake district, Lincoln county, Nevada. A. M. Gordon is president; J. H. Lovendale, vice president; Edgar S. Darling, secretary and treasurer, who, with L. E. Maxfield and Thomas L. Smith, constitute the board of directors.

The Mount Alcott Copper company of Salt Lake also filed its articles. It has a capital stock of $1,000,000 divided into $2 shares, and owns the Shamrock, Woodside, Woodside No. 1, Alice K., Pot Metal, Shoofly, Eddie, Arthur K., Copper Queen and Ina C., claims in Yellow Pine district, Lincoln county, Nevada. Oscar K. Lewis is president, John A. Street vice president, S. H. Green secretary and treasurer, who, with James D. Kenneily and Walter C. Lewis constitute the board of directors.

CALIENTE, NEVADA

TERRIFIC EXPLOSION

Nearly Two Tons of Giant Powder Set Off by Some Miscreant.

Caliente, Nev., Feb. 9.—This morning about 3 oclock this town was shaken from end to end to its very foundations by a terrific explosion of nearly two tons of giant powder. Though nearly everybody was frightened, no one was hurt. The explosion occurred just outside of town at the mouth of the Sibert mine. There are two tunnels at the Sibert mine used as powder magazines, one of which was used by the Caliente Mercantile company, containing 3,400 pounds of giant powder, and the other by the Sibert Mining company, which contained 500 pounds. The two tunnels are some considerable distance apart, but the powder in both places was exploded simultaneously. Men were working in the tunnel but were not injured.

Everything about the premises other than where the men were working in the tunnel was blown away or destroyed. This includes all of the new supplies recently shipped from Salt Lake and Los Angeles for Sibert property. From all indications the powder was exploded by some one who had it in for the Sibert company. Fifty feet of fuse, a candlestick and a candle that were left in the tunnel in which the men were working were removed by some one and it is believed that they were used in the dastardly deed. Sheriff Johnson is on the ground, and he is giving the matter his personal attention.

There is a suspicion as to who did the job and it is probable that an arrest will be made of the suspicious character unless his mysterious actions during the last few days can be explained away.

The Timpiaute Mining company, operating near Hiko, Nevada, has placed an order with the Salt Lake Hardware company for a whim and skip, and 1,200 ore sacks.

E. P. Gordon, of Pioche, Nevada, is installing a gasoline engine and an Adams electric drill at the Prince mine. The machinery was ordered from the Salt Lake Hardware company.

Henry Lowry, who is working the Magnolia mine at DeLamar, Nevada, on a lease, will soon be in the Salt Lake market with a shipment of good ore.

SLIDE ON SAN PEDRO.

Scenery Came Down on Salt Lake Route Hindering Traffic.

The Salt Lake Route was somewhat demoralized on Saturday and yesterday owing to a landslide which occurred near Caliente following the recent rains. Several tons of rock and interesting scenic bric a brac came down and piled up on the grade in a fashion which made the crew of an advancing freight train vacate the engine and caboose and take to the sagebrush. When the crash came a few seconds later the engine and several cars left the rails. Word was sent back to Caliente and a wrecking outfit and all the available help left for the scene. It was over 12 hours before the track was clear for traffic.

As a consequence the Los Angeles Limited, due here yesterday afternoon, did not arrive in this city until 1:15 this afternoon.

BANK AT CALIENTE

Articles of incorporation have been filed for a bank at Caliente, with an authorized capital of $100,000, to be known as the Lincoln County Bank.

The original incorporators are Homer C. Hansen, a Los Angeles capitalist, and Geo. C. Fetterman, the well known merchant and forwarder at Caliente, and F. R. McNamee, of Delamar, Nevada.

There will be a directorate of seven, composed of the leading citizens of Lincoln county.

DELAMAR

(From the Lode)

J. A. Denton has again secured the the contract for carring the mail between Delamar and Caliente.

Manager F. P. Swindler and Mr. Rogers, consulting engineer of the Bamberger-DeLamar Company are here inspecting the mine.

Charles Lytle of Eagle Valley arrived in Delamar on Friday with beef cattle for R. J. Gordon. He reports a great number of prospectors in the hills around Fay and State Line.

MRS. CULVERWELL MOVED FURNITURE

Suit Now Brought for Board Due Mrs. Culverwell No. 2.

COURT CASE POSTPONED

Keep of One Hotel May Have to Pay Bill Due Wife Who Took Her Place.

Republican Special.

Caliente, Nev., March 10.—G. C. Collins, proprietor of the Mint saloon, whose wife recently returned from the east, rented housekeeping rooms from Mrs. Charles Culverwell at the Caliente hotel and innocently started troubles in the Culverwell family that may be aired in court. Mrs. Culverwell, proprietor of the Caliente hotel, was divorced some time ago from Charles Culverwell, proprietor of the Culverwell hotel, of this city, and when she entered the apartments in the Caliente hotel that she had rented to Mr. and Mrs. Collins and stripped them of all furnishings in the absence of her tenants, Mr. and Mrs. Collins went to the Culverwell hotel, where they boarded at the table spread by Mrs. Culverwell No. 2. When he made the change, Mr Collins immediately brought suit against Mrs. Culverwell No. 1 for board and costs, which, if successful, will result in Mrs. Culverwell No. 1 paying Mrs. Culverwell No. 2 for the good things her former tenants say are due them from the table of Mrs. Culverwell No. 1. The case was postponed in court and Mrs. Culverwell No. 1 was placed under $250 bond to keep the peace pending the settlement of the case.

A surprise party was given to Mr. and Mrs. Keats Wednesday night by the prominent people of Caliente. After several hours of whist, high five and social chat, supper was served.

A lunch counter is being built at the end of the passenger depot in Caliente. Two young men from Denver, Colo., will have charge of the place for the railroad company.

TRAINS DELAYED BY BIG WASHOUT

Los Angeles Limited Will Arrive Forty-Eight Hours Late.

WAS HELD NEAR CALIENTE

Train Service on Other Lines Nearly Normal But Telegraph Wires Are Still Disabled.

+ + + + + + + + + + + + + + + + + + +

Republican Special.

Caliente, March 14.—As the result of the severest rain and wind storm ever experienced here, several miles of tracks on the Salt Lake Route near here were washed out and all trains are waiting on both sides of the washout with no definite assurance as to when they can move. The flats around this place are all under water.

+ + + + + + + + + + + + + + + + + + +

With the exception of the Salt Lake Route, railway traffic from Salt Lake was resumed on nearly a normal basis following the severe storms of the two previous days. On the Salt Lake Route, however, extensive washouts delayed traffic so that no trains from Los Angeles have arrived since Tuesday afternoon, when the Los Angeles Limited came in about one-hour late. At 2 o'clock this morning word was received that the damage to the roadbed near Caliente would be repaired sufficiently to allow the trains through by 7 o'clock this morning and that the Los Angeles Limited due here yesterday afternoon would probably be in early this evening. To make this possible all the men available were rushed to the scene of the washout from Las Vegas and Caliente and work was continued all night with the aid of torches.

The trains from the east over the Rio Grande Western were one to two hours late, but the trouble was on the Denver & Rio Grande, east of Grand Junction, there being no delay at this end of the line. The Oregon Short Line reported only slight variations from their regular schedule, but telegraph wires on this road as well as on the Salt Lake Route were almost entirely out of commission.

Intern-Mountain Republican (Utah)
March 19, 1906

JAPS KILLED IN EXPLOSION NEAR CALIENTE.

Republican Special.

Caliente. Nev., March 18.— Three Japanese laborers were killed by the premature explosion of a blast here today while engaged in removing a rock slide from the track of the Salt Lake Route at tunnel No. 5, twelve miles east of Caliente. Thirty tons of rock fell on the track about 3 o'clock this morning. Good progress is being made in clearing at away. Train No. 2 will probably be about two hours late and train No. 8 about twelve hours late into Salt Lake.

RAILS TO PIOCHE
UNDER DISCUSSION

President of Nevada-Utah Recalled While on His Way Home.

MEETING AT LOS ANGELES

Agreement Will Probably Be Reached With Construction to Begin on Branch at Early Day.

Advices from the Pacific coast indicate that negotiations between the officials of the San Pedro and those of the Utah-Nevada Consolidated Mining company, looking to the construction of a branch from Caliente to Pioche that shall afford the wealth of the camp an all-rail outlet to the furnaces of this valley, are to be reopened the present week at the offices of the former in Los Angeles. According to particulars, Col. John Weir, president of the Nevada-Utah, had reached San Francisco on his detour of the blockade on the Salt Lake Route on his way to the offices of his company in this city, when he was asked to return to the southern metropolis and when seen by a Salt Lake acquaintance on the Pacific, he was of the impression that terms upon which an agreement could be reached had been decided on.

In the interview and the result of it there is a great deal of interest in this locality, as not a few of the Pioche properties are controlled here, and with a line of railway such as is projected, a large tonnage is promised by them. It was said by one of these interests during the day that Col. Weir has signified his company's willingness to provide the money with which to construct the link but that the principals have been unable thus far to agree on the tariff on ores and supplies. It is known that the Nevada-Utah is financially prepared to execute its portion of any agreement to which it shall subscribe and in the meeting the present week local interest is quite acute.

Meanwhile, the development of the company's properties in this state and Nevada, is progressing with the most satisfactory results.

JAPS KILLED ON SALT LAKE ROUTE.

Three Men Blown to Pieces While Blasting out the Rock Slide.

NEAR TUNNEL NUMBER SIX.

Their Bodies Brought Into Salt Lake For Burial—Tourist Dies on Train.

During the operations yesterday in cleaning up the rock slide at tunnel No. 6 near Caliente, a big blast was touched off and after the smoke, dirt and rock settled it was found that three Japanese section hands had been blown into eternity and several others had been hurt. The bodies of the unfortunate men were brought into Salt Lake on the delayed train this morning and turned over to the local Japanese colony here for burial.

Passengers coming in this morning over the Salt Lake Route report that the rockslide was a big proposition but it has now been cleaned up sufficiently to permit the passage of trains. At the places where the bad washouts occurred trains proceed at snail's pace. A big force of available laborers is at work and it will be some time before repairs of a permanent nature will be completed. To add to the embarassment of the operating department, one of the trains while passing a soft spot had the misfortune to derail two cars and in consequence trains due to arrive from the west this afternoon and tomorrow morning will be late.

The body of James A. Owen, a tourist who was accompanied by his mother, was shipped from this city last night to Port Amboy, N. J. The gentleman was traveling for his health and while returning home got caught in the washout tie-up below Caliente and succumbed before the train could be released.

Salt Lake Route Trains Reach Point Ten Miles From Caliente.

SAVE PERISHABLE GOODS

Road Will Not Be Open For Through Traffic Until May 1 at Earliest Date.

Repairs on the Salt Lake Route were completed as far west as Minto, ten miles this side of Caliente, yesterday, five miles being the result of the days' work. The train that left at midnight last night will run as far as Minto as No. 1 and return as No. 2 today, carrying passengers for all intermediate points.

A stage line has been established for the ten miles from Minto to Caliente that will be in operation until the repairs are completed to Caliente which, with no further delays, will be accomplished April 7. The length of time that will be necessary to complete the next ten miles of repairs southwestward is explained by the fact that the condition over that part of the tracks is the worst in the remaining sixty miles that are out of commission.

No Through Traffic Before May 1.

In this short distance between Minto and Caliente there are several bridges washed away, and about one mile of track in the ten will have to be rebuilt entirely. It will be impossible to restore the tracks so as to allow through traffic before May 1, and it is believed that the first through train will not reach Salt Lake from Los Angeles before May 10.

In this short distance between Minto and Caliente there are several bridges washed away, and about one mile of track in the ten will have to be rebuilt entirely. It will be impossible to restore the tracks so as to allow through traffic before May 1, and it is believed that the first through train will not reach Salt Lake from Los Angeles before May 10.

The completion of the work on this ten miles means much to the company, as then trains can be run to Caliente, large amounts of stores at that point will be available for further repairs and a considerable amount of rolling stock and bridge supplies will be available from that point.

Save Trainload of Oranges.

The traffic department reports that the train of nineteen cars of oranges and one car of olives caught between two washouts a few miles east of Caliente will be saved through the efforts of the company in opening the doors of the cars and affording ventilation. This train will be moved northward Monday and will be transferred on its way east the following day in good condition.

Several carloads of potatoes, eggs and other perishable freight that were stalled for a few days have been sold to Caliente merchants at current market prices, relieving the railroad of the danger of loss on them and netting the owners as good prices as they would have received had the cars continued to their destinations without delay.

From the south end of the road trains were run out of Las Vegas on time last night, going as far west as Galt, fifty miles from Las Vegas. This point is fifty-two miles from Caliente, leaving a length of track of sixty-two miles still "off the map" so far as present service is concerned. In this distance, however, the length of track actually washed away will not exceed ten miles.

The company was fortunate in having a pile driver and two engines at Caliente that can be worked in the middle of the damaged track, and it now has one on the west end, and another on the east end of the trouble.

Restore Telegraph Service.

Telegraph service on the road, which has been badly crippled since the washouts, has been resumed as far south as Las Vegas and dispatches from that point received yesterday said no condition of famine or serious shortage of supplies had existed so far, either there or in the towns in the vicinity that depended on Caliente as their base of supplies. It is expected that telegraph service through to Los Angeles will be restored today.

Inter-Mountain Republican (Utah)
April 5, 1906

ORANGE TRAIN RELEASED.

Salt Lake Route Completes Repairs to Side Track at Eccles.

The force of 300 men working on the repairs on the Salt Lake Route west of Minto completed the work of raising the tracks over the washouts by means of cribbing as far as Eccles at 8 o'clock last night and a few minutes later the train of nineteen cars of oranges that had been stalled there since March 24 was started east. The train passed Minto at 8:30 and is due in Salt Lake at 4:30 this afternoon.

It was only a few minutes' work to attach engine No. 614 to the train as it was waiting on a side track at Minto, ready for the train, since Sunday.

Another trainload of supplies reached Minto from Salt Lake yesterday afternoon. It is expected that the two engines that brought the orange train as far as Eccles when it was abandoned ten days ago, will be released this morning as there is only one washout of less than 100 feet between them and Eccles. The work of getting into Caliente will have to proceed with wonderful rapidity if that place is reached Friday as there are several washouts in the remaining six miles that are worse than any encountered between Minto and Eccles.

Gangs are working from both ends of the stretch between Eccles and Caliente, however, and dispatches received at the local offices of the road from General Manager Wells at Caliente yesterday said that place would be reached Friday night. Mr. Wells also said he expected that the road would be open for through traffic between Salt Lake and Los Angeles April 11.

SALT LAKE REPAIRS

Road Open to Cana, Ten Miles From Caliente

Surgeon H. L. Hewetson came in from the front Thursday and stated that the construction train was then at Boyd, and will move forward to Cana by tonight.

General Manager Wells, with 1000 men, is pushing the work of reconstruction. With good luck, says Dr. Hewetson, the line will be open to Caliente by the end of next week.

Considerable sickness results from constant exposure of the men, but no serious accidents have occurred.

The entire construction force and trains of the L. V. & T. have been sent to the assistance of the Salt Lake and work on the new line is suspended.

LANDSLIDE SOUTH

Thursday's Salt Lake train from Los Angeles was delayed several hours by a landslide on the Santa Fe tracks between Daggett and San Bernardino.

Deseret News (Utah)
April 7, 1906

STILL STORMING NEAR CALIENTE.

Operations on Repair Work on Salt Lake Route Are Hampered Thereby.

ARE THREE MORE WASHOUTS.

Freshet Came Down the Canyon Yesterday Damaging the Repair Work Already Completed.

Operations on repair work on the Salt Lake Route in the vicinity of Caliente have again received a setback occasioned by rains and accompanying freshets which came down the canyon causing three washouts of the dirt dumped into the grade following the trouble of March 24. Accordingly communication with Caliente was not re-established today as anticipated. The work train at this end was caught between two washouts between Acoma and Minto and the gangs today are patching up the breaks. Some small washouts are also reported in the Meadow Valley wash where there is a large force of men working to meet the gangs pushing west.

Reports from Caliente this morning state that it is still raining but it is believed that the worst is over.

The fact that both men and material for the Las Vegas & Tonopah, now pushing on to Bullfrog, have been pressed into service to repair the break will delay the completion of that important feeder.

All railroads are encountering trouble and according to dispatches from Orville, Cal., the recent storms have been so severe that it has been impossible to reach some of the construction camps by team and in consequence provisions are scarce and men are quitting their work and coming out. Landslides and washouts are in order on practically every big western road this week.

Deseret News (Utah)
April 10, 1906

INTO CALIENTE TONIGHT.

Repair Gangs Expect to Reach That Point This Evening.

Work on repairs on the washouts on the Salt Lake Route is being rushed harder than ever. From a dispatch received at the Clark road headquarters from Supt. Van Housen who is at the front, it is learned that the forces at work are straining every muscle to have the line opened to Caliente by this evening. It is a safe proposition that by the time it is necessary to handle the dozen or so Shriner special trains that the line will be open for through business and the Los Angeles limited will be making trips both ways.

Deseret News (Utah)
April 11, 1906

NOW INTO CALIENTE.

First Train Gets in After a Period of Sixteen Days.

The first train to reach Caliente since March 24 pulled into Caliente last evening, and the road is now declared open to that point. There is yet considerable work to be done on the washout repairs, but it is hoped that the worst is now over. With gangs working night and day it is anticipated that the midnight train leaving Salt Lake on Friday night will be able to pull right through to Los Angeles. All energies are being concentrated in the direction of temporary repairs so as to get the trains through, but work will be pushed until the roadbed is brought up to a condition where washouts in future will be practically impossible, owing to the system of rock rip-rapping and concrete culverts.

Deseret News (Utah)
April 12, 1906

CALIENTE, NEVADA

Three Days Downpour Again Floods Country and Much Damage is Done.

Caliente, Nev., April 11.—For 60 hours rain has been falling without cessation, and it is still coming down in torrents, flooding the main business streets, which are all under several inches of water. Business is at a standstill, prospectors are seeking the warmth of saloons, while the railroad tracks are bare of equipment and repairs recently made to the tracks after the big washout are being swept away in the new flood. The damage inflicted by the recent washout is being repeated all along the line of the Salt Lake Route, and attempts to repair tracks and roadbed are meeting with a decided setback by the down-pouring rain.

Emery County News (Utah)
April 14, 1906

Rainfall in Nevada Makes More Trouble for Salt Lake Route

Salt Lake City—Rains falling in Nevada have delayed the work of repairing the Salt Lake Route's tracks near Caliente. Local officials are unable to furnish any information as no news is coming from the scene of the washouts. General Manager R E Wells of the Salt Lake Route is quoted by the Los Angeles papers as saying that the rains have delayed work and undone some of the repairs already made

Salt Lake Mining Review (Utah)
April 30, 1905

Henry Lowrey, of DeLamar, Nevada, leasing at the Magnolia mine near that place, recently sent out a carload of ore that assayed $186 in gold to the ton, the lot bringing him $1,773 above all expenses. Mr. Lowery has two more carloads sacked ready for shipment.

Las Vegas Age
May 12, 1906

AGAINST VEGAS

Las Vegas Times Pulls for Caliente

In Las Vegas Times Jim Blowhard is boosting Caliente at the expense of Las Vegas.

The following paragraphs are taken from the last issue of the Times:

"As a railroad point it (Caliente) is the most important and lively along the whole line, with the exception of Los Angeles and Salt Lake.

"The mineral resources surrounding it are of such an incalculable sort as to make one wonder at the immense possibilities.

"Caliente will be the largest and most thriving town in the State of Nevada before many years. It has the resources. It has the push and the vim to win."

Will the people of Las Vegas continue to support Blowhard at his two-faced game?

Salt Lake Mining Review (Utah)
May 15, 1906

Word comes from DeLamar, Nevada, that a new ore chimney has been found in the Bamberger-DeLamar mine workings that assays from $15 to $300 in gold to the ton.

Deseret News (Utah)
May 16, 1906

CALIENTE, NEVADA

PERISHED IN DEATH VALLEY.

Two Young Eastern Prospectors Die For Want of Water.

Caliente, Nev., May 14.—Joe Constantine, an old prospector of Nevada, who has just returned from a three months' trip into the depths of Death valley, told the Tribune correspondent a gruesome tale of deprivation and death which overtook two young eastern men who preceded him into the death-trap lying at the foot of the Funeral range in the dread valley.

The young fellows, whose names are unknown, but whose trousers are marked, "Walsh, The Tailor," lost their lives somewhere close to the range mentioned and nearly 20 miles from water.

Their animals have not been found, except one pack horse which was partly covered by sand and nothing but skin and bones. The older of the men had evidently gone crazy before dying, his fingers being worn away to the bone on both hands. Near where he was found by Constantine and party he had dug a three or four-foot hole in the sand, and with his naked hands vainly tried to reach water.

The bodies of both were nearly nude, and the younger, a man not over 25 years of age, with gold-filled front teeth, had on him a handsome gold watch of Elgin movement, marked with a monogram ", G. H.," and a seal ring with the letter "H" on the seal.

The bodies were brought out of the valley of death by Constantine and his partners and buried near Carroll Springs.

Copper Near Caliente.

J. T. Wood called on the Express Sunday. Mr. Wood has several prospects about twelve miles from Caliente and three miles from the Clover valley wash. Mr. Wood has a shaft 100 feet down on the Mammoth No. 1 of the Blue Bell group. One of the pleasing features of the property is that the ore is clear across the bottom of the shaft, and thus far Mr. Wood has found neither foot nor hanging wall. The average assay from a sample of the ore across the face of the lead returned $12.90 and that was the very lowest assay ever taken from the lead, and that, too, when copper was selling at only 12 1-4 cents, says the Express of Caliente, on the San Pedro Route.

HAS BIG DEAL ON IN COPPER MINES

Colonel John Weir to Decide the Fate of Another Undertaking.

LEAVES FOR WEST TODAY

Will Return to Devote Much Time to Interests in This State and Over the Line.

Colonel John Weir, under whose intelligent and masterly endeavor the work of the Nevada-Utah Mines & Smelters corporation in this state and Nevada is reaching a point where it must begin the reimbursement of all who are following him, leaves for California today where he will pass on another proposition which has been commended to him and of which the preliminary examination is about to conclude. While the distinguished miner would not divulge the whereabouts of the property it is among the copper-bearing camps of that state and one over which there has been not a little rivalry in the past. Returning from this pilgrimage he will remain in the saddle for a month or more, alternating between the various camps in which his company has acquired interests, and before leaving for the east will have added not a little to their prestige, no doubt.

While the colonel does not believe it discreet at this time to discuss the status of the proposed branch of railway between Pioche and Caliente on the main line of the San Pedro, there is no more doubt of its ultimate consummation than is there that under his touch, Pioche is to be made to repeat the stories of an earlier period.

In the latest development at the properties of the Utah Con., Bingham, in which camp his big company is the possessor of the Last Chance group, Colonel Weir was very much interested as he has all the while contended that intelligent researches in new territory would add immeasurably to the resources of a region that is yet in its infancy. He will visit the camp and spend not a little time there on his return from the west.

HOW JAPS KILLED DEPUTY SHERIFF

Additional Details of His Murder At Caliente Received Today.

VICTIM WAS AN OGDEN MAN.

Collision of Trains Caused the Attack Upon Train Crew and Officer Was Summoned.

Stones and Clubs Were Thrown and When the Officer Responded to Call for Help He Was Shot.

AFTER JAP MURDERER

One Who Killed Deputy Monahan at Caliente Thought to Have Gone East.

Deputy Sheriff J. J. Monahan of Caliente, Nevada, was shot and instantly killed in a fight with a gang of Japanese railroad laborers Tuesday night. A Jap named Fugita, who is supposed to have done the shooting, has left town and is believed to have gone East. Descriptions have been furnished the police authorities throughout the West and it is hoped by the officers at Caliente that he will be arrested.

The row arose when the Japs were on the train and a drawhead was accidentally pulled out and the cars bumped violently, shaking up the Japs. They got very angry and jumped at the train crew with clubs, knives and guns. The sheriff's force was called upon and in suppressing the mob Deputy Sheriff Monahan was shot and killed by some member of the mob.

This is the same gang of Japs that held up a train at Caliente and drove the crew away about one year ago.

The peace officers are doing all in their power to preserve order. Deputy Sheriff Murphy and the district attorney have arrived from Las Vegas to investigate the matter and Attorney Whittemore of the railroad company is now in Caliente looking after the interests of the company.

ANOTHER SMELTER

New York Paper Builds One at Caliente

New York Evening Mail says: No more welcome news has recently come to those interested in Southern Nevada mining properties than that which the Mail is now able to give of the intention of the American Smelting and Refining company to erect a great smelting plant in that section.

At the New York office of Senator W. A. Clark and his San Pedro, Los Angeles and Salt Lake railroad, it is learned that this smelter is to be built at Caliente, Nev., about one hundred miles northwest of Las Vegas, the point from which the Clark branch has been built to Bullfrog.

BLOODY RIOT

Deputy Sheriff Monahan Killed at Caliente

Deputy Sheriff J. J. Monohan was killed at Caliente Tuesday night by a rioting Japanese railroad gang.

The trouble occurred about 10 o'clock. The Japs were riding in freight cars, when the train broke in two, shaking them up. This incensed the foreigners, and they swarmed from the cars, attacking the train men and driving them from their posts. Deputy Sheriff Monahan was summoned and upon attempting to restore order was shot and cut by the rioters. He was removed from the scene and died 20 minutes later.

A vigilance committe was formed and the mob subdued. During the night three of the principal offenders escaped, but were overtaken next morning by an engine with a posse and taken into custody.

Sheriff Johnson was out of the county, and Deputy Sheriff Murphy and District Attorney Horsey, who was in Las Vegas, left for Caliente Wednesday morning to assist in restoring order.

Railroad men are worked up over the outrage and it would not take much to precipitate further trouble.

Salt Lake Telegram (Utah)
July 20, 1906

FINE PERCHERONS FOR NEVADA STOCK FARM

J. P. Gardner is the proud owner of seven head of high-class Percherons, which he has purchased from the pedigree stock farms of Samuel Bishop and Frank Fork, at Lewistown, Ill.

Percherons are regarded by horse fanciers as being among the best animals, and those now in the possession of Mr. Gardner are of the best of their class. Of the seven four are brood mares, the two older ones weighing 1600 pounds each. One is a yearling and one a three-year-old, one an eight-year-old and one a nine-year-old. One is a stallion weighing 1900 pounds. The other two are stallion colts 3 months old.

The pedigrees have not yet arrived, but Mr. Gardner has written his brother, Frank L. Gardner, that there is no better stock in the country.

The animals arrived yesterday and are being stabled on Market street. Saturday morning they will be taken to the Gardner Ranch company's ranch of 8000 acres in Pahranagat valley, Nevada.

Inter-Mountain Republican (Utah)
August 12, 1906

The Road to Pioche Is Positively Assured

Senator Clark Advises Management of Nevada Over His Personal Signature

A cable dispatch to The Republican from Liverpool during the night says that John Weir, president of the Nevada-Utah Copper company, has just received a message from Senator Clark of the San Pedro system which assures him that construction on the long-projected branch from Caliente to Pioche is to begin at once. Perhaps no information will appeal to the interests of that region as does this from Liverpool. It is not necessary, perhaps, to exploit particulars, as they have appeared hitherto in print with such frequency. It means undoubtedly the reclamation of another great mining camp on the margins of the San Pedro system, which has exercised so liberal a policy toward its wards, and that it will be abundantly compensated by the mines of Pioche the Senator, as well as his field representatives, has learned to appreciate after personal investigation.

Eureka Reporter (Utah)
September 14, 1906

The Bristol Mining company operating in the Bristol district in Nevada has shipped a great deal of rich copper ore to the Salt Lake valley smelters and when the railroad is built from Caliente to Pioche the company will become a constant shipper of large consignments

Salt Lake Mining Review (Utah)
August 15, 1906

Fred Faulkner has accepted a position as superintendent of the Bamberger-DeLamar mines at DeLamar, Nevada.

Las Vegas Age
September 15, 1906

CALIENTE'S CANDIDATE

Deputy Sheriff Taylor, of Caliente, candidate for sheriff, is in Las Vegas viewing the political landscape.

CALIENTE CONVENTION

Democrats Name a Strong Ticket With Harmony and Enthusiasm—W. E. Hawkins, of Las Vegas, for Commissioner.

The Democrats of Lincoln county, in convention at Caliente Monday, nominated the following candidates:

THE TICKET

FOR ASSEMBLYMEN

Frank Williams.............Good Springs
Levi Syphus.........................Panaca
J. H. Vaughan ....Searchlight

RECORDER AND AUDITOR

Henry Lee............................Panaca

TREASURER

Ed. W. Clark ....Caliente

CLERK

Wm. E. Orr........................Pioche

PUBLIC ADMINISTRATOR

James Lemoine....................Caliente

DISTRICT ATTORNEY AND SUPT. SCHOOLS

Chas Lee Horsey...................Pioche

SHERIFF

Phillip K. Smith.............Dutch Flat

ASSESSOR

John F. Roeder.....................Pioche

COMMISSIONERS

W. E. Hawkins (long term)...Las Vegas
Geo. T. Banovich (short term)..DeLamar

The convention was called to order at 10:30 o'clock by Chairman Denton of the County Central Committee. Senator Denton made a brief, but forceful, address on Democracy and the duties and opportunities confronting the convention, arousing great enthusiasm.

Levi Syphus, of Panaca, was elected temporary chairman and Wm. E. Orr, of Pioche, temporary secretary. The chair appointed committees on credentials, organization and platform and the convention adjourned until two o'clock p. m. Committees were made up as follows:

Credentials—A J Roeder, H Olson, A O Lee, E T Maxwell, H H Sparks.

Permanent Organization and Order of Business—J A Clark, J H Vaughn, Chas C Corkhill, H P Henniger, E E Smith.

Resolutions and Platform—Frank Williams, F L Reber, J A Denton, J A Nesbitt, Geo Baldwin.

Upon reconvening the credentials committee reported favorably on all delegates and proxies present.

ORGANIZATION

The committee on order of business reported as follows:

We recommend C. C. Corkhill as permanent chairman and Wm. E. Orr as permanent secretary of this convention.

That the chairman appoint one sergeant-at-arms to be allowed the sum of $5; that the secretary be allowed the sum of $10.

That each candidate nominated shall pay the sum of $5, except public administrator, from which no fee shall be collected, and commissioners, who shall pay the sum of $2.50.

That the order of nominations shall be as follows: Assemblymen (three), Recorder and Auditor, Treasurer, Clerk, Public Administrator, District Attorney, Sheriff, Assessor, Commissioner (long term), Commissioner (short term); township officers to be nominated by each delegation.

The report being adopted, Chas. C. Corkhill assumed the chair. Josh Oliphant was appointed sergeant-at-arms.

Following the report of the committee on platform (published below), nomination of candidates proceeded in the order named, all nominations being made by acclamation and with much enthusiasm. Each candidate addressed the convention, pledging loyalty to the ticket and faithfulness to their constituents if elected. Ed. W. Clark, for Treasurer, and Phil. Smith, for Sheriff, received ovations as they took the floor. All received loud applause.

It was ordered that an executive committee of seven be elected by the convention, with a chairman and secretary, to be selected by the nominees, to be thereafter added. The following were elected to the committee: C. A. Rucker, Las Vegas; E. E. Smith; J. A. Clark, Pioche; J. A. Denton, Caliente; C. W. Thomas; A. O. Lee, Panaca; J. I. Earl, Bunkerville. It was ordered that each precinct name five members of a committee to act in conjunction with the executive committee as a county central committee.

CENTRAL COMMITTEE

Selections were made by the delegations present as follows:

Caliente—C Culverwell, Jr, Frank O'Shea, Tim Harrington, George Warren, Joseph Canoway.

Crescent—Andy Short, P O Chilstron, C M White, George Morgan, Carl Larson.

Panaca— A V Lee, Phillip Mathews, N J Wadsworth, D I Findlay, Geo Syphus.

Searchlight — John Wheatley, John Howe, J C Walters, Frank J Wardlow, Wm Allison;

CALIENTE CONVENTION

(Continued from page 1)

Pioche—J A Nesbitt, Jas Wheeler, Wm Wheatley, Chas Garrison, E F Freudenthal.

St Thomas—Martin A Bunker, Harry Gentry, G L Whitney, Ed H Syphus, Jno F Perkins.

Las Vegas—E T Maxwell, H A Barker, Frank M Grace, D D Hickey, E J Roselle.

Good Springs—Wm Cooper, J C Armstrong, C M Over, John Fredrickson, Bart Angell.

De Lamar—Geo A Williams, Geo T Banovich, Ed Lemon, J P Henniger.

TOWNSHIP OFFICERS

The following township nominations were submitted and ratified:

Las Vegas—Passed.

De Lamar—Justice of the peace, Louie Chancellor; constable, Ed Lemon.

Good Springs—Justice, C M Over; constable, J C Armstrong.

Pioche—Justice, C W Garrison; constable, Ed Deck.

St Thomas—Justice, Martin A Bunker; Constable, Samuel B Gentry.

Searchlight—Justice, Frank L Wardlow; constable, Lon Cromer.

The convention extended a vote of thanks to the people of Caliente and to the chairman and secretary of the convention and adjourned sine die.

In the evening a largely-attended dance was given in Denton hall in honor of the visitors.

PLATFORM

The Democratic party of Lincoln

lican party being the organization through which corporate influence and corruption dominates national affairs, deserves the chastisement of the people, and this convention urges the voters of Lincoln county to aid us in repudiating this party at the polls.

This convention pledges its representatives to the enactment of legislation that will tend to the betterment of the condition of the wage worker; to safeguard the eight-hour law; and we favor such additional legislation as will require adequate provision to be made by the railroad interests of Nevada for the safety of employes and the traveling public.

We commend the attention of the public to the salient features of the Democratic platform, which is hereby endorsed in its entirety and will further emphasize that portion of the State platform which demands the establishment of a terminal or common point in Nevada by all interstate railway lines, in compliance with the interstate law, so that merchants, consumers and users may have non-discriminating passenger and freight rates and such traffic advantages as will facilitate the development of Nevada's immense resources.

We further pledge the Democratic legislators in the forthcoming legislature to support a measure for the refunding of the present indebtedness of Lincoln county on a basis that will be just and equitable to the interests involved and to the end of being a saving to the tax-paying portion of Lincoln county. This commendation is deemed wise inasmuch that the present unsatisfactory basis of this indebtedness is a menace to the progressive interests of the county, a discouragement to capital seeking investment in the great natural possibilities and rich resources that endow Lincoln county.

We demand the enactment of a banking law for the protection of depositors and for the punishment of those who loot the moneys of the people.

We favor adequate compensation for all county officers and pledge the Democratic representatives, if elected, to bring this matter before the forthcoming legislature.

We favor a sufficient appropriation to continue the present Experiment Farm station in Lincoln county with provisions to improve and demonstrate the best calculated successful scientific methods for the benefit of our husbandry.

We cordially congratulate Governor Sparks upon his renomination and particularly call the attention of the voters to the splendid record of his conduct of State affairs, and earnestly commend his associates on the State ticket as worthy of the support of all the voters of Nevada.

We are unalterably opposed to the juggling of State and county funds for the benefit of individuals; if there is to be any source of gain by the deposit of such funds with any banking institution we demand that the people receive such benefit.

· Public office being a public trust, we pledge that the candidates this day selected will so conduct themselves as to give force and effect to the declarations made by this convention.

We denounce the unseemly action of that boss-ruled convention of the Republican party, which, under the whip lash of a masterful boss, recorded a boss' edict at the Las Vegas convention and rode rough shod over the majority of the actual delegates present in that convention. And for a further warning to such boss domination, this convention invites the free and untrameled Republicans to support the principles and candidates this day presented to the voters of Lincoln county.

Inter-Mountain Republican (Utah)
October 10, 1906

MURDERER IN CUSTODY

Korean Who Killed Comrade at Caliente, Nev., Will Be Tried.

H. A. Bucheneau, city marshal of St. Anthony, Idaho, arrived in Salt Lake yesterday having in custody a self-confessed murderer named S. K. Park. Park, who is a Korean, killed a fellow countryman named Y. Jung on September 5, at Caliente, Nev. Both men were working as laborers for the railroad company at the time of the murder. Park was in debt to Jung for $65, and Jung was having a hard time to collect it. The two men had fought about it several times. On September 5 both men disappeared, and a week later Jung was found under the railroad bridge shot through the heart. A search for Park was then begun, and through other Koreans it was learned that he left Caliente and had gone north. Park was traced to a place in Idaho called Egin bench, about seven miles west of St. Anthony, where he was working in the beet fields. He confessed to the murder, and also to robbing his victim of $27.50. Park was held at the county jail in this city last night awaiting the arrival of Jake Johnson, sheriff of Lincoln county, Nevada.

Registration by Precincts

The number of registered voters in the precincts from which returns have been received is given below:

Las Vegas	320
Searchlight	320
Crescent	36
El Dorado	18
Moapa	16
Logan	17
Pioche	132
Caliente	176
DeLamar	114
Good Springs	30
Overton	20
Lake Valley	13
Sandy	11
Spring Valley (Newlands)	9
Deerlodge (Fay)	30
Stewart (Alamo)	20
Eagle Valley (Ursine)	13
St. Thomas	25
Panaca	50
Hiko	30
Stine (Power Plant)	12
Acoma	17
Bunkerville	30
Mesquite	20

Other precincts will be added as received.

Caliente Murder

The Salt Lake Tribune says a Korean named S. K. Park has been arrested in Idaho and taken to Pioche for murdering a companion at Caliente about Sept. 25th. Park had a quarrel with his friend Junz about money, killed him and threw his body under a bridge near Caliente, after taking $25 from the dead man's pockets.

MISSING MINER FOUND.

Man Believed to be Dead Turns Up in California.

Salt Lake City.—E. H. Lee, formerly a prospector for the National Development company, who was lost while prospecting in Nevada last spring, has been located in Bakersfield, Cal. Lee left Salt Lake on April 23, and two letters were received from him from Caliente, Nev., dated April 25. Nothing more was heard from him and he was finally given up for dead.

Lee writes from Bakersfield that before he left Caliente he had been sick and feverish, but that he had gone on purchasing some burros and supplies and started for Las Vegas. That was the last he remembered until he found himself in a hospital at Los Angeles, Cal.

He had been taken with typhoid fever and lost his reason, wandering for days alone on the desert. Finally he was found by an old friend who was prospecting in the Johnnie and Indian Wells country.

MINES LONG CLOSED WILL BE BONANZAS

This Virtually the Situation in Old Camp of Pioche, Nevada.

CLEARING OUT WORKINGS

Utah-Nevada, Ohio-Kentucky and Others Preparing for Large Production.

E. A. Hedges a merchant of Pioche, Nev., who is in the city purchasing goods, declares that the old camp is already giving much evidence of the rejuvenation which is bound to follow the building of the branch railroad from Caliente. While the work of laying track has not begun, enough steel has been delivered at Caliente to build the entire line, and the ties are expected to begin arriving in a few days. Mr. Hedges declares that there is more activity in the camp today than has been seen there at any time since the palmy days of the "seventies," and he predicts that the best of those days will be speedily outdone very soon after shipping facilities are provided. Speaking of some of the activities to be noted, Mr. Hedges said:

"The Utah-Nevada Mines & Smelters corporation has retimbered its Meadow Valley No. 5 shaft to the depth of 1,000 feet, and it is the intention to continue the timbering to the 1,300-foot level. Much work is being done on the 1,000-foot in the way of getting the property in shape to begin shipping.

Old Times and the New.

"Lloyd & Cook are shipping ore from the Poorman property. Mr. Cook is now on the way to Salt Lake to purchase a gasoline hoist for the Mendha mine. This last property is a valuable one and contains an immense tonnage of ore. The mine was worked in the old days, but under conditions then existing ore running $40 a ton could not be shipped with profit. The ore now being taken out goes 1 1-2 ounces of gold 10 per cent lead and 16 ounces of silver, and there is 1,000 tons of this ore on the dump now. Twenty-five to 30 men can be put to work in this mine, and every man can work on ore. Where in the old days is used to cost $25 a ton for smelting the charge is now around $6.

"The Ohio-Kentucky people are now working three shifts of men and are sinking a shaft. They expect to encounter ore at a depth of 200 feet, which it will probably take them about 60 days to make. This property was also a mine in the old days, but on account of the expense of working was abandoned. Supt. Earls has just completed the installation of a new skip and recently installed a new hoist. With the additional facilities afforded by this new machinery work will progress rapidly.

NEAR DE LAMAR

Discovery of Rich Ore Close to Camp Causes Genuine Excitement.

WHOLE COUNTRY LOCATED

SHIPMENTS MADE FROM THERE MANY YEARS AGO.

A genuine mining excitement is reported to have broken out at DeLamar, Nevada, the home of the Bamberger-DeLamar gold mines. It is not gold, but silver that is causing all the excitement, however, and reports coming from camp indicate that the district is going to shine as a producer of the white metal as well as the yellow.

"Dick" Phillips, an old time prospector of DeLamar and at one time sheriff of Lincoln county, walked into camp a few days ago with samples of silver ore that assayed all the way from 10 to 1,000 ounces per ton. Little attention was at first paid to Phillips and his find, but finally George T. Benovich, always looking out for something new and good, sent an expert out to make an examination of the Phillips discovery. The expert returned and reported that the strike was bona fide. Then came the fireworks. Men rushed out to the scene of the discovery and locations have since been made over a wide range of country.

The Phillips discovery is located about two and one-half miles south-east of DeLamar. The group of claims are known as the new DeLamar and undoubtedly cover ground from which silver ore was shipped as long ago as 1892 by an old man named Gilbert. He sent out 1,000 pounds of the rock, according to the word of the camp and got returns from the smelter here on the basis of 800 ounces to the ton. The following year the slump in silver came and, as it was then impossible to ship even 1,000-ounce ore at a profit with a wagon haul of more than 100 miles, the ground was abandoned.

It is now believed at camp that the belt will prove an extensive one and that some good mines will be opened up. The advancing price of silver will stimulate development as will also the better facilities for getting ore to the market and the greatly reduced costs of smelting.

Material is being assembled at Caliente Nevada for the Pioche branch of the Salt Lake route. About half the rails are already unloaded at Caliente and enough ties will be on hand within the next sixty days or so to cover the line

Emery County News (Utah)
December 1, 1906

Material is being assembled at
Caliente Nevada for the Pioche
branch of the Salt Lake route About
half the rails are already unloaded at
Caliente and enough ties will be on
hand within the next sixty days or so
to cover the line

Salt Lake Herald (Utah)
December 15, 1906

DELAMAR, NEVADA, IS IN PULBIC EYE

San Francisco, Dec. 14.—James R. De-
Lamar, the well known mining man, was
a witness yesterday before Judge Seawell
in his own defense.

The Utah-Nevada company is seeking
to obtain judgment declaring it to be
the owner of forty-nine per cent of the
stock of the DeLamar Nevada Gold Mining company, an organization which is
said to have taken $13,000,000 worth of ore
out of the properties acquired from an
option holder whose interest has been purchased by the plaintiffs.

DeLamar denied that he was under any
obligation to hand over forty-nine per
cent, or any other percent, of his stock
to anybody, and the litigation promises
to be protracted, as about $2,000,000 is at
stake.

A. F. Schneider, general manager of the Nevada-Utah Mines & Smelters corporation, has returned to the city after several weeks occupied principally by a holiday visit to his home in New York. Mr. Schneider is well pleased with the situation as affecting the affairs of his company, which has mapped out for the new year a campaign of unusual activity in the development of properties and the increasing of production. The favorable situation is reflected to some extent in the action of the company's stock in the market centers, an advance of more than a dollar a share having been scored in the last week or two on the Boston exchange.

Toward the close of the old year the Nevada-Utah brought in a new shipper in the Last Chance mine at Bingham, which is already giving a good account of itself, and during the present year, with the completion of the branch railroad from Caliente to Pioche, which is to be pushed through as rapidly as possible, the company will greatly extend its operations at Pioche and Royal City, Nev. The work of opening the ore bodies in the mines at both places is being carried on vigorously, and they are now only awaiting transportation facilities to begin making regular shipments. The company is also opening the old Comet mine at Newhouse, which there is excellent prospect of making a good producer.

Inter-Mountain Republican (Utah)
January 29, 1907

CALIENTE IS GROWING

Prosperous Nevada Town Is Pushing Rapidly Ahead.

Caliente, Jan. 28.—Owing to the rapid strides which Caliente is making along all lines of commercial and industrial activity, a call is being made upon the business men of the town to consider the establishment of a chamber of commerce. The matter of incorporating the town is also being agitated. Relative to this matter the Press says:

"At the rate Caliente is growing it will not be long before our people will by crying for incorporation. During dull times in Nevada it was all well and good to let the towns take care of themselves, any old way. Now, however, it is different, and our people are as enterprising as any, therefore, it behooves us to prepare a way for the future. In order to get ourselves in shape it will not come amiss at this time, to call the attention of the business men to the fact that all other towns worthy of mention have already organized either a board of trade or a chamber of commerce and Caliente with her bright future cannot afford to be left in the rear ranks. Such a body is an absolute necessity for the welfare and advancement of any community."

Deseret News (Utah)
February 7, 1907

CALIENTE & PIOCHE R. R.

Surveyors Are Making Final Trip Over The Proposed Route.

Surveyors are going over the line of the Salt Lake Route's Pioche branch from Caliente, and as soon as the weather clears up construction on this long looked for road will commence. Division Engineer Lanthrop has a camp of engineers in Round valley and this gang is covering the route for the last time. The Caliente Express says the line is to be known as the Caliente & Pioche railroad. The branch is to follow the old grade with the exception of a short stretch in the valley just above its lower terminus. The old line takes the road right to the Pioche smelter. The route to be adopted from the smelter to the mines has not been mapped out in detail yet. Material is arriving at Caliente daily and 30 men are engaged in sorting the consignments in the material yards. Had it not been for heavy rains, construction would be now on, but with the ground in present condition nothing can be done.

SALT LAKE ROUTE IS TIED UP AGAIN

Wash-outs Just West of Caliente Stop All Traiffic Completely.

WIRES ARE DOWN NEAR MINTO

Local and Los Angeles Officials Are At the Scene—Travel Being Carried Over Southern Pacific.

The Salt Lake Route celebrated Washington's birthday by becoming tied up. Washouts occurring yesterday just west of Caliente have stopped traffic completely. Little is known here regarding the extent of damage done to the tracks as wires are down this side of Minto, about nine miles east of Caliente. The company experienced a tie-up of three weeks last winter on account of wash-outs in the Meadow valley region, but local officials do not believe the present trouble will be of any such duration. R. E. Wells, general manager of the road; H. E. Van Housen, division superintendent; R. K. Brown, division engineer, maintenance of way and other officials, are on the ground and are directing the work of repair personally. Mr. Van Housen and Mr. Brown left this city early yesterday. Mr. Wells was on his way east from Los Angeles. He reached Caliente just in time and immediately assumed charge of affairs.

WIRES ARE DOWN.

Further than the wash-out is somewhere just west of Caliente, its location even is not known. The local offices have been endeavoring to reach the scene by wire, but no word is expected until the wires at Minto are put up again. It is not expected this work will consume much time and communication between Salt Lake and Caliente or at least Minto, may be restored during the day. Wrecking crews are moving towards the hole in the tracks. All movement between Los Angeles and Salt Lake is to be carried ahead over the Southern Pacific's line while the Salt Lake Route is out of order. The Los Angeles Limited, leaving here daily at 6:45 p. m. did not go out yesterday. No. 1, leaving for Los Angeles at 9 o'clock every evening was held here also. In fact no trains have left this city over the Clark road since day before yesterday evening. No. 2 came in yesterday morning. Trains moving towards this city from Salt Lake were stopped and sent back.

LONG TIE-UP A YEAR AGO.

Until wire communication can be received here little definite information about the washout or washouts can be obtained. The Salt Lake Route's tracks pass through what is known as the Meadow Valley Wash, in the Caliente division. The road-bed runs at right angles with the gullies between the side hills. Water rushes down these at a fearful speed, and in striking the tracks sweeps them away, piling them up with the debris and wreckage over the level stretches along the line. The thaw of the past few weeks is believed to have melted the snow in the hills rapidly, creating early spring torrents. The company has spent thousands of dollars in repairing damage wrought by last winter's floods and in strengthening the line through the wash. Culverts of unusual size and strength have been installed so the company attaches here do not anticipate any long tie-up from the present trouble.

Deseret News (Utah)
February 28, 1907

WRECK AT CALIENTE.

One Man Killed and Many Injured on San Pedro.

Las Vegas, Nev., Feb. 28.— One man was killed and many injured in a collision today between two work trains engaged in repairing a washout on the Salt Lake railroad south of Caliente. A special train bearing medical aid has left Las Vegas for the scene. The washout will probably be repaired so that trains can pass through Sunday.

DEADLY CRASH

Salt Lake Work Train at Washout Collides With Tie Car

FOUR KILLED FIFTY INJURED

About eight o'clock Thursday morning four flat cars loaded with men and timbers were backed into a car of ties and a box car that had been left near the washout by another gang, 20 miles south of Caliente. One of the injured men informs The Age that the train was backing around a curve at high speed without a brakeman or conductor on duty to watch for obstacles.

Had the train not struck the cars it would have plunged into a washout a few yards ahead.

KILLED AND INJURED

Just before the crash some of the men jumped from the cars and got off with slight injury. Timbers piled on the cars rolled down on the workmen sitting around them, killing two men, horribly mangling others, injuring in all about fifty.

RELIEF TRAIN SENT

Dr. H. L. Hewetson, Salt Lake surgeon in camp at the washout, took charge of the injured and gave all possible relief, with the aid of others. A relief train was sent to the scene of the wreck with Drs. Roy W. Martin and others to assist the suffers, who were loaded on the train and brought to Las Vegas, arriving about four o'clock p. m. Thursday.

FOUR MEN DEAD

Two workmen died soon after the accident, and an inquest will be held over their remains at the wreck. Two others expired on the train before reaching Las Vegas, and will be buried in Las Vegas by Clayson and Griffith, undertakers.

Leaving Las Vegas about five o'clock Thursday evening, the relief train bearing the injured arrived in Los Angeles at three o'clock Friday morning. No deaths occured on the trip, but three were very low when they reached Los Angeles, and a dozen more, horribly injured may die. Many have compound fractures of the limbs, caused by the heavy timbers rolling on them and several amputations will be neccessary. Drs. Hewettson, Martin and Wilson rendered all possible aid to the sufferers on the relief train enroute to Los Angeles.

Names of killed and injured are not given because they are nearly all foreign and difficult to obtain.

The Age does not wish to do any one injustice by commenting on the horrible accident, prefering to leave that duty to the coroner's jury. A thorough investigation should be made in the interest of humanity. It is plain that negligence on the part of some one caused several deaths and sent forty injured men to the hospital.

RAILROAD WASHOUT

The Salt Lake railroad has been out of commission for a week, caused by a big washout above Moapa, in Meadow Valley Wash. Again the river has claimed its own and ousted the railroad from its bed. The story will be repeated as long as the Salt Lake runs through the river channel. Temporary repairs will permit trains to pass through Monday or Tuesday.

Las Vegas Age
March 9, 1907

DANGEROUS CANYON

SALT LAKE RAILROAD MAY FIND ANOTHER BETTER ROUTE NORTH

WHY CLARK SURRENDERED TO HARRIMAN

60 Miles of Track Destroyed and no Trains to Salt Lake for 30 Days

LAS VEGAS MAROONED

Again 60 miles of Salt Lake track has been honey combed in Meadow Valley wash and north of Caliente. South of Las Vegas, between Otis and Daggett the Mohave river has carried away a large section of railroad. Repairs and maintenance is uncertain.

The Age has reliable authority for stating that about sixty miles of Salt Lake railroad track has been washed out in the canyons north and south of Caliente. Last March the Salt Lake was out of business 22 days, and the prospects are that no trains will run through the canyons during the present month of March. Rains and snows will make repair impossible before April 1st.

To avoid the semi-annual washouts at Meadow Valley Canyon, the Salt Lake railroad may seek another route north.

Maps and surveys show that to the west of Meadow Valley range there is a route leading north, by which the Salt Lake could avoid the dangerous river bed known as Meadow Valley Wash. Engineers and desert rats, who know elevations by the ozone in the air, have told us of railroad surveys and stakes running north from the big Muddy Spring near Moapa, to the west of Meadow Valley range; passing midway between Delamar and Caliente; northward to Pioche, cutting out the big bend and dangerous canyon above Caliente; thence north through Ely and the Copper fields to Salt Lake.

This route would leave out Caliente, Modena and a few small towns north on the present line, and tap Delamar, Pioche, Ely and other rich mining sections. Engineers say it would be a little more expensive than the Meadow Valley river bed, but fully as short.

Possibly when Harriman gets Senator Clark pinched out of the Salt Lake road he may do a little permanent work in Meadow Valley Wash, and raise the railroad from the river bed, by blasting a route along the walls of the canyon, above the reach of high waters. The grand scenery of the canyon is an attraction on the present route. Passengers can't enjoy it, however, when compelled to walk over the washouts.

Harriman dont lose much when the Salt Lake is out of commission. He sends trains over his other lines; just like taking money out of one pocket and putting it in the other. The public pays the freight.

INJURES NEVADA BUSINESS

It must be plain to the management that passengers and freight will avoid the Salt Lake in storm seasons, rather than take the risk of being wrecked in Meadow Valley Canyon. How many more lives must be sacrificed before removal of the Salt Lake track from the river bed to a safe position above high water?

CLARK-HARRIMAN DEAL

Many doubt the story that right of way through Meadow Valley canyon was the real cause of Clark's surrender to Harriman. Salt Lake was probably the Appomattox where Clark capitulated. Harriman's control of all lines east of Salt Lake probably forced the Copper King to terms. Only by allowing Harriman control of the Salt Lake could Clark get favorable freight rates east. Clark was shrewd enough to let go when he found himself in possession of a stub railroad, with Harriman demanding tribute on all through business. Perhaps it paid him to sell control to the man in the highway.

Circumstances indicate the Salt Lake railroad was built economically to sell to the highest bidder.

The Age comments only because the public is concerned in common carriers. Let our law makers apply the remedy; compel adequate service and reasonable passenger and freight rates.

LIMITED IS ANNULLED

Salt Lake Route to Devote All Energies on Repairs.

The Los Angeles Limited was annulled indefinitely by an order issued Saturday. The action on the part of the Salt Lake Route does away with all the limited passenger trains operated by that company between Chicago and southern California.

The cancellation of these trains results from the tie up of the road caused by the recent washouts east and west of Caliente. The service will be resumed when the line has been repaired. The line will be practically at a standstill, except for local traffic until the damaged roadbed can be replaced.

While the Salt Lake Route is closed for through traffic special attention will be given to local service on that line. The first of several local excursions will be run from Provo to Salt Lake March 16, when the Brigham Young University of Provo, and the Brigham Young college of Logan meet in the Y. M. C. A. gymnasium to decide the basketball championship of the state. A special train will be run, and reduced rates given.

CALIENTE

Serene by the Side of Senator Clark's Floating Railroad

The railroad shops at Caliente are busy with repair work, but nearly all train crews have been laid off indefinitely and are walking out of town.

Senator Denton, the veteran stage runner, will put on a line either to Acoma or the old stage station Modena, to carry mail and passengers around the washouts.

With the yearly washouts on the Salt Lake and the postponement of the Pioche branch, Caliente will remain a prominent stage center for some time to come.

The natives take it all serenely and start a new stage line whenever the occasion demands it.

TRAINMASTER ARRIVES.

Reports Work on Salt Lake Route Progressing Rapidly.

Trainmaster Smith of the Salt Lake Route arrived in this city Monday from Caliente and points on the line where the work of rebuilding the damaged track is being carried on.

He reports that as has been expected the line will be opened as far as Caliente within a day or two and repaired sufficiently to carry through trains by April 1. J. A. Burtner, district freight and passenger agent, stated Monday that a telegram from officials down the line had just arrived, stating that the train leaving Salt Lake Tuesday night would be able to go as far as Caliente.

Work on the damaged roadbed is being carried on as fast as possible, and efforts will not be relaxed until that work is completed. Temporary tracks are being laid at present to carry trains around the washouts until the roadbed itself can be thoroughly reconstructed at the points where it was washed away.

SALT LAKE ROUTE AGAIN WASHED OUT

Traffic Once More Stalled by Heavy Rains in the Caliente Neighborhood.

Meagre advices received at the local offices of the Salt Lake Route Thursday night were to the effect that more floods had come down from the sides of the mountains Thursday afternoon and washed out a great part of the roadbed in the Caliente district which had been filled in within the past ten days. Within a few hours the work of days was destroyed and the line is said to be in worse condition than ever. The rain which was falling Wednesday night and Thursday morning swelled the streams in the gullies, and, breaking over their channels, they swept the new grading down.

This latest news is the greatest discouragement yet to the officials of the line, who had hoped and expected to have trains running through to the coast by April 1. The time at which this can be done now can only be conjectured. All wires to the scene of the trouble were down at a late hour Thursday night and the local offices are almost entirely in the dark as to the extent of the new damage. The rain was reported falling over a great part of Nevada, and it is feared that the roadbed was still being carried away when the wires went out of commission.

The situation which confronts the Salt Lake Route is bringing nearer to realization the fact that a new line must be selected and built to replace the one through Meadow valley. The experiences of the past few weeks is believed to have convinced the officials of that line that a new route is the only solution of the difficulty.

Inter-Mountain Republican (Utah)
March 30, 1907

SALT LAKE ROUTE TO RUN INTO CALIENTE

Line Has Been Sufficiently Repaired to Do Away With Stage Ride.

It is expected that trains on the Salt Lake Route will be running into Caliente from this end of the line today or tomorrow. The large force of workmen which has been laboring incessantly for several weeks have repaired the line sufficiently for trains to pass, although it will be some time before the ballasting work can be completely finished.

Since the flooding of the roadbed, causing cessation of through traffic, trains have been running from Salt Lake to Acoma, Nevada, connecting with a stage which carried passengers on to Caliente, a distance of about 15 miles. With the opening of the line to Caliente, the stage service will be stopped.

Few details of the repair work on the damaged track have been obtainable at this end of the line, owing to the fact that the leading officials of the road have been at the point of trouble and it has therefore been unnecessary to send detailed reports out. It is understood at the local offices, however, that the line will be repaired and through traffic resumed April 10, unless some unforeseen emergency arises.

SALT LAKE ROUTE RESUMES TRAFFIC

Washouts on Line Fixed Up and Trains Will Run This Week.

COST NEARLY A MILLION

Caliente District Causes Endless Trouble to Officials and Workmen.

Entailing an expense of nearly a million, after a cessation of nearly two months, with the exception of three or four days before the second washout occurred, the Salt Lake Route will resume through traffic on its line this week. Train number 1, which leaves Salt Lake on the evening of April 12, will be ordered through to Los Angeles, and, barring unforeseen accidents, will begin the regular and permanent through service. The limited trains will run, commencing April 15.

The first serious trouble for the line this year occurred February 22, when the heavy rains, causing the melting of the masses of snow in the mountains, started down the gulches streams of water that tore out the railroad bridges and grade through Meadow valley and tied up all through traffic on the line. Two or three freight trains passing over that part of the line were ditched in the washouts, their cars being piled up in spectacular fashion. Two passenger trains, with all on board, were cut off from escape eastward or westward, and until the line was temporarily repaired these trains and passengers were stalled in and about Caliente.

Officials Rush to Scene.

When the first piece of track was washed away the wires hurried a message to both ends of the line, and officials with a large force of men and supplies hurried to the scene, for it was known that every hour of delay meant the loss of considerable money. It was thought that with their most strenuous efforts the repair gangs could get the line in shape in a short time. But continuing freshets washed out the roadbed as fast as it was piled up, and the men found themselves working against great odds. More materials and more men were hurried to the scene of trouble, and the task of repairing the line was hurried in the face of great discouragement. To add to the inconvenience and discomfort of the situation the telegraph line was washed out with the railroad track, and it was a difficult matter for the officials overseeing the work to order and receive the supplies needed. But with a temporary ceasing of the rain the force of men doubled their efforts, and soon temporary tracks were laid around the worst washouts, and the smaller ones were filled in. Word was sent to both Salt Lake and Los Angeles that through trains could be ordered out.

Work Is Again Balked.

The officials of the road had just settled back for a breathing spell and the lines of worry on their faces were beginning to be smoothed out when word came over the wires that more water had come down from the mountains and had destroyed the greater part of their work in addition to tearing out the line at other places. Through trains, including the limited from Chicago, were annulled, and the discouraging work was recommenced. More supplies were ordered. Material that had been set aside for other uses was dispatched to the scene, the force of men was increased—all means available were utilized getting the line back in shape. For more than a month that work has been carried on, and the opening of the line April 12 will be its consummation, although a great deal of ballasting will have to be done after that time.

The washouts, it is estimated, have cost the company considerably more than a million dollars, in the expense of rebuilding and the loss of business while the line has been out of operation. The agents of the company have put their attention to local traffic in an effort to get in as much revenue as possible to offset the loss. Beginning April 26 and continuing every day until May 19, the line will offer a $30 rate for the round trip to Los Angeles, the return limit being July 31.

Intermountain Catholic (Utah)
April 13, 1907

WALKED THIRTY MILES
BECAUSE OF WASHOUTS

M. Mahoney, a Well-known Mining Man, in From Railroad Cross- ing, Nevada.

M. Mahoney of Railroad Crossing on the Colorado river, twenty-two miles east of Las Vegas, arrived in the city last week over the Salt Lake Route.

In coming east from Las Vegas to Caliente he, with several others, was obliged to walk a distance of thirty miles on account of the washouts below the latter place. No such heavy rain-pours were ever known in this Meadow valley as have fallen there this spring.

The railroad company is doing heroic work in repairing the track, and with fair weather Mr. Mahoney is informed through trains will be running in about ten days.

Mr. Mahoney is one of the oldest and among the most widely-known mining men in the west.

His thirty-five years' experience has embraced the states of Utah, Nevada, Idaho, Montana and Oregon. He is now located at Railroad Crossing, in Lincoln county, Nevada, where he says many mines rich in gold and silver are being developed. There is great activity in the district, and plenty of money with which to operate.

Deseret News (Utah)
April 18, 1907

NOVELTY IN RAILROADING.

Unusual Train Hauled Over the Tracks Of the Salt Lake Route.

The citizens of Caliente were treated to a novel sight the other day, accord-ing to the Caliente Lode-Express. Eight heavily loaded freight wagons were pulling up the road, but were unable to cross the ford at the wash, owing to high water. Yardmaster Blunt, of the Salt Lake Route, saw the predicament of the teams and kindly offered to help. Under his instructions the teams were detached, the wagons coupled together and the lead wagon coupled to the yard engine. Then giving Engineer Johnson a crack of a whip purloined from George Hicks, the iron horse and its unique train started along the track, crossed the Caliente & Pioche railroad bridge and landed the outfit safely on the other side of the watercourse. Mr. Blunt has the good wishes of the peo-ple who are desirous of keeping the freight hauling business here.

Richfield Reaper
April 25, 1907

Niels Ericksen left for Hiko, Nevada, Sunday after spending several months here with his son, E P Ericksen

Las Vegas Age
April 27, 1907

Dr. W. P. Murray was acquitted at Caliente last Friday of the charge of assaulting Dr. J. W. Smith some weeks ago. Attorney Dan V. Noland of Las Vegas conducted the defense.

Las Vegas Age
May 11, 1907

Hawkins' Hoodoo

Commissioner Hawkins' Pioche hoodoo still pursues him and on this trip worked to the discomfort and inconvenience of Judge Lillis, Attorney Noland, Dr. Martin and Dr. Park, as well as himself.

When they set sail from Caliente Sunday night it was raining hard and a few miles out their driver ran into a fence, smashing up the vehicle.

They found shelter for the night with a railroad grading camp and next day took a heavy team and lumber wagon for Pioche, arriving several hours late.

On his first trip to Pioche Mr. Hawkins and companions were lost and had to seek shelter for the night on account of a blinding snow storm, and on his next was forced to make a three-day drive to get home, on account of the railroad washouts.

Las Vegas Age
May 18, 1907

Circus Day

Nearly everybody in Las Vegas went to the circus, and there were a few from outside points, but that didn't nearly pay the expenses of the big show.

It was a real circus, with a good-sized menagerie, peanuts, lemonade, and a three-ring performance, to say nothing of the side show and the gents with the husky barking apparatuses.

One pleasing feature was the fine string of horses carried by the show. A better looking lot of horse flesh could hardly be found anywhere. In the parade they attracted more attention than the ladies with the short clothes and the long stockings.

The Sells-Floto is the first circus to make the Southern Nevada desert circuit, and will probably be the last for some time. It was by far a better show than most people expected to see. The natives of the north end of the county saw it at Caliente yesterday.

Emery County News (Utah)
May 25, 1907

It is stated in what apparently is authoritative circles that as soon as the Salt Lake route completes its branch line from Caliente to Pioche it will begin immediately upon the proposed line to the Deep Creek section of Utah and Ely Nevada. This will be cheering news to the miners of that section

Las Vegas Age
June 8, 1907

F. R. McNamee, of Caliente, has established his family, a residence at Los Angeles. Mr. McNamee now holds a position with the Harriman-Clark railroad as attorney.

Emery County News (Utah)
June 22, 1907

Tracklaying on the Caliente & Pioche railroad which has been suspended will immediately be resumed

Inter-Mountain Republican (Utah)
June 25, 1907

Marriage Licenses.

E. R. Hennefer, Salt Lake City; Emma Fransen, Salt Lake City.

Fred Schiele, San Jose, Cal.; Hannah E. Ryan, Salt Lake City.

Richard B. Bowdridge, Salt Lake City; Catherine Ann Benton, Detroit. Mich.

Gurnsey B. Smith, Draper; Mabel C. Thomson, Granite.

W. Woodruff Cannon, St George; Marie K. Anderson, Salt Lake City.

Willard C. Snow, Salt Lake City; Hazel DeMars Pond, Salt Lake City.

Vestil F. Harrison, Salt Lake City; Lavena Schofield, Centerville.

Rowland Bennion, Taylorsville; Ida Stock, Hams Fork, Wyo.

William Manhart, Salt Lake City; Hannah Larsen, Salt Lake City.

Thomas J. Sweeney, Caliente, Nev.; Florence E. Adair, Caliente.

FORTIFIES ROADBED IN MEADOW VALLEY

Salt Lake Route Seeks to Prevent Repetition of Recent Costly Washouts.

"In time of drought prepare for flood" is the slogan of the Salt Lake Route just now. In putting this rule into practice it is extremely active. The center of operations is Meadow Valley, where the line has been washed out in two consecutive seasons, entailing a loss of many thousands of dollars, as well as a tie-up of several weeks for through traffic on the line.

For some time it was a question in the minds of officials of the Salt Lake Route whether or not the line through Meadow Valley should be abandoned for one on higher ground. It was finally decided that the route through the valley should be retained, and that it should be constructed in such a way as to prevent a repetition of the washouts.

Through the narrow gulches of the valley, where the line is exposed to the onslaught of surplus water from the hills each spring the roadbed is being widened and in many places the embankment is faced with stone. Where the track parallels the stream that flows through the narrow valley, cement culverts and steel bridges are being built. The roadbed is being "ripped-rapped" and outlets for excess water dug.

Laying of rails on the Caliente-Pioche branch has began. The grading for this line is complete and trains will be put in operation there as soon as the ties and steel can be laid and ballasted. Pioche and the surrounding district are at present without railroad communication.

BABE DROWNS IN CANAL ON PROVO BENCH.

Republican Special Service.

Provo, June 29.—Gerald, the three-year-old son of Mr. and Mrs. Hyrum Rice of Caliente, Nev., who was visiting with his grandmother, Mrs. Darrow, at the C. E. Crandall home on Provo bench, fell into the canal at that place this morning. The body was found three miles down stream. Nothing is known as to how the boy fell into the stream.

Las Vegas Age
July 7, 1907

Lee McGaughey is back from Caliente, where he erected J. F. Miller's concrete saloon building.

J. O. McIntosh and J. F. Miller were looking after their respective business establishments in Caliente this week.

Emery County News (Utah)
July 7, 1907

The people of Pioche do not propose to be outdone by the sister towns in southern Nevada in celebrating the advent of the railroad now building from Caliente to the famous old mining camp. It is not expected that the line will reach the town before September 1 but the citizens are already beginning to prepare for the celebration

Deseret News (Utah)
July 16, 1907

GRADING FORCE ENLARGED.

Hot weather is making progress along the Caliente & Pioche branch of the Salt Lake Route rather slow. Mendenhall and Deal increased the grading force by the addition of 40 teams last week. A new camp has been established in Round valley. Twenty-five men quit a few days ago because of the poor quality of food, so it is explained. The higher officials instructed the clerk to stock the commissary with first class provisions and the affair ended.

Inter-Mountain Republican (Utah)
July 25, 1907

CLARK ROAD WILL GIVE MINES CHANCE

To Establish Halfway Station for the Shippers of Pioche Camp.

The Pioche Record learns that it is the intention of the railroad company to establish a station at Bullionville-Panaca just as soon as the rails reach that point. From progress that is being made now it is expected that point will be reached about August 15. The determination of the railroad to build a station at that point for receiving freight was reached after the earnest solicitation of some of the leading mining companies. These companies have been extracting ore for some time and now have their ore bins filled to their utmost capacity, and it is absolutely necessary that they commence shipping as soon as possible.

The Bristol Consolidated, for instance, is shipping to Modena and Caliente and every mile that is reduced in hauling means considerable money to the company. The Mendah, the Lyndon Mines company and numerous other mines and prospects will commence shipping when the road reaches that point.

Labor Scarcity Hinders.

The one great problem which the railroad is contending with at present is the scarcity of labor and any delay in the road's completion may be assigned directly to that cause. Should it be possible to maintain the present force, the road will reach Pioche at least by the first of October, and if additional help can be secured, much before that time.

The officials in making their estimates of the probable completion of the road, always figure upon the provision of keeping sufficient help. The steel gang is laying about 2,000 feet per day, or about 12,000 feet per week; no work is being done Sundays. Deal Brothers & Mendenhall, who have the contract for the grading, anticipate no trouble in keeping the grade well in advance of the steel gang. At present there is about ten miles of rails laid and the grading force is well along in Condor canyon.

Eureka Reporter (Utah)
July 27, 1907

The people of Pioche do not propose to be outdone by the sister towns in southern Nevada in celebrating the advent of the railroad now building from Caliente to the famous old mining camp. It is not expected that the line will reach the town before September 1 but the citizens are already beginning to prepare for the celebration.

Las Vegas Age
August 31, 1907

Caliente

Two more concrete machines for use in the re-construction of the railroad arrived during the week.

The Pioche branch has reached Bullionville, says the Lode-Express.

Four Towns

No doubt four towns in Lincoln County will adopt County Commissioner government in order to secure the $500 to $1000 gambling license money that the law provides for. Las Vegas, Searchlight, Caliente and Pioche will thus draw from the county fund from $2,000 to $4,000 per month hereafter. It is natural for all to go after the money where one does.

Las Vegas Age
September 7, 1907

BASEBALL

Caliente Comes to Las Vegas Sunday

The Caliente players will come down Sunday to cross bats with the Vegas nine on the home diamond. The game will be called at 2:30. At Caliente two weeks ago Vegas lost the game by a score of 8 to 10.

PIOCHE-CALIENTE

In a close game at Caliente last Sunday Pioche took the short end of a 4 to 2 score, giving Caliente two out of three over the county seaters. O. H. Griffith of the Vegas nine played 1st for Caliente. He says it was one of the best games he has been in for years.

The Caliente baseball team failed to materialize last Sunday, as advertised. The Vegas boys say it is a case of cold feet; the Caliente bunch say that they understood the date to be the 29th. J. O. McIntosh has sent word that the Caliente team will be here on the 29th; Pioche Record says that Caliente will play at Pioche on the 29th. So the promised game seems to be in the same category with the Fairbanks cocktail and the question, "who struck Billy Patterson." In other words, the baseball game, as played by Caliente, seems to be a "shell game."

Caliente Fire

The Denton Hotel at Caliente, owned by ex-senator J. A. Denton, was completely destroyed by fire last Saturday. It will be rebuilt.

BUILDING

Some Figures For Benefit of Caliente Paper

"More buildings are being constructed in Caliente than are at Milford or Las Vegas," says the Caliente Lode-Express.

Perhaps! But more money is being put into buildings in Las Vegas than in all the rest of Lincoln County combined. The splendid Masonic building alone will probably cost as much as all the buildings that have been erected in Caliente during the year.

Below we append a list of some of the more important buildings now in course of construction and their estimated cost:

Masonic Temple, $14,000.
Stewart & Lockett hotel, $8,000.
Overland Hotel, $8,000.
C. E. Gabriel, rooming house, $2,000.
A. H. Kramer, barber shop, $1,200.
Peter Buol, residence, $1,700.
A. J. Frye, residence, $1,500.
C. E. Colson, three residences, $3000.
W. R. Thomas, residence, $2,000.
W. E. Arnold, residence, $750.

This list includes only buildings actually in course of construction or being completed at the time of writing.

Buildings previously completed since the first of the year will probably aggregate in cost between $25,000 and $30,000. Among the number are the electric light and power plant, the railroad eating house, Peter Buol's fine home, Messrs Sullivan & Wilson's several cottages and many others. A detailed list of the year's building will soon be published.

Pete Peterson plead guilty to the charge of appropriating funds of the Salt Lake railroad while in the company's employ at Caliente.

Inter-Mountain Republican (Utah)
October 16, 1907

GLASSES HAVE PART IN ROW IN BARROOM

Paul Powleuch, an Austrian laborer, aged 44, and Paul Sheenich, an Austrian bartender, aged 20, were arrested at 8:30 o'clock Tuesday night for fighting in the Caliente saloon at 263 West South Temple street. Powleuch got the worst of the encounter, as he had several scalp wounds, evidently inflicted with a glass or bottle. He was taken to the emergency hospital.

When the hostilities began, Powleuch, it is said, struck Sheenich on the head with his fist. Beer bottles and glasses were prominent in the subsequent mixup. The fight was stopped by Detective Wheeling and Policeman Curran.

Inter-Mountain Republican (Utah)
October 18, 1907

Both Austrians Guilty.

Paul Sherrick and Paul Powlitch, two Austrians, were found guilty of disturbing the peace by Judge Diehl Thursday. The trouble started in the Caliente saloon on West South Temple street October 15. As Powlitch's head was badly cut in the affray and it seemed that he had been badly punished, he was discharged from custody and the court instructed Sherrick to appear for sentence this afternoon. He was released on bail soop after the fight.

Inter-Mountain Republican (Utah)
November 12, 1907

NEVADA-UTAH MINES ACCUMULATING ORE

Pushing Preparations for Shipping From Pioche Properties.

A. P. Schneider, general manager of the Nevada-Utah company, who has been looking after his company's operations at Pioche, reports things reasonably lively in that camp. The Nevada-Utah is accumulating ore at its Day mine at Jackrabbit, to be ready to start shipping as soon as the new railroad is ready to receive freight, and is also working in ore in its mines in the Pioche camp. A few freight cars are being handled on the Caliente and Pioche line, but no attempt will be made to take ore until the grade shall have been ballasted and terminal facilities provided.

With the advent of the railroad, Mr. Schneider says, the Pioche district is in position to become very active the moment that normal conditions in the metal market are assured.

Las Vegas Age
November 16, 1907

Caliente Bank

The Lincoln County Bank has recently changed hands. Lynn Boyd is now president and O. C. Durango, cashier. Both are from San Diego, California.

Las Vegas Age
November 30, 1907

CALIENTE

(From Lode-Express)

J. O. McIntosh, of the East Side Bar, is building a storehouse and will establish a wholesale liquor business at Caliente.

The Denton Hotel is being rebuilt and will be open about Dec. 1st.

Six hundred dollars will be expended on Caliente streets during December.

Ong Loy, formerly of Vegas, is opening a new restaurant.

Geo. C. Fetterman has retired from the Lincoln County Bank.

PIOCHE

[From The Record]

Nevada-Utah Corporation shipped the first carload of ore over new Caliente-Pioche railroad, from the Day mine at Jackrabbit.

Pioche is against remitting assessment work, and also opposes a special session of the legislature.

Taxes are coming in slowly, says the treasurer's office.

Unruly pupils in Pioche school caused the teacher to resign and the school is closed.

Emery County News (Utah)
November 30, 1907

There will be several months work yet on the improvements being made by the Salt Lake road near Caliente Nevada to have the track in condition to withstand the spring flood Since the last washouts a great amount of work has been done in this district some 800 men being employed

Emery County News (Utah)
December 7, 1907

George Frisbee who fell from a train between Caliente and Moapa Nevada and had his left foot cut off probably saved his life by flagging a train which came along several hours later by setting fire to an envelope Frisbee was picked up and is now in the hospital

CALIENTE

Suit has been commenced by Geo. C. Fetterman, plaintiff, vs. The Lincoln County Bank, Inc. The suit is brought to recover certain certificates, alleged to be wrongfully withheld by the defendant corporation from plaintiff, or for their equivalent, the sum of $60,000 and costs of suit.

Caliente will build a 50,000 gallon water tank on the hill above town for fire protection.

Dave Tobin who was so badly burned by a powder explosion near Caliente Nevada when Tom Duggan was fatally burned died in a Salt Lake hospital last week. Duggan in the torment caused by the burns pleaded for some one to end his misery

CALIENTE

Death has ended the misery of Tom Dugan and D. Tobin railroad employes, who were injured in a powder explosion at Etna, near Caliente, a couple of weeks ago.

The five-year-old son of Mr. and Mrs. Ernest Keith was burned to death by exploding a can of gasoline with a lighted stick, December 4th.

Emery County News (Utah)
December 14, 1907

Elliott Keats a 6 year old boy of Caliente Nevada was burned to death last week by an explosion of gasoline The little fellow dropped a burning stick into a five gallon can of gasoline

Las Vegas Age
December 28, 1907

CALIENTE

(From the Lode Express)

The latest reports are that Sheriff Smith's brother, accidentally shot at Caliente, will soon recover. He is in the hospital at Salt Lake.

The Cedar Basin Gold Mining Company, of Gold Butte, this county, is making good headway in the development of its property and has a large quantity of free-milling gold ore on the dump. The company has mill construction under consideration.

Much progress is being made on the Caliente water system. The ditches have been dug for the pipe and 2000 feet of iron and redwood pipe will be on the ground soon. The 50,000 gallon water tank has been built on the hill back of town, the five horse power gasoline engine has been placed and is ready for use. As soon now as the pipe can be laid Caliente will be equipped with an adequate water system. The work will be completed in about two weeks.

Inter-Mountain Republican (Utah)
January 1, 1908

NEW RAILROAD BRANCH FORMALLY TRANSFERRED

At midnight last night the Pioche branch railroad from Caliente to Pioche was transferred by the contractors to the operating department of the San Pedro, Los Angeles and Salt Lake railroad and a new train schedule went into effect. Train 401 will leave Caliente at 5 p. m. and will reach Pioche at 7:30 p. m. The return trip will be made in the morning; leaving Pioche at 10 a. m. and arriving at Caliente at 12:30 p. m. This train although scheduled to leave Caliente at 5 o'clock in the afternoon, will wait for No. 1, making direct connections for travelers from Salt Lake and the east.

Las Vegas Age
January 4, 1908

CALIENTE

(From Lode-Express)

J. O. McIntosh and wife have been visiting friends in Las Vegas.

Hon. F. R. McNamee is spending the holidays with his family in Los Angeles.

The Christmas tree given in connection with the Union Sunday School for the children of Caliente on Christmas eve was a tremendous success.

John Smith, brother of Sheriff Phil Smith, who was accidently shot last Sunday, the 22nd, from reports recently received at the hospital in Salt Lake where he was taken, is getting along nicely and will recover. The bullet struck the right groin far enough out so that it plowed through fleshy wall of the body, coming out at the back.

Mr. Martin Hamilton came down to Vegas Friday from Caliente to enjoy a day in Nevada's garden.

Mr. and Mrs. J. O. McIntosh, accompanied by Miss McIntosh, came down from Caliente and spent a few days in a live town last week. Mac says 1,000 men are still repairing the railroad on both sides of Caliente.

F. Chopetal came down from Caliente with a bad case of pneumonia but soon recovered at Las Vegas Hospital.

CALIENTE

(From Lode-Express)

Caliente and Pioche train leaves Caliente at 5 o'clock in the afternoon, connecting with No. 1 from Salt Lake and No. 2 from Los Angeles, arriving in Pioche 7:30 p. m. A train leaves Pioche daily at 10 o'clock in the forenoon, arriving in Caliente 12:30 in the afternoon.

Arthur McIntosh, brother of J. O. McIntosh, had his leg broken by being run over by his delivery wagon.

John Smith, brother of the sheriff, who was accidently shot a few days ago, is reported to be rapidly improving.

Senator Denton's hotel is now open for lodgings.

Miss Mae Wadsworth, formerly of Vegas, is assistant in the Caliente postoffice.

The district attorney objected to the allowance of all bills incured by the Board of Fire Commissioners of Caliente upon the ground that said Board is without any legal authority whatever to incur any indebtedness but on the contrary are merely vested with an advisary authority to reccommend to the County Commissioners the purchase of what is necessary for a proper fire system in the town of Caliente.

The county advertising for the year 1908 was awarded to Caliente Lode-Express and the county job printing contract to Pioche Record, the only bidder. [The Age bids were not received in time to be considered—Ed.]

Chairman of the board was authorized to extend lease for ground occupied by branch county jail at Caliente.

A petition from Caliente requested the lease of the Caliente fire system to individuals. Laid over.

The Sheriff was authorized to purchase and have installed an additional cage for the branch County Jail at Caliente.

Emery County News (Utah)
January 11, 1908

After practically a year s unremit
ting work the newest branch of the
Salt Lake Route the Caliente Pioche
line was turned over to the operat
ing department of the system at mid
night Tuesday December 31

Las Vegas Age
February 8, 1908

CALIENTE

John Smith, brother of Sheriff Phil
Smith, who was shot last December
under circumstances unfortunate for
those interested, died in the Salt Lake
hospital January 28th. The funeral
services were held in Panaca January
30th.

The deceased was a twin brother of
Sheriff Smith, and both have lived in
this section for many years.

COMMISSIONERS

County Debt Not Quite So Big
Tax Rate $2.00

Commissioner Hawkins returned from Pioche Wednesday night and reports a long and busy session. All members were present.

Court judgments produced by Salt Lake railroad representatives in closing up the refunding deal showed the amount of the county debt to be only $429,000, which is $30,000 less than the amount previously claimed. This fact will also reduce the figured accrued interest something like $1200 per year. A resolution was passed by the board absolving Treasurer Ed. W. Clark from being responsible for causing any delay in closing up the bond matter; this in reply to certain unjust intimations.

The county tax rate for 1908 was fixed at $2.00 on the $100, 10c less than the 1907 rate. The reduction was made on the county debt interest fund which has a surplus.

Petitions for county hospital were received from Las Vegas and Caliente. Caliente was also on hand with an offer of land for the purpose and a schedule of costs for doctor's and nurse's services. The matter was laid over to advertise for offers from other towns interested.

Changes in the Las Vegas town ordinances recommended by the advisory board were approved. The ordinances will appear in the Age next week.

Moapa road fund received an appropriation of $500.

Two petitions were presented from the town of Las Vegas, one requesting an ordinance restricting gambling to block 16, and the other protesting against the same. Both petitions were liberally signed, so liberally in fact, that they both contained the same identical names, with a few exceptions. The board decided to let the industry flourish unrestricted.

Salt Lake officials, H. I. Bettis, F. A. Waters and F. R. McNamee were present in the bond matter.

Inter-Mountain Republican (Utah)
February 8, 1908

Robert Burns was granted a divorce from Eleanor M. B. Burns and the custody of the child was awarded to the grandmother, after Burns had relinquished his rights. Burns sued on the ground of desertion, saying that his wife had gone into a house of ill repute. They were married July 13, 1900, and two years later his wife left him, going to Milford and then to Caliente, Nev.

Washington County News (Utah)
February 20, 1908

Alma Wakeling of Lund, Nevada, and Miss Rhea Higbee of Toquerville were united in marriage here the 12th inst We congratulate the happy couple and wish them all happiness,

Inter-Mountain Republican (Utah)
February 25, 1908

KILLED BROTHER; MIND NOW BLANK

Caliente Sheriff Holding Himself Without Bail to Answer in Court.

SHOOTING WHILE DRUNK

Jack Smith Brought Here and Died in Holy Cross Hospital

In order to determine the exact cause of death of Jack Smith of Caliente, Nev., brother of Phil K. Smith, sheriff of Lincoln county, Nev., Charles Lee Horsey, district attorney, whose home is at Pioche, Nev., was in Salt Lake yesterday and held a conference with Dr. A. J. Hosmer.

Jack Smith was shot by Sheriff Smith on a street in Caliente, December 22, 1907, so Mr. Horsey stated, and when the Lincoln county grand jury convenes on March 10 the facts in the case will be presented.

In the meantime, on a complaint charging him with murder, the sheriff, as an officer, is holding himself, as an individual, in custody without bail. The case is one of the most peculiar in criminal annals that has ever come up in Nevada.

Sheriff Smith, it is alleged, had been on a protracted spree and had fallen in a stupor in a street. His brother, seeing his plight, went to pick him up. The sheriff drew his revolver and fired. Jack Smith was brought to Salt Lake, placed in the Holy Cross hospital, where Dr. Hosmer treated him. He died about three weeks ago.

Sheriff Smith is popular in Lincoln county, having been elected two years ago by a big majority on the Democratic ticket. Mr. Horsey stated that the sheriff remembers nothing of the tragic affair and is in a mental state of mind that cannot be described.

The laws of Nevada provide for additional sheriff appointments in case of a civil action against the sheriff, but in a criminal procedure the judge may only appoint a sheriff to summon the jurors. Consequently Sheriff Smith is still in office and the court has appointed no special sheriff for jury duty. The case is attracting attention throughout Nevada.

Inter-Mountain Republican (Utah)
February 27, 1908

One-way colonist rates from the East are announced on the railroads that will give a slight reduction to Salt Lake, and a proportionately larger decrease in rates the farther west the colonist comes. On the Salt Lake Route the tickets call for the allowance of five-day stopovers at Clear Lake and Milford, Utah, and Caliente and Las Vegas, Nev. The tickets will be on sale from March 1 to April 30, and special equipment is being arranged for on the various trunk lines to handle the traffic.

Las Vegas Age
February 29, 1908

CALIENTE

Caliente is nothing if not a community of consumers. It now has three liquor cold storage plants.

The Lode-Express announces that it is non-partisan in political matters. Good policy.

A good sized railroad payroll is Caliente's principal support. There is little mining activity there at present.

Deseret News (Utah)
March 6, 1908

SHOOTING AT CALIENTE.

None of the Salt Lake hospitals knew at noon today anything about Engineer Card, who was shot in a reported accident at Caliente, Nev., yesterday. Card was shot by Conductor C. ? Knox. Both men have families in Caliente and both are well known and highly respected. They were the best of friends and were playing with revolvers when the one Knox held in his hands, went off, the ball striking Card's head. The injured man was said to have been placed on the Overland passenger due in here at 6:30 o'clock this morning, but he has not reached any of the hospitals. It was thought Knox might have died while on the train, but none of the undertaking establishments had received any body from the west.

Emery County News (Utah)
March 7, 1908

Diphtheria has been quite prevalent in Caliente Nevada several cases and one death having occurred It is thought the Indians have spread the contagion It is known that an Indian child died with the disease before it appeared among the whites

COMMISSIONERS

Pioche, the Famous "Health" Resort, Gets County Hospital

The board of county commissioners met Monday March 2nd., 1908 at 10 o'clock. Present: J. A. Nesbitt, Chairman, W. E. Hawkins and Geo. T. Banovich members; Chas. Lee Horsey, district attorney and Wm. E. Orr, Clerk.

Minutes of February meeting read and approved.

Monthly reports of the various county officers, filed, read and approved.

Salary and general county bills, allowed as per Register Claim Book.

The board having inspected the steel work in the county jail and having found the same to be in full compliance with contract, it was ordered that said jail be accepted and that the contract price for such construction be paid.

Ordered that the amount heretofore allowed for the services of an extra jailer be discontinued.

In response to the advertisement caused to be made by the board for the submission of proposals for the caring of the county indigent sick, to be submitted at this meeting and proposals for the donation of ground etc. for the erection of county hospital, proposals were received from Dr. T. O. Duckworth of Pioche, Dr. J. W. Smith and Dr. W. P. Murray of Caliente and Buol & McPherson of Las Vegas. After due consideration of the different proposals submitted, the board deemed that submitted by Dr. T. O. Duckworth as being the more advantageous to the county, whereupon it was ordered that the contract for caring of the County indigent sick be let to said Dr. T. O. Duckworth for the sum of $350.00 per month. Said contractor to care for such sick and furnish all necessary supplies.

Applications for engineers, license were received from Henry C. Detmers and Nelson Baker. Granted.

Upon request of the deputy state school superintendent, it was ordered that the boundaries of the Goodsprings School district be changed to conform to the following description.

Commencing at a point eight miles directly north of Good Springs Post office; thence fourteen miles directly east; thence sixteen directly south; thence sixteen miles west, thence sixteen miles directly north; thence two miles directly east back to the place of beginning.

It was ordered that there be transferred from the general county fund to the salary fund the sum of $2,000.00

It was ordered that there be a special levy of six mills on the dollar of the assessed valuation of all sheep in Lincoln County.

A communication was received by the board asking that the liquor licenses issued to J. O. McIntosh and A. J. Hansen to conduct a saloon business in Meadow Valley Wash be revoked for the reason that said saloon was being conducted in violation of law. Said petition was laid over until April meeting for action.

No further business appearing the board adjourned

FATAL FUN

Practical Joke Results in Tragedy at Caliente--Engineer Card is Victim

Caliente, Nev., March 5—Engineer Osman Card was shot and killed today by Conductor G. T. Knox in a saloon where they were engaged in a game of cards. In a spirit of fun Card and Knox were to scare Engineer Davis and as the latter entered Card and Knox begun wrangling at each other and instantly pulled their guns. In a moment of excitement Knox accidentally pulled the trigger and Card dropped mortally wounded. Its the old story: "Didn't know it was loaded."

Card was put on No. 2 for Salt Lake, but died near Lund Utah. Both parties are well known railroad men and Card has a wife and child at Nephi, Utah.

Intermountain Catholic (Utah)
March 7, 1908

The construction work on the new Catholic church at Caliente, Nev., will soon be begun. Residents, both Catholic and non-Catholic, have subscribed liberally to the fund and the structure is now assured.

Inter-Mountain Republican (Utah)
March 8, 1908

DIED.

CARD—In Caliente, March 5, Osmond Card; in his 41st year. Funeral services will be held from the S. D. Evans mortuary chapel, 48 South State street, Monday, March 9, at 12 noon. Interment in Mt. Olivet.

Emery County News (Utah)
March 14, 1908

While Engineer Card and Conductor
Knox were fooling with a pistol at
Caliente Nevada the weapon was ac
cidentally discharged and Card was
shot in the head and fatally injured

Inter-Mountain Republican (Utah)
March 14, 1908

SHERIFF IS INDICTED FOR KILLING BROTHER

Phillip Smith of Caliente Hold-
·.·ing Himself on Charge of
· Voluntary Manslaughter.

Republican Special Service.

Pioche, Nev., March 13.—Phillip
Smith of Caliente, sheriff of Lincoln
county, was yesterday indicted by the
grand jury now in session for the killing of his brother. John Smith, on the
street in Caliente last December. At
the time of the shooting it is alleged
Sheriff Smith was on a protracted
spree. He fell in a stupor on the street
and his brother ran to pick him up.
The sheriff failed to recognize his
brother, pulled a pistol and fired on
him.

John Smith was taken to Salt Lake
and placed in the Holy Cross hospital,
where, after lingering about three
weeks, he died. Sheriff Smith claims
that his mind is an absolute blank on
the shooting. The prosecution of the
sheriff will be conducted by Charles
Lee Horsey, who, with Sheriff Smith,
was elected by a large majority on the
Democratic ticket two years ago. Smith
is popular in Lincoln county, where he
was well known as a ranchman long
before he sought political preferment.

The most peculiar feature of the
case is the fact that Smith as sheriff
of Lincoln county is responsible as an
official for the return of himself, as an
individual, to the trial court.

Deseret News (Utah)
March 17, 1908

CALIENTE TO BE DIVISION POINT

Salt Lake Route To Be Divided In Two On and After April 1.

The Salt Lake Route will be divided into two divisions on and after April 1, with Caliente as the dividing point. Everything east of the west switch in the Caliente yards will be Salt Lake division and everything west of it, will be the Los Angeles division. The Los Angeles division now contains Las Vegas at which point the Las Vegas & Tonpah branches off to the north. At first thought it would appear the western division is much longer, but there is quite a stretch of Santa Fe in use by the Salt Lake Route on the western end and this must be deducted, of course. The change was made for convenience, solely. The two men in charge of the line are H. E. Van Housen, superintendent of the Salt Lake division and T. T. Cullen, of the Los Angeles division. They have their headquarters at the eastern and western termini respectively.

RAILROAD

Las Vegas Not Effected By Change of Division

The Salt Lake has made a change in the division of territory between its superintendents, to take effect April 1st. On the west end the jurisdiction of Supt., Cullen has been extended to Caliente, while Supt. Van Housen retains jurisdiction of Caliente and east from that point. The change is made merely to equalize the mileage between the two officials and will not change the runs of any of the train crews now laying over in Las Vegas.

Over a million dollars have been expended to put the Salt Lake road above high water in Meadow Valley wash, but no floods this year to test the efficiency of the work. An army of laborers will soon break up camp.

Eastern and western railroads have concluded to make 2 cent rates and less to conventions and excursions, but the the local rates in Nevada remain from five to seven cents per mile. Lower rates would bring more business.

At Parker on the Colorado, below the Needles, the Santa Fe is building a big bridge for the railroad cut-off, which opens a new mining country.

Speaking of the proposed change of division from Las Vegas, to suit the 16 hour law, a railroad man said his life was something like that of the farmer's chicken. It had been moved so often that it sat down and crossed its legs to be tied every time Mr Hayseed came to the barnyard.

CALIENTE

Mr. Martin Hamilton came to Vegas Tuesday to enjoy metropolitan life for a day. He says McIntosh and Miller are doing well, but the town is quiet, because many men' working on the railroad have been let out.

Political Potpie...

Voting precincts should be made at Arden and Sunset.

Nearly all the boys now holding office in this county desire a continuance.

Senator Newlands was in Reno last week and announced his desire for re-election to the Senate.

Republicans of Las Vegas will meet Tuesday evening to organize a Republican Club. Officers will be elected.

John Howe of Searchlight and Senator Denton of Caliente are mentioned for Sheriff. Phil Smith will not again seek the office.

Senator Newlands, booster on the Inland Water Ways Committee, seems to have forgotten that the Colorado river once carried steamers to within 25 miles of Las Vegas. Nevada statesmen should remember their home State if it is off the champagne route at present.

RAILROAD

Supt. Cullen, Master Mechanic Lundholm and other Salt Lake officials were over the line from Vegas to Caliente arranging for the extension of Cullen's division to Caliente April 1st. This has caused more men to make headquarters at Las Vegas.

Railroad mountain time is now dead at Las Vegas and we are working under Pacific time. Mountain time has been shoved up to Caliente—thanks. Don't get up in the middle of the night now for breakfast.

April 1st saw an increase in railroad men at Las Vegas. Ten crews of locomotive men and ten crews of trainmen began making headquarters at Vegas.

We have good authority for saying that railroad machine shops will be built at Las Vegas soon as money becomes a little easier.

More cottages are wanted for railroad men and the company contemplates the construction of a few.

Manager Hedden of the Tonopah & Goldfield railroad has resigned and will go east, while an eastern man, named Hamlin has taken his place.

PRETTY NEAR THE LIMIT.

On Sunday last the Tribune stated, by way of proving the incapacity of Postmaster Thomas, that a mail pouch had been lost on the way to the depot, directed to Caliente, and had been taken into a saloon and kept until next day, when it was "returned" to the postoffice.

Here is the truth. A mail bag containing newspapers from the Tribune office was dropped FROM THE TRIBUNE'S OWN WAGON Saturday night. It was taken into a saloon, and was later sent on its way. It never had been in the possession of the postoffice before its loss from the Tribune wagon. The wagon is the private conveyance of the Tribune, the driver is their employe, and the contents of the mail bags are Tribunes exclusively.

Postmaster Thomas never had anything to do with that lost bag. It never was in the Salt Lake postoffice before it was found in the street and carried to the saloon. It was in no possible way then connected with the mail service of Salt Lake or the United States government.

Yet that paper declared the postmaster had lost the bag, that he had caused the making up of a "dummy" bag for Caliente to take the place of the one he had lost, and that he was an incompetent official, and dishonorable man.

There is a pretty fair sample of the Tribune's method of warfare.

Loses its own mail bag from its own wagon, and then blames the postmaster.

Hereafter, when you read that paper's condemnation of Arthur L. Thomas, you will know it is another story of its own mistakes charged against a man the Tribune owner hates.

CALIENTE

The Lode Express says Hans Olson of Caliente is a candidate for Sheriff; also Smith of Searchlight, Sam Blunt of Caliente, Jake Johnson of Delamar and Sam Gay. Ed. Clark and Frank Williams for State Senate.

COMMISSIONRS

The Board of County Commissioners of Lincoln County, Nevada, met Monday, April 6th, A. D. 1908 at 10 o'clock a. m. present: James A. Nesbitt, Chairman; Geo. T. Banovich, member; Chas. Lee Horsey, district attorney and Wm. E. Orr, Clerk.

Minutes of March meeting read and approved. Salary and General County bills allowed as per register claim book.

The Clerk was instructed to advertise for new water mains for Pioche.

Deputy Sheriff for Royal City ordered at salary of $50 per month.

That salary of Deputy Sheriff at Panaca be discontinued.

Petition for W. J. McBurney for Deputy Sheriff, Muddy river, laid over.

That C. W. Patterson be appointed Supt. of Fire and Water, with bond, at $50 per month at Caliente.

Petition of Frank Bonelli, J. I. Earl and Frank Miller granted to act as locators of county road from Moapa to Wise ranch.

David Boyer appointed road supervisor of Eldorado district.

Geo. C. Baldwin appointed road inspector for the Upper Muddy.

Bunkerville petition for $500 for road to Moapa laid over.

A communication from the School Trustees of Good Springs for an appropriation of $500 was laid over.

It was ordered that a school tax of $4.50 per hundred be levied on the Good Springs school district.

Adjourned to Monday, May 11th.

RAILROAD NEWS

All freight and passenger crews will probably make headquarters at Vegas soon. A liberal legal construction of the law will do it.

The widow of Claude Bailey is suing the Salt Lake for damages for the death of her husband in an explosion near Arden last August.

Again the Railroad Commission is after the big railroads in California for rebating. Even the rich have troubles.

Another change is expected in passenger railroad runs May 1st, which may favor Caliente or Otis. Under the law the roads are having difficulty to adjust their business.

An electric railroad to the Colorado river from Vegas, and another down the Muddy to St Thomas and Bunkerville are probabilities.

Las Vegas Age
April 25, 1908

CALIENTE

New Catholic church building.
Senator Denton may run for Sheriff.

Las Vegas Age
May 2, 1908

CALIENTE

The County Commissioners certainly
feel proud of the appearance of their
official newspaper.

Mr. Carl Schmidt and Miss Lizzie
Hansen were married at Panaca.

Las Vegas Age
May 9, 1908

Wedding at Caliente

On Monday last Rev. Dr. Bain took a
trip to Caliente to officiate at the Denton Foster wedding. He reports a fine
occasion. The groom is J. Lester Denton, nephew of ex-Senator Denton, and
the bride one of the fair daughters of
Caliente—Miss Hazel May Foster.

At 7 o'clock on Tuesday evening, at
the home of the groom, the contracting
parties appeared and the ceremonies
were solemnized.

Following the ceremony refreshments
were served to the vast crowds who
came to congratulate the happy pair.

Las Vegas Age
May 16, 1908

CALIENTE

It is said that many people in Caliente favor county removal or division.

Emery County News (Utah)
May 16, 1908

An Indian called Keno while on a drunken debauch became entangled in a barb wire fence about ten miles from Caliente and was out all night in the snow and rain When discovered and taken to town for treatment he was in such condition that he has small chance of recovery

Las Vegas Age
May 23, 1908

CALIENTE

Hans Olson will be back from Sweden before the convention.
Sam Blunt also wants to be Sheriff.

Las Vegas Age
May 30, 1908

PIOCHE

Pioche baseball team recently beat Caliente 11 to 10,

Reported that Newhouse will build a smelter at Pioche.

Pioche proposes to bond and build a $15,000 school house.

Political Potpie...

Senator Denton is Chairman and Ed. Clark Secretary of the Democratic Central committee.

Searchlight, Caliente and other sections should organize political clubs and communicate officially with Vegas Club.

Searchlight has a candidate for Congress, Mr. Wright, but we do not know him. His home town will probably endorse him for support.

Many names are mentioned for the Senate or Representative—Judge Lillis, W. R. Thomas, Frank Williams, Levi Syphus, John Shier, Senator Campbell, Ed. Clark, Sam Yount and others.

Ex-Senator J. A. Denton of Caliente and Frank Williams of Crescent were in Las Vegas Friday on their way to the Democratic State convention at Carson. They will work for Ed. Clark for delegate to the National convention at Denver. In the anticipated fight over instructions and endorsement of U. S. Senator the Lincoln delegation will stand for Bryan and Newlands.

RAILROAD

Mr. J. H. Burtner of the Salt Lake railroad was in Vegas Monday.

Division changes will cause some new railroad men to move from Caliente to Las Vegas soon.

J. F. Bragelton, Chief Clerk to Salt Lake Supt. of Machinery, was in Vegas Wednesday on business.

Las Vegas Age
June 6, 1908

BASEBALL

Vegas local teams will play Sunday at 2:30, the Caliente club having backed down, fearing defeat. So say the boys.

Len Stewart of Caliente was married recently to Miss Jennie King. And Paul Shirley recently arrived with his bride. Both railroad boys.

Peter Hopley of Lewis, Ida., an importer of heavy thoroughbred horses, is at the Kenyon. He has in the past shipped many horses to Utah.

Bishop Scanlan has returned from a week's visit through the mining camps of southern Nevada. He officiated at the dedication of the Caliente Catholic church.

George Roberts of this city has gone to Bews, Nev., to work for the Nevada Construction company until the opening of the fall term at the state university, when he will return to Salt Lake to resume his collegiate studies.

C. G. Lundholm has been over the Salt Lake route from Otis to Caliente during the past week. He reports an improvement in business.

PIOCHE

Pioche baseball club was defeated by Caliente 18 to 13.

It is reported that Senator Clark will extend the Pioche railroad branch on to Ely soon.

CALIENTE

We understand that Hans Olson expects to arrive home at Caliente from a trip to Sweden about July 6th. Mr. Olson has announced himself as a candidate for Sheriff of this county.

The attendance at the Episcopal services held by Rev. H. G. Gray on Tuesday evening was large and an interesting service was enjoyed. There is some talk of organizing a church here.

Regular services will be held every two weeks hereafter.

Judge H. M. Lillis made a business trip to Caliente Thursday.

Mr. and Mrs. J. O. McIntosh of Caliente are in town for a few days greeting old friends with smiling faces. It seems quite like old times to see "Mc" and his estimable wife on our streets again.

Las Vegas Age
June 27, 1908

County Division?

With symptoms of great nervousness and in words which fairly make the type tremble with excitement, our good friend the Caliente Lode Express fearfully inquires:

"Who is this Beal doing so much mouthing about the division of Lincoln county? We don't hear him say anything about the county getting out of its big debt and becoming a little easier financially while he is harping division. Who are you Mr. Beal, anyway?"

Now don't be impatient, brother. Of course, with the weight of County governmental and political affairs resting heavily upon your shoulders and bearing the brunt of the tremendous battle for supremacy now waging between Caliente and Pioche, as you do, it is not surprising that you have momentarily overlooked the fact that there is at least a small and unimportant fraction of the world outside of Caliente.

As to the county "getting out of its big debt and becoming a little easier financially" our brother seems very hard to please. Surely under the management of our northern statesmen, the County has long been about the easiest thing, financially, on record.

It appears, however, that the debt is so securely fixed that there is no "getting out" of it except—to pay up.

We hope you won't think us impertinent, brother, if we should ask which of two horns of the dilemma you would prefer. Shall we leave the county as it is and move the County seat to Las Vegas, or would you prefer to divide the County and leave the old County seat in the hands of Pioche, your deadly rival? We wish to be accommodating, so just let us know which you prefer.

As to "this Beal"—if you should ever visit these foreign parts we would be glad to introduce you to a man—and a gentleman.

Las Vegas Age
July 4, 1908

LINCOLN COUNTY REPUBLICANS

Perfect Organization and Select Delegates to State Convention

In pursuance to a call issued by the Republican County Central Committee, representatives of the Republican party of Lincoln County convened at Las Vegas, June 30th. The meeting, which took place at the headquarters of Las Vegas Republican Club, resulted in the perfection of the organization of the Republicans of this County and the selection of eight delegates to the State Convention at Goldfield on August 27, 1908. Harmony was the keynote of the meeting and there is no doubt but what the Republican Party of Lincoln County is now in a position to make a strong fight for first honors in the coming campaign.

The preceedings were opened by A. W. Jurden, Central Committeeman from Las Vegas, with representation from eighteen precincts out of a possible twenty-five on the floor before him. In the absence of John G. Brown, chairman of the Central Committee, who was unavoidably absent on account of illness, A. W. Jurden was selected as temporary chairman and Eugene Goodrich of Pioche, secretary, performed his duties as such in his usually capable manner.

(Concluded on last page)

REPUBLICANS

(Concluded from first page)

The first business before the meeting was the filling of vacancies existing in the County Central Committee, which was accomplished with the following result.

List of members of the Republican County Central Committee by precincts.

Alamo, J. E. Allen.

Arden, J. A. Sumner.

Barclay, Albert Woods.

Bristol, Charles Fernander.

Bunkerville, Ezra Bunker and Ed Cox.

Caliente, George E. Coxe, W. P. Murray and A. Springall.

Crescent, M. H. McClure.

Delamar, George W. Nesbitt, Bert Pace and H. W. Turner.

Eagle Valley, J. M. Hollanger.

Fay, Henry Bennett.

Goodsprings, S. E. Yount and C. E. McCarthy.

Highland, J. W. Taylor.

Hiko, David Service.

Las Vegas, W. J. Stewart, W. R. Bracken, F. W. Manuel, J. D. Kramer and A. W. Jurden.

Logan, H. H. Church.

Lake Valley, ----

Mesquite, Nephi Johnson and W. F. Abbott.

Moapa, F. F. Gunn.

Nelson, E. P. Jeans.

Overton, John W. Bunker and Maudus Cooper.

Panaca, A. G. Bladd and Chris Ronnow.

Pioche, Eugene Goodrich, John G. Brown, M. L. Lee and W. W. Stockhan.

Potosi, W. E. Smith.

Power Plant, George Baker.

Sandy, Walter McCuen and Jesse Jones.

Searchlight, Howard Perkins, W. T. Kennedy, H. A. Perkins, F. A. Doherty, Wm. Colton, H. A. Walbrecht, G. E. Burdick and Leon French.

Spring Valley, Henry Rice and A. Delmue.

Sunset, John Burns.

St. Thomas, Frank Bonelli.

As delegates to the State Convention at Goldfield to be held August 27th the following were selected:—George Baker, Delamar; A. Bladd, Panaca; H. H. Church, Logan; F. A. Doherty, Searchlight; Eugene Goodrich, Pioche; C. E.

McCarthy, Goodsprings; Dr. W. P. Murray, Caliente and C. C. Ronnow, Las Vegas.

As alternates to the State Convention the following were selected:—J. G. Brown, Pioche; Stephen Bunker, Bunkerville; George Coxe, Caliente; H. A. Perkins, Searchlight; W. Geer, Hiko; H. M. Lillis, Las Vegas; George W. Nesbitt, Delamar and S. E. Yount, Goodsprings.

Ordered that the County Convention be held at Caliente on Thursday, September 17, 1908.

Ordered that the representation at the County Convention be on the basis of one delegate at large from each precinct and one additional delegate for every 15 votes and major fraction thereof cast for Oscar J. Smith for Congress in the election of 1906.

Ordered that the primaries to select delegates to the County Convention be held on Thursday, September 3rd, 1908, between the hours of 1 p. m. and 8. p. m.

Election officers to serve at the above

Election officers to serve at the above primaries in the various precincts were selected as follows.

List of precinct election officers and polling places for primaries, Sept. 3, 1908:

Alamo: J. E. Allen, W. T. Stewart, A. Niebecker; school house.

Arden: J. A. Sumner, A. Simmons; boarding house.

Barclay, Albert Woods, J. Woods, H' Empy; school house.

Bristol: C. Fernander, A. Bishop, A. VanEmon; Fernander's.

Bunkerville: J. S. Abbott, Frank Cox, Ed. Bunker; school house.

Caliente: J. W. Smith, George Coxe, O. M. Moody; Ward's Hall.

Crescent: H. M. McClure, J. S. Morgan; McClure's.

Delamar: J. Johnson, Bert Puce, H. W. Turner; school house.

Eagle Valley: J. M. Hollanger, Ed Lytle, Wm. Werem; school house.

Fay: Henry Bennet, E. H. Hackett, O. Stokes; school house.

Goodsprings: O. E. McCarthy, Harvey Hardy, Jr., P. H. Springer; school house.

Highland: J. W. Taylor, I. Hinkle; Menduli Mine office.

Hiko: David Service, Lewis Stern,

A. W. Gear; school house.

Las Vegas: A. W. Jurden, H. M. Lillis, C. C. Ronnow; Republican Club Rooms.

Logan: H. H. Church, W. T. Bowman, J. Wells; school house.

Lake Valley: School house.

Mesquite: Nephi Johnson, W. F. Abbott, Allen Waters; school house.

Moapa: A. T. Sharp, F. F. Gunn, W. C. Bowman; Bowman's Hotel.

Nelson: H. Spanogle, E. P. Jeans, J. Smith; Vanna's.

Overton: S. A. Angel, T. J. Jones, Maudus Cooper; school house.

Panaca: A. G. Blad, Chris Ronnow, H. Mathews; school house.

Pioche: Jesse Peaslee, F. W. Dickle, H. E. Freudenthal; Hotel Cecil.

Potosi: W. E. Smith, Clayton Smith, J. Poznasky; mine office.

Power Plant: George Baker, M. Matasky, J. Jones; school house.

Sandy: Walter McCuen, Jesse Jones, Nickolas Kuntz; McClanahan's.

Searchlight: F. A. Doherty, Wm. Colton, H. A. Perkins; Doherty's office.

Spring Valley: Henry Rice, Chas. Millet, A. Delmue; school house.

St. Thomas: Frank Bonelli, Jacob Bauer, W. Murphy; school house.

Sunset: John Burns, L. Butterfield, Wm. Bright; mine office.

Adjourned subject to call of chairman of County Central Committee.

PIOCHE

The Pioche Weekly Record contains an account of a rare and racy rumor to the effect that R. D. Montgomery, station agent at Pioche, was recently obliged to take a hasty departure from that growing city owing to the discovery of his intimate relations with the wife of Brakeman Garrison.

Pioche is now enjoying the luxury of a real "phone" system with a central station. A long distance line connecting Vegas with Caliente, Pioche and the Muddy Valley would be a great convience.

Las Vegas Age
August 1, 1908

Mrs. F. R. McNamee and children passed through Vegas Wednesday. They were met here by Mr. McNamee and after a short visit in Caliente will return to their summer home in Los Angeles.

A washout near Caliente Tuesday delayed all trains for a short time.

Inter-Mountain Republican
August 6, 1908

WASHOUT RESULT OF CLOUDBURST

Salt Lake Route Tied Up, but Will Reopen This Afternoon.

PASSENGERS AT CALIENTE

Present Trouble Is First Real Test of Reconstructed Track.

About two miles of track on the Salt Lake route near Acoma, Nev., was partially washed out and rendered unsafe for travel Tuesday night and it will be at least 24 hours before temporary repairs are completed for through traffic between Salt Lake and Los Angeles. The washout was the result of a cloudburst near the top of the highest point on the railroad and about ten miles east of the serious washouts of one and two years ago. First reports of the trouble indicated that the railroad would be tied up for three or four days and agents of other lines were instructed to sell no tickets over the Salt Lake route until further notice. Reports received at the local offices last night changed the prospects for the better and it was announced that the line would be opened for through traffic early Thursday afternoon.

This announcement led to a change in plans in Salt Lake and Los Angeles and trains east and west were started out last night with prospects of getting through with little delay.

Two trains each way were held up by the washout and these will arrive in Salt Lake and Los Angeles 24 to 36 hours late. The washout was discovered by an inspector and serious trouble was avoided by holding the trains at each side of the washout. Passengers bound for Salt Lake sent telegrams from Acoma saying they were delayed and then their train was taken back to Caliente, where good accommodations for the passengers were provided. The west-bound trains were held at Modena, Utah, so that little discomfort was experienced except for the delay.

The experience of the Clark road during its first two years of existence resulted in practical rebuilding of the roadbed through the Meadow Valley wash and more than $1,000,000 was expended in this work. The bed of the wash was straightened and heavy stone and concrete protecting walls were built. New bridges were substituted for the temporary structures.

The cloudburst of Tuesday night, being near the summit above the extensive repair work in Meadow Valley, this reconstructed portion of the track has had its first real test since its completion last spring.

Lund, Nevada, August 10.—We are having rain every two or three days. The crops are growing very fast, the second crop of alfalfa is being cut.

Bishop O. H. Snow, his children, mother and sister, Mrs John H. Gardner, have gone to Pine Valley, Utah, to attend the Snow family reunion, to be held at that place.

Willard Burgess has returned from Gridley, California. He has come on a visit.

George E. Burgess is getting ready to move to Alpine, Utah, he will go in September.

The school trustees are talking of bonding the district to build a school house.

Some of our first crop of hay is being hauled to Ely where it brings $23 per ton.

Miss Mary Sinfield is going to Ely to work for Mrs Miles for a few weeks.

Martin Peterson and Dan Nicolns of Preston were over here yesterday.

A number of our boys have gone to Lake valley to help put up hay.

The two large smelters at McGill's have been running.

DISTANCES

In Lincoln County, to Pioche and Las Vegas

Mileage given is by ordinary conveyance route. Note the remarkable equalization of distances in the proposed division on the Third Standard Paralell.

Township	Miles to Pioche	Miles to Las Vegas
Searchlight	233	77
Nelson	257	101
Crescent	219	63
Jean	187	31
Goodsprings	195	39
Sandy	207	51
Potosi	195	30
Las Vegas	156	...
Moapa	107	49
Logan	119	61
Overton	122	64
St. Thomas	131	73
Bunkervill	147	89
Mesquite	152	94
Gold Butte	157	99
Caliente	33	
Ursine (Eagle Valley)	16	
Newlands (Spring Valley)	22	
Fay (Deer Lodge)	22	
Barclay (Clover Valley)	55	
DeLamar	68	
Alamo	98	
Hiko	100	
Panaca	12	
Geyser (Lake Valley)	60	
Stine	41	
Jack Rabbit	18	
Bristol	23	
Tem Piute	130	

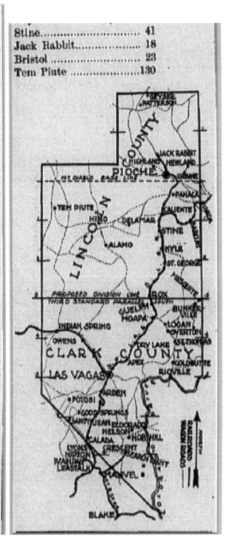

We are informed that Harry W. Preston, Editor of the Caliente Lode-Express has been arrested on a charge of criminal libel on account of an article published in the Lode Express Aug. 22d with regard to Eugene Goodrich, Editor of the Pioche Record. It is also reported that in retaliation Eugene Goodrich will be made the defendant in a similar suit on account of the publication in the Record of alleged libelous and slanderous matter relating to Jake Johnson, ex-sheriff.

REPUBLICAN STATE CONVENTION

NOMINEES

Congressman—Col. H. B. Maxson of Washoe County.

Supreme Judge—Hugh Brown of Nye County.

Surveyor General—Con. A. Ahern of Storey County.

Presidential Electors—W. R. Thomas of Lincoln County, J. G. Thompson of Esmeralda, H. A. Comins of White Pine.

Regents—A. A. Codd of Esmeralda, H. A. Comins of White Pine, H. S. Starrett of Lander.

State Chairman—W. J. Humphreys of Washoe.

Patrick L. Flanigan was endorsed for United States Senator.

Lincoln County was represented by a strong delegation consisting of Joseph Ronnow of Panaca, John Shier and W. P. Murray of Caliente, Geo. Baker of Stine, H. H. Church of Logan, C. C. Ronnow and H. M. Lillis of Las Vegas, C. E. McCarthy of Goodsprings, Frank A. Doherty of Searchlight.

John Shier was appointed a member of the Committee on Credentials, W. P. Murray on Platform and Resolutions and Geo. Baker on Permanent Organization. As a result of the active work of the delegation the claims of the south were recognized by the nomination of Hon. W. R. Thomas of Las Vegas as a Presidential Elector.

Col. H. B. Maxson, Congressional nominee, is an able and versatile man. He has a very wide acquaintance throughout the State and will prove a most successful campaigner.

The challenge of the supporters of U. S. Senator Francis G. Newlands, that the names of the Senatorial candidates appear on the ticket in order to secure an expression of the will of the people, was accepted by the Hon. P. L. Flanigan and endorsed by the convention. Mr. Flanigan has worked his way to his present position of prominence by his square dealing and his staunch integrity and force of character. He is said to be an educated, polished and versatile gentlemen of high standing in the communities where he is best known.

Our delegates returned with high praises for the open-handed hospitality of the people of Goldfield, where everything possible was done to add to their pleasure and comfort. The closing feature of the visit was an elegant banquet given the delegates at the splendid new Goldfield Hotel, at which the beauty, wit, wealth and wisdom of the State were represented.

Adolph Levy and J. F. Fox last week visited Caliente and Delamar and secured many signatures to the County Division petitions. They report that in every case a clear presentation of the facts would gain a convert to the cause and that they were received by the people in a spirit of fairness and neighborly feeling.

Mrs. T. H. Sharp and Mrs. M. B. Goodwin enjoyed a visit with Mr. and Mrs. J. O. McIntosh at Caliente last week. Among other pleasures, they attended the picnic given by the railroad men at Panaca, in company with Mr. and Mrs. McIntosh. The picnic was a grand success and a royal good time enjoyed by all fortunate enough to be present.

Washington County News (Utah)
September 10, 1908

Mrs. Lucy Oxborrow and Mrs Earl Ashworth arrived here Monday from Lund, Nevada, to visit relatives.

Davis County Clipper (Utah)
September 11, 1908

The little daughter of Mr. and
Mrs. Tennish of Caliente, Nev,
who was suddenly taken ill in
Salt Lake, while on the way to
her home in Caliente, Nevada, is
much better and it is believed
she will be able to accompany
her mother home in a few days

Davis County Clipper (Utah)
September 14, 1908

Saturday as Mrs. Ruth Tennish of Caliente, Nev., who had
been here visiting with her sister, Mrs. H. J. Harrison, reached
Salt Lake on her way home, her
little girl developed a bad case of
typhoid fever so she was obliged
to remain in the city. She is
stopping with her mother, Mrs.
Acocks with whom she had also
spent part of the month she was
up here.

Lund, Nevada, Sept. 14.—It has rained almost every day during the past week and the harvesting of grain and cutting of hay has been delayed as a result   The threshing machine started threshing yesterday.

Lund and Preston have organized a farmers' institute and they have contracted the present crop of hay and grain at Ely, the price for hay being $21 per ton and $40 per ton for grain   The potato crop is not contracted yet but the prospect is good.

E. A. Hendrix took four of his sons to Ely this week to start them for Provo, Utah, where they will attend school. They are Edmund A., Gideon, Ray and Philo.

Last Friday the Preston baseball team came over and played the Lund team for a dance, the result being the Lund boys got a free dance in the Preston hall.

Gomer Nicholas, a resident of Sanpete, has started a saloon here. Our worthy fathers and mothers are hoping it will last soon and live a short life.

Geo E Burgess will start with his family for Alpine, Utah, the 15th inst. to make his home at that place

Elder Ernest H Burgess left last week for Salt Lake City, where he will attend school the coming year.

George, Wilford and Elby Terry have returned from Sunnyside, where they had been working.

Mrs Heber C. Smith has gone to Lake valley to visit with relatives for a few days.

The WASHINGTON COUNTY NEWS is a welcome visitor at Lund. Long may it live.

Jack Frost paid us a visit the other night but did not do much damage.

Dan Nicholas and Ed Funk of Preston were in town today.

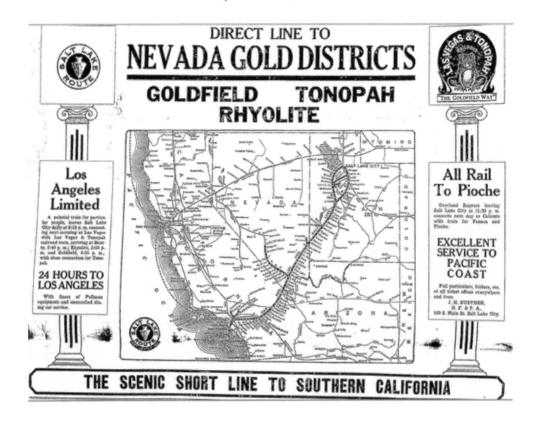

Las Vegas Age
September 29, 1908

DR. W. P. MURRAY

Dr. W. P. Murray of Caliente is known as an able, energetic and progressive citizen. In politics he is known to be opposed to any form of graft or political jobbery. He was one of the first in the north to come out frankly and openly in favor of County Division and if elec- ted may be depended upon to help carry this issue to a successful conclusion and one fair to all sections.

Las Vegas Age
October 3, 1908

The light of journalism in Caliente recently flickered over much and went out, leaving our sister city to group in the dark. Perhaps the injection of an excess of personality in the Lode-Express is in a measure responsible for this or perhaps the lack of support on the part of Caliente people, or again perhaps the one is responsible for the other.

Be this as it may, any town the size of Caliente should have a live paper and give it hearty support.

The newspaper of a town is the light by which the world may know it is alive. If the people support the paper the light burns brightly and attracts many from afar.

Don't expect your paper to be perfect for an editor is only human. But do expect and insist that your paper shall be an optimist and a booster. Each place has its own peculiar advantages. Insist that your paper shall work to build up, not to pull down. Support it with your business, assist it with information and a good live paper will make a city of any town.

Here's hoping, Caliente that your next newspaper may be a success.

Lund, Nevada, Sept. 27.—The people of Lund are favored with the presence of Apostles Geo. A. Smith and Anthony W. Ivins, Pres. Ed. H. Snow of the St. George Stake and Stake Clerk David R Forsha. Our ward conference was held today, the speakers being Pres E. H. Snow and Elders Smith and Ivins There will be another meeting held this evening.

We have had a cold rain storm ending with a frost, which killed our gardens and injured some hay. Our threshing machine had to lay off on account of the rain.

Jacob Schmutz and Mr. Bearlocker from Washington were here the past week with Dixie fruit.

Our primary school will start tomorrow morning with Mrs. Earnest H. Burgess as teacher.

A goodly number of the Preston people were over to attend conference.

The frost caught some of the late oats, also some of the last crop of hay.

Our late grain is not all harvested yet.

ITINERARY

Democratic Meetings

The Democratic Campaign has opened in ernest and from now on candidates will go sleepless. Meetings have been arranged as follows:

Oct.
17 Overton
18 St. Thomas
19 Bunkerville
20 Mesquite
21 Caliente
22 Delamar
23 Alamo
24 Hiko
25 Delamar
26 Panaca
27 Eagle Valley
28 Spring Valley and Fay
29 Pioche
30 Jack Rabbit
31 Las Vegas

The meeting at Las Vegas Oct 31st will be an enthusiastic wind up of the campaign and the feature of great interest will be the grand ball at which the candidates will do the honors.

Las Vegas Age
October 24, 1908

Brotherhood of Locomotive Engineers

A new division of the Brotherhood of Locomotive Engineers will be organized on Sunday next in this city, to be known as "Mt. Charleston No. 766"

A number of members from Caliente, Los Angeles and other points will be present to assist in the installation ceremonies, among them being Messrs Mason and Diffenbaugh of Los Angeles and Wills of Chicago.

This order is probably the most effective organization in existence and has done more to advance the interests of its members than any other. Yet, through its conservatism and fairness, it retains the confidence and respect of both employers and employees. Would that the same were true of all similar organizations.

Inter-Mountain Republican (Utah)
October 27, 1908

GOOD STRIKE OF GOLD NEAR CALIENTE, NEV.

Salt Lake Man Opens Promising Prospect Overlooking Town.

Caliente, Nev., according to Joseph T. Jenkins, who came up from the south Sunday, is in the throes of a gold excitement on account of a strike made in the property of the Caliente Gold Mining company, overlooking the town. The stock of the company is nearly all owned by Charles E. Rives of this city and Los Angeles associates.

Mr. Rives is confident that he has a bonanza. From the surface he has stripped a zone 20 feet or more in dimensions and in that quarry-like cavity he has exposed nine feet of ore which he says will average better than $26 a ton in gold, while not a little shows free gold. He has on the ground a supply of sacks into which he is throwing the high grade stuff and it looks as though the proposition would be made to pay its way from grass roots. The vein has been traced for more than 3,000 feet and it is said that at frequent intervals ore is found showing as much free gold as that in the main workings.

Women as well as men were trooping up to the scene of the strike Sunday, Mr. Jenkins says, and the little city was congratulating itself that it is yet to be the center of a gold-producing district.

The ore taken from the prospect is not unlike the high-grade product of Goldfield, some of the richest of it consisting of a talcose gangue with granulated quartz, and the showing at least warrants the performance of sufficient work to determine the presence of the ledge with its ores in place at greater depth.

Richfield Reaper (Utah)
October 29, 1908

Miss Maggie Erickson Married

Mr. and Mrs Sydney Pace arrived here from Delamar, Nevada, last Saturday on a honeymoon trip among the friends and relatives of the bride. Mrs. Pace was Miss Maggie Erickson up until the 18th inst, when she was married to Mr. Pace in the Nevada town A reception was tendered the couple at the home of the bride's parents, Mr. and Mrs. E. P. Erickson, and the friends of the bride gave her a splendid greeting and many wishes for future happiness The couple will continue their honeymoon trip down to St. George before returning to Delamar. Mr. Pace is a prosperous young business man of the latter place and that will be their home for the present. Mrs. Pace is one of Richfield's prettiest and most accomplished young ladies.

Lund, Nevada, Nov 1 —It is expected that work on the foundation of a meeting house for this place will be commenced next week. It is the intention to erect a cement building, part of the cement for it being here.

Most of our farmers are hauling hay, grain, and potatoes to Ely. Our cattle are not looking as well as they usually do at this season.

People here are busy digging potatoes, which the frost caught in the ground, resulting in some loss

The grammar grade school started last Monday with a Mr. Williams of Ely as teacher

Heber C. Smith has gone to Smelter to work.

John Shier of Caliente spent election day in Vegas, keeping his eye on the political game.

Inter-Mountain Republican (Utah)
November 7, 1908

CAN'T FULLY INDORSE CALIENTE'S BIG STRIKE

Alleged Rich Find Lacks Signs of Permanency, Says Engineer.

W. C. Marshall, mining engineer, who upon the way home from the Irish Mountain district took occasion to examine the reputed big gold find at Caliente, has to report that in his opinion it has been greatly overrated. He found that instead of there being eight feet of rock showing free gold, as had been reported, the free gold showing was limited to about eight inches. And aside from this the ore is found in a big lense—indications of permanency are lacking.

But further back in the country, about three and one-half miles northwest of the original strike, he says that he found a formation altogether favorable for the making of permanent ore bodies. The formation there includes diorite, andesite, biatite, rhyolite, all cut by the different classes of porphyry.

On account of the strike at Caliente the country has been staked from that point right up to the line of what Mr. Marshall regards the really promising mineralized section, and for about five miles northeast and southwest. But no one has yet got over onto the ground where he expects mineral to be found in paying quantities.

Mr. Marshall found considerable activity in the Irish Mountain district. Easterners are doing good work on the Illinois and Indiana claims, and the Prohilo company, formed by Provo and Salt Lake people, is sending in a hoist and a force of men to start active development.

The Bamberger-De Lamar mine is running at full blast turning out 400 tons daily of ore that averages from $3 to $3.50 a ton in gold. In the mill an adaptation of the usual process is being worked successfully; this consisting of the full strength of the cyanide solution being applied at the crusher.

Inter-Mountain Republican (Utah)
November 11, 1908

SAY CALIENTE STRIKE LOOKS LIKE WINNER

Is Promising Gold Prospect, Declare Bransford and Farrell

James Farrell and Mayor Bransford are favorably impressed by the new gold strike at Caliente, which they took occasion to examine when on the way home from Pioche. The strike is only a half mile from the depot at Caliente, so that it is an ideal situation as to transportation facilities and other conveniences in the event that a mine should be opened.

"I regard it a fine looking prospect," said Mr. Farrell. While virtually nothing but quarry work has been done so far it has exposed a four-foot vein of ore with free gold showing all through it.

"There are two veins, as a matter of fact, and outcroppings some distance up the hill from the surface workings indicate that the two veins come together there. A tunnel is to be driven to tap the theoretical juncture of the veins at considerable depth and if promising indications do not fail a good body of ore will be opened. It is as good a showing for the amount of work done as I have seen anywhere."

Emery County News (Utah)
November 14, 1908

A mining engineer who has recently investigated the reputed big gold find at Caliente Nevada finds that the free gold showing is limited to about eight inches of the eight feet of rock On account of the strike at Caliente the country has been staked for miles

BIG STRIKE AT CALIENTE

Rives Brothers Srike It Rich on Old "Caliente Gold Mining" Property

Conductor R. T. Rives, of the S. P. L. A. & S. L. R. R. and his brother C. E. Rives have opened up a body of ore on their property at Caliente which is creating considerable excitement in that section. Within 600 feet of the railroad, opposite the depot, they have at last succeeded in locating the ledge which has been the object of search by successive owners of the property for several years.

The development work done by Geo. Fetterman in 1905 was quite extensive and included running a tunnel into the mountain for 310 feet in the expectation of cutting the vein. It now appears that for almost the entire distance the tunnel was running parallel with the vein and only 30 or 40 feet from it.

In prospecting the surface the present owners, Rives Bros. discovered the ledge and are now sinking a shaft which has reached a depth of 30 feet. The pay streak is 18 inches wide and assays from $120 to $800 per ton, much of the ore containing free gold plainly visible without the aid of a glass. Considerable rich ore has been sacked and has to be guarded against the depredations of ore thieves who have already robbed the mine of considerable values.

One significant feature of the property is the fact that the ore appears to be in "alunite" and is very similar to that found in Goldfield, Cripple Creek and the rich Railroad Pass district near Vegas, now known as Alunite. Whenever found in quantities, alunite has always proven an index to ore bodies of wonderful richness.

Rives Bros. have many warm friends in Las Vegas and vicinity who rejoice with them in the good fortune which has attended their persistent efforts.

LUND

Lund, Nevada, Nov. 15 —The speaker at our Sunday service to-day was Elder Charles Sullivan of St. George, who was here in the interest of religion class work.

A fine character ball was given by the Y. M. & Y. L M I A last Friday week. The proceeds, $23 75 went to the meeting house.

Our meeting house foundation is nearly completed The cement blocks for the building are being made here

A. R. Whitehead and M. W. Harrison went to Preston as home missionaries today.

Weather is fine, and farmers are busy hauling their produce to Ely.

ELK'S ENTERTAINED

One of the most delightful social events of the season was the party given by Mr. and Mrs. Arthur Frye to the Elks and their wives on the 340th night and 20th hour, which being interpreted means Saturday night at eight o'clock. The early part of the evening was spent at cards. The tally cards were decorated, with pen and ink sketches of Elk's heads. Mr. Watson won 1st prize; Mrs. Watson 2nd prize; A. N. Pauff, booby prize. At eleven o'clock a toast was given "To Our Absent Brothers," by Mr. Badenhousen after which delicious refreshments were served. Later dancing was indulged in. On departing the guests were unanimous in voting the Fryes ideal entertainers.

Those present were:

Mr. and Mrs. Rives of Caliente, Mr. and Mrs. Jurden, Mr. and Mrs. Watson, Mr. and Mrs. Pauff, Mr. and Mrs. Bracken, Mr. and Mrs. Cherette, Mr. and Mrs. Frank Buol, Mr. and Mrs. Badenhousen, Mr. and Mrs. Pyles, Mr. Mrs. and Beale, Misses Rives, Ager, Eason and Olive Cavelaria.

FUNERAL NOTICE.

SPRINGALL—The funeral services of A. D. Springhall, who died from scald, received at Caliente on Christmas day, will be held from the Woodmen hall, corner Second South and West Temple streets, at 2 p. m. Sunday, January 10, 1909. All members of the Woodmen of the World, Brotherhood of Locomotive Firemen, Machinist's union and friends are invited to attend. Interment City cemetery.

Sheriff Orrin H. Smith has appointed W. L. Colton his deputy for Searchlight, Trembly for Caliente, Fitzgerald for Pioche, and Gay for Vegas. The deputies for Jack Rabbit and Moapa have not yet been named.

Inter-Mountain Republican (Utah)
January 9, 1909

YOUTHFUL BURGLARS CAUGHT WITH TOOLS

Detectives Bring in Complete Paraphernalia for Shady Night Work.

Following the breaking open and rifling of the trunk of A. H. Day, a Garfield smelter worker living at 205 West Second South street Thursday afternoon, two boys were arrested yesterday afternoon by Detectives Burt and Schultz, in the rooming house where the theft took place. In their possession was found a complete set of tools familiar only to the burglar. Bill Smith, aged 18, and John Moore, aged 16, were suspected immediately after the theft.

When the arrests were made a search was instigated and it was found that the personal effects of each young man were confined to two cheap telescopes. In one was wearing apparel, butter, salt, etc., and in the other two revolvers, a jimmy, a brace and bit, files, skeleton keys, felt soled shoes, cartridges, etc.

The two boys say that they are from Caliente, Nev.

Day has not yet been to the police station to identify his property.

Emery County News (Utah)
January 16, 1909

Arthur D Springall a former resident of Utah who was seriously scalded at Caliente Nevada on Christmas eve by falling into a pit of boiling water died in a Salt Lake hospital last week

Lloyd Denton and wife removed from Caliente to Las Vegas. They will give their attention to farming in the artesian belt, having moved onto the Passno ranch south of town, where they are engaged in building a cottage and making other necessary improvements.

Joseph Conoway, of Caliente, was a welcome caller at The Age office Wednesday. Mr. Conway is one of the Assemblyman from this County and left Thursday to enter upon his duties at Carson City. He is one of the "Old guard" of the Democratic party in Lincoln County.

HOWELL GETS DAMAGES FROM SALT LAKE ROUTE

J. F Howell, who was injured in a wreck on the Salt Lake Route near Caliente, Nev., February 26, 1907, received damages amounting to $2,475 from a jury in Judge M. L. Ritchie's court yesterday. Howell was riding on a construction train, as other trains had been stopped on account of washouts, and in the crash near Caliente he was badly injured. The contention of the railroad company was that Howell was not a passenger on the construction train, but was simply riding at his own risk. The jury, however, decided Howell was a passenger and awarded damages accordingly. Howell sued for $15,200.

Train number 1 was delayed five hours Thursday by a land slide this side of Caliente.

J. O. McIntosh of Caliente was a visitor in Vegas Wednesday and Thursday. He left for Los Angeles on the Thursday evening train.

OLD GOLD MINES ARE TAKEN OVER

Chief Properties Near Pioche to Be Worked by Big Company.

OPENED IN EARLY DAYS

Present Gigantic · Cyaniding Proposition Under Present Conditions.

Operations of great importance to Pioche section are forecasted by the taking over by A. B. Lowis, B. F. Freudenthal and New York associates of the Panaca and other gold properties in the Chief district about midway between Pioche and Callente and only three and a half miles from the railroad. To work the properties a $3,-000,000 corporation is being formed to be called the Goldmant Gold Mining company.

The Chief, or Goldmont mines, are pronounced by experts who have examined them—including A. Chester Beatty and W. A. Parish—one of the greatest cyaniding propositions in the country. On a contact between quartzite and lime is a great vein carrying from 15 feet to 56 feet of ore which, according to the most rigid sampling, carries gold values of $8 a ton and better all the way through. The values are evenly disseminated throughout the mass and the ore is so soft that in mining it augurs are used instead of drills. It is said to be susceptible to a simple cyaniding process, with a close saving of values assured.

The Panaca mine was worked to some extent in the old days. Ore averaging around $24 a ton was shipped from it, but on account of the long haul to railroad and the high treatment charge it would not pay. Under conditions of today, mined on a large scale and with a mill on the ground, there will, of course be a large profit in ore that averages $8 a ton.

Average Values Are High.

Old workings in the property attained a depth of 300 feet, and at that depth Mr. Lewis says that he sampled 5 feet of ore from which the assay returns were $14.50 a ton, while it is not uncommon to get samples clear across the big vein that runs $20 and $30 a ton. Aside from the contact vein are numerous parallel and cross fissures, so that the indications are that greater results will be attained at depth. The new company will own from 4,000 to 5,000 feet on the big vein. The contact is one that, experts now concede, extends from near Callente to Pioche and thence through the Bristol district with the possibility that it continues through the Snake range all the way to Ely.

On account of the failure of the Chief mines to pay in the old days, it was only recently that their value under changed conditions began to be appreciated. The Guggenheims and one or two eastern syndicates have been anxious, it is said, to take over the properties, but Lowis and Freudenthal have for some time had the call upon them and have just succeeded in rounding out plans for operation upon scale which the proposition warrants.

Inter-Mountain Republican (Utah)
February 28, 1909

LARGE OPERATORS GO TO SEE PIOCHE MINES

Colonel J. B. Hackett, A. H. Gulbe and E. L. Gulbe, who, with Samuel Newhouse form the heavy interests in Ohio Kentucky Mining, left last night for Pioche, accompanying George A. Learnard, president of the Nevada Utah company who passed through on the Los Angeles limited train. The party will be carried from Caliente to the mines by special train. The visit to Pioche at this time of these officers of the two long contending companies, it is believed, will be followed by the closing of the consolidation deal already tacitly agreed upon. Mr. Learnard desired to make a personal inspection of the mines involved before the deal should be finally closed and the Ohio Kentucky people were highly gratified on account of his decision to visit the camp.

Inter-Mountain Republican (Utah)
March 16, 1909

RICH STRIKE AT CALIENTE.

Sensational Showing Is Made in Rives Property.

Caliente, Nev. March 15.—Another rich strike was made in the Caliente mine Saturday. Shots tore down a hanging wall, disclosing a ledge about forty feet across and eight feet high, which is seamed and lined across the entire face with free gold in large quantities. The rock is so rich that gold can be obtained with the crudest methods.

The new strike is only a few feet west of the former workings. More excitement is manifest than has occurred for years in this part of Nevada. Every foot of available ground is being staked. That the ore body continues through the mountain is shown by numerous samples taken from various points.

Manager Rives, of the Caliente mine, has been negotiating for the erection of a mill for some time and it is now expected that the deal will be immediately closed.

Miss Wadsworth and Mrs. Norris, of Caliente, are visiting at the home of Mrs. C. C. Ronnow.

Miss Lena Rives of Caliente, was a visitor at the home of Rev. H. G. Gray, this week.

Hemstreet and Mitchell have opened a first class grill room in Caliente.

Caliente Now has Newspaper

"The Prospector" is the attractive title of the newspaper just started at Caliente. The first issue appeared March 20, with the name Robert Graham, at the head as editor and owner. Caliente should be able to support a newspaper if the citizens show the right public spirit. The Age extends its best wishes.

The people of Las Vegas are making an effort to change the name to Vegas. Out of courtesy to the wish the Prospector will in the future refer to that city as Vegas.—Prospector, (Caliente)

DEPUTY MAXWELL

Handcuffed and Robbed by his Prisoners

Deputy Sheriff Maxwell of Moapa, had an experience at Crestline, a small station on the Salt Lake Route, near the Nevada-Utah line, Thursday night which he will not forget very soon.

On March 26th two hard looking characters stole three horses from a ranch near Moapa, and the thieves were traced to Parowan, Utah, where with the assistance of Utah officers, they were arrested by Maxwell last Sunday morning. The men had the horses with them and having been interrogated gave their names as Bert West and Cooper Davis.

The prisoners consented to return to this state without the formality of requisition papers; whereupon, Maxwell started for Pioche. Arriving at Crestline shortly before sunset, it was decided to put up for the night, instead of moving on to Caliente, where good jail facilities could be had. Right here is where Maxwell blundered.

Evidently, the thieves had friends in that vicinity; for in some inexplicable manner, the outlaws procured a gun while Maxwell slumbered and disarmed him, deprived him of all the money he had with him, applied the handcuffs, and then feeling quite secure, bid Maxwell adieu, mounted the horses and rode away.

Yesterday morning the sheriff's office was notified of what had occurred and in a short while a posse was organized at Caliente to scour the country for the fugitives. Two deputies were started from Pioche and telegrams were sent to various points in this state and Utah where it is possible that the men might put in an appearance.

Up to this writing the thieves have successfully evaded the searchers and Deputy Sheriff Fitzgerald is of the opinion that they have made their way into Arizona, while others express the belief that they have gone back into the wilds of southern Utah.

One of the men is described as being five feet ten inches in height, very shifty eyes, wears a dark hat, coat and overalls. The other man is slightly taller; has a dark moustache, with very cool dark clothes.—[Pioche Record.

Las Vegas Age
May 1, 1909

John Berry, who had the distinction
of running the first train into Caliente
when the railroad was first completed
to that place, passed through Vegas
Tuesday.

Las Vegas Age
May 8, 1909

SALT LAKE ROAD

Officials Make Tour of General Inspection

Messrs. R. E. Wells, general manager;
T. P. Cullen, superintendent; W. C.
Frazier, general foreman; Mr. Jessup,
superintendent of bridges and buildings,
and Mr. Hitt, roadmaster, composed
the party of officials of the Salt Lake
road which has been making a tour of
inspection this week.

The party arrived in Vegas Wenesday
morning and after looking over the railroad property in this city, embarked in
motor car No. 100 in which they made
the trip to Caliente.

We are glad to note that business is
picking up for the R. R. boys. Two
work trains were put on this week between Vegas and Caliente.

Intermountain Catholic (Utah)
May 29, 1909

CALIENTE, NEV.

Little girls dressed in white closed in around the altar of the Blessed Virgin and one of them, Miss Helen O'Shea, crowned the statue with white and purple flowers. Mrs. Frank Boudreau and her daughter Alice, of Modena, Utah, assisted the regular choir, and the clear voice of Mrs. Hemstreet, who was principally instrumental in building the church, could be heard above the rest. The church is almost finished and cost $2,225. The gold chalice and white silk vestments, sent by the Tabernacle society of Philadelphia, Pa., were objects of much interest.

Inter-Mountain Republican (Utah)
June 8, 1909

UNCOVER SECRET OF OLD TUNNEL

Rich Ore Body Is Found in Working Caved by Explosion.

Miners at work in the Rives mine at Caliente last week broke into the old Fetterman tunnel, whose portal was some years ago obliterated by a giant explosion, according to the Caliente Prospector, and in the abandoned working have found an ore body of unknown dimensions, to hide which, it is now believed, the explosion was purposely perpetrated.

"There has always been a suspicion," says the Prospector, "that the Fetterman tunnel hid some great secret, for peculiar circumstances surrounded the explosion which filled the mouth. The discovery Thursday proves that a rich lead was struck and the explosion was the work of individuals who wished to hide the discovery.

"When the old tunnel was entered it was found to be in terrible shape. The car rails were bent and in some cases were almost tied in knots from the force of the explosion. Great masses of debris were heaped along the track and great chambers were stoped down where the 55 boxes of dynamite had been stored.

"For two hundred feet along this tunnel a vein of quartz has been exposed which carries high values in gold, but as no assays have been made it is impossible to state the value of the rock. Lying in heaps along the floor are masses of talc which, where in place, covers the vein like a blanket hung along a wall. The talc ranges from 18 inches to two feet in thickness. The dimensions of the quartz are not to be estimated by the present exposure. The quartz is of the white and mottled pink variety, pitted with 'bugholes' and seamed with brown scales that cover filmy flakes of gold."

HIDDEN TUNNEL SHOWS RICHES

Surprising Disclosures in Rives Mine at Caliente

Miners working in the tunnel at the Rives mine broke through into the old Fetterman tunnel Thursday and found a body of ore so immense that it is impossible to define its dimensions.

The Fetterman tunnel has been hidden for about four years. There has always been a suspicion that this tunnel hid some great secret as peculiar circumstances surrounded the explosion that filled the mouth. The discovery Thursday proves that a rich lead was struck and the explosion was the work of individuals who wished to hide the discovery.

When the old tunnel was entered it was found to be in terrible shape, the car rails were bent and in some cases almost tied in knots from the force of the explosion. Great masses of debris were heaped along the track and great chambers stoped down where the 85 boxes of dynamite had been stored.

For two hundred feet along this tunnel a vein of quartz has been exposed which carries high values in gold but as no assays have been made it is impossible to state the value of the rock. Lying in heaps along the floor are great masses of talc which, where in place, covers the vein like a blanket hung along a wall, the talc ranges from 18 inches to two feet in thickness. The dimensions of the quartz are not to be estimated by the present exposure. The quartz is of the white and mottled pink variety, pitted with "bugholes" and seamed with brown scales that cover filmy flakes of gold.—(Prospector, Caliente.

Inter-Mountain Republican (Utah)
June 15, 1909

CALIENTE MINE IS PROVING UP WELL

Vein Outlined 200 Feet Is Strong on 120-Foot Level.

Work of developing the Rives mine is being continued with the view of determining the extent of the vein and opening enough ore to justify the building of a mill, according to the Caliente Prospector. A crosscut has been carried nine feet into the vein, about midway between the extreme openings north and south, with no change of formation.

The rose quartz vein, which carries the stronger values, has been outlined for 200 feet in length and about 120 feet vertically, with no indication of its limits, and there is every indication that it extends through the mountain and through adjoining claims in a northerly direction.

Outcroppings show that the ore body is unbroken to the 120-foot level, where it is now being crosscut. At that depth is encountered four and five feet of talc, which is shot full of kidneys of quartz carrying values estimated by four figures. The main vein appears to average from $38 to $100 a ton, and it is becoming richer as depth is attained.

Married

At Caliente, Wednesday June 23, 1909, Charles A. Thompson, of Pioche, to Miss Louise Fieldson of Caliente, Rev. Harry G. Gray officiating. The ceremony was performed at the home of Hon. John Shier. The bride was attended by Miss Chanclor of De Lamar and was given away by her brother, Herbert Fieldson. Fred Thompson, brother of the groom acted as best man. The wedding march was played during the ceremony by Miss Rives.

The bride was beautiful in a wedding gown of white decorated with orange blossoms and carried a large bridal bouquet. The house was handsomely decorated with flowers and an elaborate wedding breakfast was served following the ceremony. The wedding was a very quiet one, only the relatives and a few intimate friends being present.

The happy couple left on the afternoon train for an extended bridal tour which will include Yellowstone Park and other points of interest.

The contracting parties have hosts of friends throughout the county, with whom the Age joins in most hearty congratulations.

Las Vegas Age
July 3, 1909

LIMITED DERAILED

Narrow Escape of Fast Train From Serious Damage Near Galt

On Sunday morning last as the limited passenger train on the Salt Lake road, west bound, was rounding the curve at Galt siding, between Moapa and Caliente, one of the journals of the tender broke. The tender jumped the track tearing up the ties for a distance of several hundred yards. Fortunately the heavy pullmans kept the track and engineer Holland succeeded in bringing the train to a standstill without serious mishap. Nobody was injured and the damage was light. After a delay of about eight hours the train was able to proceed to its destination.

TALK OF MINERALS AROUND CALIENTE

Mining Engineer Tells of Resources About Nevada City—Declares Some Of Rarest Metals In Vicinity.

Although many mining men of ability pass through Caliente every day, the people in that vicinity assert there has been but little done there in a mining way, although it affords some of the rarest metals. F. L. Wilson, a mining engineer, has the following to say of the district after making an examination of it:

"It has long been a question with the people of Caliente why they could not secure mills and smelters," said Mr. Wilson, "they have a great deal of undeveloped ore indications of sufficient richness, however, to indicate large deposits. There is plenty of water here to furnish power for a large mill six months of the year. There are natural reservoir sites in the vicinity for storing this water which could be perfected at small cost which if properly handled would supply a mill all the year round with power.

"There are a few gold, silver, lead or galena and copper mines in the vicinity that have proven beyond a doubt their permanency, aside from these I find that there really has been no prospecting that has been done in a systematic way. The prospector who "goes it blind" in this district stands a poor chance of ever getting beyond his first samples. There is no section of the state where he needs the knowledge of geology and assaying more. Nature has placed some of the rarest metals close to Caliente, Some of these metals seldom, if ever reach a western assay office and the average assayer seldom in a life time.

"Some of the largest bodies of low grade gold ore in the state are at the very door of Caliente awaiting development."

NICKEL IN COBALT.

"Cobalt carrying nickel is abundant. Nickel is found in genthite, gannierite and noemite. These minerals are analogous to copper silicate, known as chysocolla and it is possible they run more into copper values.

"I also find some cinnibar in this vicinity, but as no work has been done on this it is hard to determine its future. Metacinnabarite or black sulphide of mercury exists in paying quantities near Elgin, 20 miles south. This mineral greatly resembles graphite in appearance.

"There is scarcely a rock found in this vicinity that does not show tungsten.

"Acid aluminum is present in large amounts. Many mineral streaks show chalcopyrite in small pyrites. Above Caliente opals are plentiful they are small but there is nothing to show that any one has ever tried to find larger ones.

"A few miles south are bodies of onyx which if opened up may prove sufficient to work. Last but not least I will call your attention to the great beds of magnesium minerals, the New York quotations on these is $1.25 per pound.

EXPERT DEVELOPMENT.

"What is needed is expert development of these resources and then all that will be needed will be the capital. You have the stuff, what you lack is men with push who will show their own confidence by developing. It will not be out of place here to advise the prospector in this district not to overlook the fact that certain rocks and earths in this vicinity though not generally reckoned among minerals have not infrequently proved the foundation of large fortunes and for that reason are worthy of the time of locating and investigating."

TINTIC QUEEN INCORPORATES.

(Special to the "News.")

Provo, July 5.—The Tintic Queen Mining company has filed articles of incorporation with the county clerk. Provo is named as the principal place of business. The capital stock is $100,-000, in shares of the par value of 10 cents each, based on the valuation of Tintic Queen mining claims 1 to 16, both inclusive, situated in North Tintic mining district. The directors and officers are. W. D. Rawson, president;

Andrew Madsen, vice president; Alfred L. Booth, Leroy Rixon, secretary and treasurer.

COLE-RYAN CROWD INTERESTED

Probably Behind Road Proposed from Goldfield to Camp of Ely.

The announcement made on reliable authority that the Cole-Ryan interests are identified with the proposed Ely-Goldfield road means that the Ely district is about to realize another of its hopes, says the Ely Expositor. The reputation for doing things which the Cole-Ryan people have so firmly established must be taken into consideration with the announcement of this fact. With these progressive capitalists behind the scheme it is not too much to expect to see the new road built and in operation months before it likely would have been otherwise. And even though the Giroux should decide to erect only a concentrator here and ship its concentrates to the new International smelter at Tooele, Utah, the extension of the new road through to Salt Lake will mean to the district much more than the erection of a single smelter. Ely will then have realized its ambition to be on a direct line of railroad. The realization of this hope will in itself mean more activity and development in all parts of the district and throughout eastern Nevada than would have followed through any other means. The resources of the country to the south and west, known to be great, though as yet scarcely estimated, will be developed and the products of this development brought to the railroad. And

Ely is the natural center of this great and growing country.

CONCENTRATES.

The new mill of the Bingham-New Haven company is ready and should start operations today. Henry Thomas, an experienced mill man formerly of Montana but more recently from the Minnemas mill at Bingham, will be in charge. The mill is able to care for 125 tons of ore a day.

It is understood that the properties owned by J. P. Gardner and Paul Rodenhouse in the Deep Creek district are now being thoroughly examined and it is probable that they are now under option to a large eastern concern. The large area of low grade porphyry developed by Mr. Gardner and his associates, it is said, will establish another Bingham in Utah.

A dispatch from New York says that the Cupric Mines company has purchased of the Horn Silver Mining company a group of claims at Grantsville, Nev., known as the Alexandria group. The Horn Silver company has held the property as collateral for some 22 years. The Cupric Mines takes over the property for $400,000 of its treasury stock.

According to a statement made by A. H. Howe, secretary and treasurer of the Goldfield Consolidated Mines company the estimated June production of the company was: Tons produced, 19,410; estimated net values recovered, $457,000; estimated total cost of production, $150,000; estimated net profit, $397,000. The shortage in tonnage was due to the lack of power, caused by the washout on the Little Bishop. The company has also adopted a new policy to ship the high grade and low grade at the same time and thereby avoid the handling of the ore twice and lengthen the life of the mine. This will also cut down the revenue slightly.

Las Vegas Age
July 10, 1909

Salt Lake Mining Review (Utah)
July 15, 1909

The Bamberger-DeLamar Mining company of DeLamar, Nevada, consigned a lot
of bullion, valued at $40,000, to the mint a
few days ago. The shipment represented a
fifteen-day run.

Eureka Reporter (Utah)
July 16, 1909

A mining engineer who has been in
vestigating the mineral resources of
the region about Caliente Nevada
says some of the largest bodies of low
grade gold ore in the state are at the
very door of Caliente awaiting deve
opment Cobalt carrying nickel is
abundant Nickel is found in gen
thite gannierite and noemite

Emery County News (Utah)
July 17, 1909

A mining engineer who has been in vestigating the mineral resources of the region about Caliente Nevada says some of the largest bodies of low grade gold ore in the state are at the very door of Caliente a vaiting deve opment Cobalt carrying nickel is abundant Nickel is found in gen thite gannierite and noemite

Las Vegas Age
July 24, 1909

A Strenuous Day

Some people have been heard to kick abut Caliente being so quiet. What do you want for excitement anyway? Take Monday for instance. Sheriff Trimble started things off by cuffing a rowdy's ears, Bert Lowell by kicking the same guy between the depot and the lunch counter, Lon Manners slapped the same fellow in his jaw. Two railroad men got mixed up in a family row shortly afterwards and made such a noise they scared the deputy's sorrel horse so he ran away—the horse, not the deputy—the horse was caught before any damage was done to the rig he was hooked to. Things quieted down in the evening until Bert Hamerton began to sing and Denton's bull dog went out and killed a cat to get even. About bedtime the editor took off his glasses and nearly swallowed a hatpin which he mistook for a black pill—It is nobody's business where hat pin came from— Then just as most honest people had gone to sleep the fire company was called to put out the roundhouse, after the fire skinner came near getting shot in mistake for a burglar. When things quited down some son-of-a-gun broke into a box car and stole a lot of merchandise, then right after breakfast Tuesday, George Fetterman washed his store windows. Talk about excitement —Well!—[Prospector, Caliente.

Dr. W. P. Murray has closed his branch office at Pioche and will hereafter give his entire attention to his Caliente practice. The Doctor has just returned from the east where he took a course at the famous Mayo hospital at Rochester, Minn.

Robert Graham, guiding spirit of the Caliente Prospector, was in this city this week making the acquaintance of some of our people.

Miss Minnie Wadsworth, of Caliente, is visiting her sister, Mrs. C. C. Ronnow. Miss Wadsworth has just returned from a trip to the coast.

The Prospector, Caliente, in speaking of Lincoln County's lack of a county commissioner, hopes that by August first "Ed Clark will have told the Governor just who to appoint as W. E. Hawkins' successor." Who would have thought that those Lincoln County fellows were too much discouraged to pick out their own commissioner, or that our busy county treasurer was going around all the time with a governor under his thumb?

Pioche, Caliente and Vegas are all anxious to secure the location of a smelter. We can safely assume that the powers that be will settle the question to suit themselves without consulting the wishes of any of us.

Henry Ingram, of Caliente, was in this city Monday last on legal business. Mr. Ingram is one of the pioneers of Vegas, having been located here for several months before and after the opening of the townsite in 1905.

Rev. Father Reynolds was the guest of honor at a surprise party at the residence of Dr. W. P. Murray in Caliente last week. Towards the close of the evening a handsome token was presented to Father Reynolds as an expression of appreciation of his services.

PROSPECTOR PERSPIRES

Haunted by Malign, Malicious and Mysterious Specter of Clark County

Did you ever awaken, terror stricken, in the dead of night, cold perspiration standing in beads upon your brow, helpless and transfixed by some nameless and unknown horror? If not, read the following article headed "The People be d——d Sentiment of Governor" in the last issue of the Caliente Prospector and you will know just how it feels—at least you will know just how those Lincoln county politicians feel under the awful and dominating influence, which, in their hideous political nightmare, they imagine this sturdy young county of Clark wields.

Let us hope that with returning consciousness they will realize that it was only the cat tipping over the milk bottle, and that there are probably not a dozen people in all Clark county who care a whoop in purgatory who was appointed commissioner in Lincoln county, or whether they ever had a commissioner or not.

The Prospector says:

Thos. Stewart of Alamo, has been appointed by Gov. Dickerson to succeed W. E. Hawkins as commissioner of Lincoln county.

The news of the appointment comes as a surprise to every one and has aroused considerable and decided dissatisfaction throughout the entire county. The general sentiment is the Acting Governor allowed Clark county to dictate the appointment, for it is certain that no other influence was evidenced.

There were a number of candidates but all had conceded the lead to James Ryan, of Caliente, who was endorsed by the leaders of both political parties and by popular sentiment all over this county. The radical action of Danny Dickerson in ignoring the express desire of the people entitles him to the full measure of caustic criticism that has been heaped upon him.

It appears that "Denver" is anxious to succeed to the real title of Governor and is willing to play into the hands of any ring, party or combine if he can receive their assurance of a nomination. By his action he evidences a inefficiency of judgment indicative of general incompetency.

Mr. Stewart, the appointee, is an old landmark in the county. An able man, honest and competent—by report. And he is accredited with a steadfastness of purpose that if exercised will dominate the future actions of the Board. Being a member of the same church as his brother commissioners is indicative of harmonious unity and accord. In view of the fact that a number of fellow Saints reside in this county it is certain that the appointment of Ex-Bishop Stewart will meet with considerable favor even though it comes as a surprise to many who not aware of his candidacy were supporting others. The only

(Continued on Page 8)

PROSPECTOR PERSPIRES

(Continued from Page 1)

censure from Caliente comes in the point of fact that an expression of the desires of the people had been given and utter disregard of this by the Governor is outrageous.

A just cause for complaint is the fact that the greater number of the population of Lincoln county have no voice in the administration.

There is one thing that is most forcibly demonstrated on this occasion that it will be well for our citizens to consider and that is the power resulting through concentration of forces and unity of action. Had this end of the county united in promoting the claims of one candidate and saw to it that these claims were presented to the Governor, instead of trusting to Clark county to do the square thing—which would have been to mind their own business— if, we had stood up ourselves for our rights, it is probable the state at large would have been spared the spectacle of the chief executive making an ass of himself.

Inter-Mountain Republican (Utah)
August 8, 1909

Acoma, Caliente, Pioche.

Excursion, round trip Acoma $11.40, Caliente $12.65, and Pioche $14.65. Salt Lake Route. Return limit 10 days.

Las Vegas Age
August 8, 1909

Leo McNamee of Caliente, was in Vegas Thursday on business, returning home Friday morning.

Inter-Mountain Republican (Utah)
August 11, 1909

RIVES MINE TO BE PROVEN AT DEPTH

Owners Will Open Big Body of Ore to the Water Level.

For years the old Siebert mine at Caliente was worked in haphazard fashion. Following the explosion in the tunnel of ninety-five boxes of dynamite, which, of course, completely wrecked and closed the workings, there was a long period of inactivity. About a year ago the Riveses took hold of the property and have been conducting work along new lines. They have opened a body of rich gold ore four feet wide, which is in a vein thirty-six feet wide, all of which is said to carry milling values. The work now in hand is the exploring of that ore body to water level to determine definitely the kind and capacity of mill required to treat the ore.

An interesting feature was brought to light a few weeks ago when the old tunnel was tapped, some distance back from the caved portion, by a new tunnel. The discovery was then made that the old tunnel had been driven for 200 feet against the hanging wall of the vein, presumably without the operators having become aware that they were next to ore.

Judge W. D. Maynard of Caliente, who is in the city attending the encampment, declares that for the 200 feet the wall of the vein shows as smooth in the tunnel as the wall of a building; and that one can scratch the wall almost anywhere and bring free gold to view.

Judge Maynard owns ground adjoining the Rives mine, so that he is particularly interested in the work that is being done in the Rives, for the reason, that it is proving his own property as well as the others. He has done enough prospecting on his own account, however, to bring to light what appears to be an important contact vein. He is confident that Caliente will soon be heard from as one of Nevada's best gold mining camps.

Eureka Reporter (Utah)
August 20, 1909

In the old Siebert mine at Caliente Nevada there has been opened a body of rich gold ore four feet wide which is in a ven thirty six feet wide all of which is said to carry milling values The work now in hand is the exploring of that ore body to water level to determine definitely the kind and capacty of mill required to treat the ore

According to information received

Salt Lake Mining Review (Utah)
September 15, 1909

The Bamberger-DeLamar mine and mill, at DeLamar, Nevada, have been closed down, and it is reported that the property of the company will be dismantled.

Las Vegas Age
September 18, 1909

Brakeman Exonerated for Shooting a Hobo

Harry Rickey, who is alleged to be a professional hobo, was shot at Caliente last Sunday morning by C. D. Rountree, a brakeman on the west bound Los Angeles limited, just as the train was leaving the Caliente station. Upon arriving at Las Vegas, Rountree was placed under arrest, but was allowed to return to Caliente on his run. According to testimony brought out at the preliminary hearing Wednesday, Justice Maynard deemed the shooting justifiable and ordered Rountree discharged.

It appears that Rickey had "beat" his way into Caliente and had made brags that he would leave town as a free passenger on the train upon which Rountree was employed. After having been ordered off and warned to keep away from the train unless he produced a ticket, Rickey began throwing rocks at conductor G. A. Goodwin and other train officials. He let one go at Rountree, who was on the rear platform, whereupon the latter responded with a bullet fired from his revolver which entered Rickey's breast. The ball struck a bone, deflected and emerged under the left arm.

The injured man was given medical attention and taken to Los Angeles Thursday evening. He is now in the county hospital there.

Washington County News (Utah)
September 30, 1909

Cards are out announcing the wedding of Miss Clara Fawcett of Lund, Nevada, and Mr. Ernest Larson of Bloomington, next Tuesday, Oct 5th

New Partnership

J. O. McIntosh has joined forces with Al. James in the business of the Arizona Club, of this city. The wholesale liquor business of Mr. McIntosh, now located at Caliente, has been transferred to the new firm and will now be carried on here.

Mr. McIntosh was the original owner of the handsome Arizona Club, which was planned and built under his direction. Both Mr. James and Mr. McIntosh will now devote themselves to the management of the business.

Big Time At Bloomington Wedding

Bloomington, Oct. 6.—Ernest Larson and Miss Clara Fawcett were married at the home of the groom's parents at 5 o'clock p. m. October 5th by Elder John E Pace. The reception was given at the home of Mr. and Mrs. J. M. Larson early in the evening. The happy young couple were the recipients of many useful and valuable presents and hearty congratulations. There were forty relatives and friends present from St. George and Washington, besides all the home people. A grand supper was served early in the evening, after which the guests assembled at the school house where dancing interspersed with songs and recitations lasted until two o'clock a. m. Feasting was then again indulged in, after which the guests departed for their respective homes, having had a very enjoyable time. The groom is the son of L. J. and Isadore Larson, and the bride is a daughter of George W. and Louisa Fawcett of Lund, Nevada. Ernest Reber and Company of Santa Clara furnished the music for the occasion.

District school commenced on the 4th inst. with Miss Edna Cragun of St. George teacher.

J. O. McIntosh closed his business in Caliente on Friday and will remove to Vegas in a few weeks and take charge of the Arizona Club. Mr. McIntosh has been an esteemed and valued citizen for over two years, maintaining an enviable reputation for integrity. He will be much missed in Caliente where he has not a single enemy among the population.—[Prospector, Caliente.

Henry Ingram, of Caliente, was in Vegas on business before the county commissioners this week.

F. R. McNamee, the Caliente attorney, was in this city Monday and Tuesday on business before the county commissioners.

County Clerk Woodbury issued marriage licenses on Oct. 4th to the following couples: Aaron Larson of Bloomington and Miss Clara Fawcett of Lund, Nevada; James W. Hunt and Miss Rozilla Pulsipher, both of Gunlock.

Las Vegas Age
October 23, 1909

DALE SUICIDES

Month of Reckless Carousal Ends in Self Destruction

Tom P. Dale, only a few short weeks ago respected and trusted, with friends by the hundred, a loving wife and helpless infant depending on him for all that makes life worth the living, lies today in a suicide's grave, disgraced, his friends and family heartbroken.

Dale was married to an estimable woman only a little over a year ago and as a result of the union a baby was born about a month ago. Since the arrival of the little stranger, Dale, so it is said, has been drinking heavily. He arrived in Vegas last week and while here continued his carousal. His money being gone Dale borrowed $40 from J. W. Horden of the Las Vegas hotel on Monday.

Tuesday morning he induced Mr. Horden to endorse a check for $100 drawn on the First National bank of Rhyolite, with the understanding that he would return the $40 borrowed upon cashing the check. He secured the money on his check and took the train at once for the north, leaving word that he was called suddenly to Salt Lake City, and failing to leave the $40 as agreed. A wire to Rhyolite disclosed the fact that Dale had no money there to meet the check. Mr. Horden immediately placed the matter in the hands of the officials and Dale was arrested at Caliente by Deputy Sheriff John Trimble. Dale induced Trimble to spare him the disgrace of the jail and made arrangements to stay that night with the officer at his house.

Waking up about six o'clock next morning, Dale remarked to Trimble that he had a sore throat and would take some medicine for it. Reaching into his pocket he produced a small vial, raised it to his lips and drained the contents. Then he said good bye and within two or three minutes was dead.

The deceased has been for some time superintendent of the Pahrump ranch. He formerly lived in Denver, where the Dale family is well known. He leaves a brother, Frank Dale, living in Pasadena, Cal.

Las Vegas Age
October 30, 1909

F. R. McNamee, of Caliente, was on hand to attend to legal matters before the district court this week.

Salt Lake Mining Review (Utah)
October 30, 1909

According to advices from the east a complete re-organization of the Bamberger-DeLamar Gold Mining & Milling company will be made next June, when the receiver for the company will retire. The property of the company is at DeLamar, Nevada, with which, it is stated, adjoining properties are to be merged.

Las Vegas Age
November 20, 1909

RAILROAD TIME CARD

Little Change Beyond Addition of Trains 3 and 4 on Main Line

According to the present plans of the railroad officials, the new time card will go into effect December first. So far as is known at this time there will be little or no change in the time of the present trains.

The new limited trains, Nos. 3 and 4 will begin operation with a 24 hour schedule between Los Angeles and Salt Lake. The train will be handsomely equipped and the through cars between Los Angeles and Denver and Butte will prove a great convenience to travellers.

The schedule will be as follows:

Number 3. Leave Salt Lake City, 9 a. m.
Arrive Las Vegas, 10:35 p. m.
Leave Las Vegas, 10:45 p. m.
Arrive Los Angeles, 9 a. m.

Number 4. Leave Los Angeles, 2 p. m.
Arrive Las Vegas, 12:15 a. m.
Leave Las Vegas 12:20 a. m.
Arrive Salt Lake City 2 p. m.

On the Caliente and Pioche branch, the train will leave Caliente in the morning after the arrival of number seven from the east and will return to connect with number two the overland from Los Angeles, in the afternoon.

The Las Vegas and Tonopah road will in all probability make no change in the present schedule. The advisability of changing time to make connections with the new trains 3 and 4 on the main line has been seriously considered, but it is thought at this time that no change in the present runs will be made.

Las Vegas Age
November 27, 1909

Senator J. A. Denton, of Caliente, has established a stage line between Pioche and the new camp of Atlanta, and will carry the mail between those places.

Washington County News
December 2, 1909

Jos W. Carpenter got a returned letter from the postoffice here one day last week that was mailed in the St. George postoffice June 18, 1905, addressed to Manse, Nevada. It bears the St. George postmark June 18, 1905, and the last legible postmark on it is Hiko, Nevada, Nov. 1909.

Gunnison Gazette (Utah)
December 3, 1909

Frank Smith and Simon Levin, two youthful bond jumpers, charged with assaulting Frederick Fougler in Salt Lake City because he refused to buy a paper, beating him in such a manner that his life was despaired of for some time, were captured in Caliente, Nevada.

Emery County News (Utah)
December 4, 1909

Frank Smith and Simon Levin two youthful bond jumpers charged with assaulting Frederick Fougler in Salt Lake C ty because he refused to buy a paper beating him in such a manner that his life was despaired of for some t n were captured in Caliente Nevada

Las Vegas Age
December 11, 1909

Dr. W. P. Murray, of Caliente, passed through Vegas Tuesday evening, enroute to Los Angeles where he will spend some time for the benefit of his health.

Deseret News (Utah)
January 4, 1910

NO CHANGE REPORTED ON SALT LAKE ROUTE

General Manager Wells Says Messenger Sent From Acoma—No News From Front.

"So far there is no change in the flood situation," said General Manager R. E. Wells of the Salt Lake Route today. "The wires are still down west of Caliente and we have not yet heard from the messenger despatched from Acoma, a distance of 25 miles, with messages for the agent at Caliente. The messenger cannot get back before late this afternoon. We wish to get word through and learn the situation at the front. Train No. 3 which passed Caliente at midnight, Jan. 1 reported the track safe in the Meadow Valley wash, but that vast quantities of water were coming down the canyon. Train No. 4 due at Caliente at 4:10 is doubtless stalled there. The passengers are being cared for, and everything is being done to facilitate their passage to their respective destinations. There is no danger of loss of life or property, except the damage done to the railroad property by the washout. We are doing everything possible to get the damage repaired, but snowstorms and floods are difficult to handle, and we cannot say when through traffic will be restored."

CALIENTE UNDER SAND AND WATER

Flood Three Feet Deep Cause of Much Suffering Among The People.

MANY ARE IN NEED OF FOOD

Courier Tells Graphic Story of Distress —Salt Lake Route Passengers Are Safe.

Devastation has been wrought in Caliente by the floods, according to information received in this city. Mounted couriers are just beginning to arrive in southern Utah towns from the stricken region and their travel has been accomplished only at the risk of their lives. The first news from the stricken center was brought to Modena by Benjamin Wadsworth from Panaca, Nev. He declares that water three feet deep is now covering Caliente and that the misery and suffering accompanying the flood are intense. There is dire need of food for the stricken men, women and children at that point. Mr. Wadsworth declares that sand and mud washed into the roundhouse to a depth of three feet and at times the water was higher than the driving wheels of the engines. The station is flooded to a depth of several feet, the water pouring into it and into homes over the window sills. Doors were calked with paper and rags in the hope of resisting the water, but the rapid rise made all attempts futile. Many buildings have been wrecked, some of them floating down the new-made lake like houseboats. Every wagon and railroad bridge is gone and not a building of any kind, on high or low ground, but what has been flooded and is now covered on the ground floor with from one to two feet and more of water, sand and mud.

Editor Graham of the Caliente Times was Mr. Wadsworth's informant and he said that at the Hot Springs of Caliente that the water poured into the bathrooms over the transoms. His picture of the misery of the place was graphic, but he declared that words could not tell all of the suffering being visited upon the unfortunate residents of the place.

Loss of life is feared at Muddy River, though no communication with this section has been possible as yet. The section house at Big Springs has gone in the flood and much suffering is being endured there, but no loss of life is yet reported from actual physical violence, but the conditions are such that pneumonia may seize the victims who are battling against it as their chief enemy. Lack of food is causing much suffering.

The thermometer at Modena registers 18 degrees below zero. The sheriff of Lincoln county has been appealed to to send help to Caliente, but whether any assistance can be sent is doubted, as the place is almost impossible to reach from the outside.

PASSENGERS ARE SAFE.

General Manager R. E. Wells of the Salt Lake Route has left this city to attend personally to the work of relief. Before leaving he said:

"The passengers from the delayed train, nine in number, are well on the way by wagon to Barclay, where they are expected to arrive Thursday afternoon. The train will be held till they arrive and they will be brought on at once to Salt Lake, where they will arrive Friday morning.

"We expect to get them into Salt Lake Thursday morning, making the ride across country in the wagon in one day, but the weather has been too cold and they had to lay over. They will no doubt start late in the forenoon after the weather warms up somewhat, as there is no especial need of haste. They are being well cared for at the expense of the road and everything possible is being done for their comfort. All are well. There is not the slightest occasion to worry over their position from the point of personal safety.

"Investigations are being made concerning the extent of the damage to the road itself. Just what the damage is we do not know, but it looks as if we could be in fair shape in a couple of months. The damage will not be as

great as might be expected from such
a flood. The road is well built, and
although washed out in part, much of
it remains in place.

"The flood was something no human
wisdom could forsee. It reached higher
by far than the highest known water
mark, and we had our road well above
the line where the water had ever come
before.

"So far as we know tonight only
one railroad life is lost, a track walker
near Caliente. We have not yet received any details about it and as the
wires are in such bad shape we cannot find out any more about him. Except this one we look for no more loss
of human life. The loss to the railroad
is severe, but is far less than it might
have been, especially if the line had
not been so solidly built in the worst
places. In many places where the
roadbed did go out the whole side of
the hill went with it, so that was beyond human power to prevent, like an
earthquake.

"All trains in Utah are running as
usual and will continue to do so. We
will have a through train over the line
within a couple of months at the most.
The disaster might have been far worse
than it is. Fortunately no lives were
lost except that one and that is what
we care the most about, the safety of
our passengers."

TRAINS LATE WITH MAILS.

Los Angeles Sacks Arrive in Salt Lake 100 Hours Behind Time.

The postoffice department has been
notified that the Los Angeles mail over
the Salt Lake Route will be in some
time Friday, after having been delayed
for 100 hours or more. The postmaster
has received an intimation that there
has been much teaming done in getting
the mail out of Caliente and that it
will be brought from a near station on
a morning train which is all made up,
and waiting for mail and passengers.

The weather man and the postmaster
have evidently been working together,
the blocking of trains giving time to
clean up the aftermath of the holiday
rush. Everything is in good shape at
the federal building, and for the first
time in a month the employes have
been given time to take a breath.

All trains are reported late to the
postmaster. The eastern mails over the
Rio Grande are coming in from 6 to 12
hours late, and from the west on all
lines it is the same. The Butte and
northwestern mails are six hours late

The Union Pacific coming from Ogden
have practically the same time limit.

The business men of the city are accepting the situation with resignation,
realizing just what has happened, and
the postoffice department is not being
hampered with strenuous "kicks."
From the information obtained by the
federal officials, the tracks are being
cleared in every part of the intermountain west and in a few days at the utmost with no great change in weather
conditions, all mails will arrive practically on time.

TWO CARS OF HORSES LOST NEAR CALIENTE

South Dakota Men Sustain Heavy Losses In Washout—Pitiable Case Of Agent's Wife.

M. H. Helmere of South Dakota and partner passed through Salt Lake today, having had experiences in the washouts down near Caliente that they do not care to repeat. They had two carloads of horses on a freight train. The train was turned over in one of the washes west of Elgin and every horse in the two cars lost, so they are returning home minus stock and cash.

They say the tracks are almost completely gone for a distance of 17 miles between Caliente and Barclay. Then west of Barclay it is reported that over 20 miles more of the track is gone, making a total distance of nearly 50 miles of washed out tracks the rip-rapped track was carried away for miles upon miles. Passengers who left Los Angeles on Dec. 31, have been marooned on the desert at various points in Nevada, some of whom are just reaching Salt Lake. Some of the men have walked as far as 40 miles in order to catch a train at the Salt Lake end of the line near Barclay and get through. The wagon roads between points are all gone. One newsboy and a passenger started across the hills from Eccles at 10 a. m., reaching Barclay last night. Many have walked from Caliente to Barclay, a distance of 22 miles. One party of passengers secured two conveyances at Acoma and went up into the hills, and will come through another valley, in a roundabout way, thus being able to escape the washed region and catch a Salt Lake train at Barclay.

One of the saddest features of the catastrophe is the experience of the wife of the railroad agent at Elgin in Rainbow canyon. At the time of the flood she was in a delicate condition. The track being washed out she could be taken no where for treatment, and to make things so much worse, the floods actually washed away the station. The agent and his wife were compelled to flee to the hills. Here a dugout was hurriedly constructed and a little later their child was born.

Those who have been over the grounds say it will be perhaps a month or more before the trains can possibly be running again through Meadow Valley wash.

CALIENTE EDITOR

Risks Life to Secure Aid for Flood Stricken People

Robert Graham, editor of the Caliente Prospector, figures in the despatches as a hero of the flood. He secured a horse when the rush of waters was threatening to wipe the town out of existence, and after desperate efforts succeeded in crossing the river, the horse losing its life in the swirling torrent. Graham then made his way on foot to Panaca, sixteen miles distant, from which point the news of the condition of Caliente was taken to Modena by B. Wadsworth.

Graham reports that the water stood four feet deep in the round house at Caliente, that the depot was undermined and several buildings swept away. A deposit of mud and silt a foot deep was left in every house by the receding waters, and much distress ensued. One life is reported lost.

At Round Valley, on the Caliente and Pioche road, water stood two feet deep over the track, and in places ice covered the track four feet deep.

A stage line has been established from Pioche to Modena.

Mr. Bailey of Caliente and Mr. Trieck of Los Angeles assisted in furnishing the music for the B. of R. T. ball New Year's Eve.

Number four passenger train which left Vegas east bound early Saturday night was marooned about six miles east of Caliente, the passengers being unable to escape for four days. They were finally taken to Modena by wagon by way of Panaca, a trip of two days through snow covered mountains.

RAILROAD SITUATION

Salt Lake Road Will Probably Abandon 100 Miles Track in Meadow Valley Wash

A hundred miles of road wiped off the map is the summary of the situation which confronts the officials of the Salt Lake road. For the third time since the completion of the line, five years ago, the flood waters have nearly obliterated the road from a point about 30 miles east of Caliente to a point 10 miles north of Moapa. When the full extent of this appalling disaster was revealed to the officials, all construction crews which had been sent to the front in the hope of quickly reopening the line were recalled and the work entirely abandoned.

At the earliest possible moment the directors of the road will meet for the purpose of deciding what shall be done in the way of rebuilding. It is the consensus of opinion among railroad men that the line will never be rebuilt in its former location. Many old surveys are discussed, and it is thought that the most feasible plan would be to leave the present main line near Molena, Utah, and build southerly on a location some 50 miles east of the old line, approaching the main line again near Moapa by way of the Virgin and Muddy valleys. This, it is believed, would be the cheapest route to construct and would have the advantage of opening a rich agricultural country. Another possibility is the old survey west from the main line passing through Panaca, Delamar, the Pahranagat valley, and again joining the present road near Dry Lake. It is thought, however, that the latter route would be the less feasible.

In any event, it seems certain that Caliente and the other points through Meadow Valley wash will be left far from direct communication with the

Continued on Page 4)

RAILROAD SITUATION

(Continued from Page 1)

outside world. Orders have been received by Agent T. E. Newman of this city, to close both the Caliente and Pioche offices of the Wells Fargo Express company at the earliest possible moment. In case the railroad is rebuilt in a new location the Caliente & Pioche railroad will possibly have no connection with the outside world. The situation, so far as the towns of Caliente and Pioche are concerned is very serious and it earnestly hoped that some means will be found to give them railway communication with the outside.

Bad at Caliente

A wire from Caliente from Mrs. J. O. McIntosh to her husband in this city reports that conditions there are bad. All railroad work has ceased and many of the employees are leaving the town. It is reported that the railroad people have definitely decided to abandon the line through the canyon entirely.

Difficult Trip

Mrs. J. O. McIntosh, who resides in Caliente, was in this city at the time of the recent flood. Full of fear as to the condition of the people and property in Caliente, Mrs. McIntosh left Vegas on the second going by rail to Monpa. There she procured a four horse team, and notwithstanding the fact that roads through the mountains had been practically obliterated by the floods, she pushed on fearless of obstacles. After a four days trip full of hardships, through the mountain snows, with the thermometer often below zero, Mrs. McIntosh succeeded in reaching Caliente, being the first from the outside world to reach the place.

A telegram from Mrs. McIntosh brought the first direct news to this city from stricken Caliente. It was sent by team to the end of the telegraph line 25 miles above Caliente and thence by wire, and reports their property not badly damaged.

Wire Through

Friday the last link in the telegraph line reconstructed between Las Vegas and Caliente was closed and the northern city is again in communication with the world. For 14 days there was no wire working out of Caliente, and for several days following the floods grave fears were entertained for the safety of its people.

Flood Victims

The bodies of two unfortunates who met death in the floods have been found in the debris below Caliente. One was that of a Japanese section hand and the other body is that of a Swede named Johnson who was employed in the round house at Caliente.

Mail Contracts Awarded

Chas. Culverwell, Jr., has been awarded the contract for carrying mail between Caliente and Acoma, a distance of about 30 miles, three times each week. Between Pioche and Modena the contract was awarded to T. J. Montgomery and the service on this route will also be three times a week. Mail for Panaca will possibly be routed by way of Pioche. It is understood that the tri-weekly service will be maintained until the reconstruction of the railroad.

Brother Graham, of the Caliente Prospector, is viewing the results of the recent floods with a faith and enthusiasm that is infectious. That he is no quitter is evidenced by the issue of the Prospector of January 8th, printed on a 9x12 sheet of colored poster paper, the only stock left after the flood. This issue, printed under so many difficulties, is full of news of the great flood and encouraging words for the people of Caliente. On the 15th the paper was increased to a four-column, four-page issue, without a groan in it. Here's wishing you success, Brother Graham, and the same to Caliente.

PROSPECTOR

Waxes Sarcastic at Expense of Pioche

Brother Graham of the Caliente Prospector does not view with equanimity the efforts of the Pioche crowd to help themselves to the railroad. Note the delicate sarcasm of the following from the pen of the Caliente editor.

"Pioche As a Pointer Pup

"To the Honorable Board of Selectmen of the City of New York: Gentlemen, you may not have noticed an article entitled 'Pioche Points the Way,' that has lately been given world wide attention. We beg to call your attention to same and offer it as our reason for making the following request: Will you kindly and immediately pass an ordinance to move the Brooklyn bridge to Caliente? We have natural piers for said bridge in the form of mountains on each side of our city:—There are other important reasons but surely this will be sufficient."

Las Vegas Age
February 12, 1910

Mrs. J. O. McIntosh arrived from Caliente Tuesday. She came by way of Meadow Valley wash. After spending a few days in this city she will visit Los Angeles.

Deseret News (Utah)
April 13, 1910

COME TO UTAH WITH TEN THOUSAND DOLLAR CAR

Shipment of Fifty-five Tons From Lucky Boy Will Net Company Small Fortune.

Accompanying a carload of high grade ore that will net their company not less than $10,000, J. H. Miller, president and general manager, and J. E. Adams, secretary of the Hawthorne Lucky Boy Mining company and the Goldfield Alamo Mining & Leasing company, which own 260 acres of mining property on the old Bodie road six miles southwest from Hawthorne, Esmeralda county, Nevada, arrived from there this morning and are registered at the Wilson.

"Our greatest depth is 650 feet, and the Lucky Boy mine has produced $1,200,000 in the last 15 months," said Mr. Miller this morning. "Our main shaft is sunk on a fissure vein between lime and granite, and is one of the prettiest fissures in the state of Nevada, and we have traced and prospected the vein for thousands of feet without a fault. We have followed a vein of ore varying from half a foot to seven feet of solid ore. This vein runs from 100 to 4,500 ounces silver, and from 10 to 60 per cent lead, and we think we have the second richest silver-lead proposition in this country, and our shipments have proven it.

"This seven feet of ore averages 300 ounces in silver alone. The carload of 55 tons we brought with us will run $10,000 to $15,000. We have shipped 19,000 tons that averaged $45.50 to the ton.

"We are now employing a force of 45 men, and the Lucky Boy is averaging us $20,000 in ore per month. Most of it is being shipped to the U. S. smelter here in Utah. Twice that company has attempted to secure control of the property on account of the richness and desirable character of the ore.

WILL RUN NEW TUNNEL.

"We are now arranging to start a 7,000 foot tunnel in the vein at the foot of the grade. This will cost $10 to $20 a foot, and will follow the vein, prospecting the two properties and giving us a depth of 1,700 feet, and tapping five ore shoots opened up above. Our intention is to carry this tunnel a mile and a half along the vein, which will tap the first ore chute at 1,000 feet.

"J. C. McCrystal of the Lucky Boy Leasing company returned this week from an inspection of our property, and was much pleased with it."

Las Vegas Age
April 22, 1910

RAPID PROGRESS

Railroad Crews Now 25 Miles North of Moapa

Reports from the front indicate that construction work is progressing very rapidly at this end of the line. Large quantities of material are constantly going forward and additional gangs of men are being employed. At this time the construction crews are working at a point above Hoya, 25 miles north of Moapa.

Work has also been begun south from Caliente and will now be pushed diligently from that end. Between Acoma and Caliente, however, there has been nothing done as yet. This is ascribed to two reasons, either of which may be the true one. The first reason is that the material which was being hurried to the scene over the Southern Pacific railroad was appropriated by that company for use in repairing the severe flood damage on its own lines, leaving the Salt Lake road out and injured. The other reason given is that it is the intention to build an entirely new line from a point near Acoma to a point on the Pioche line about six miles above Caliente. Surveying parties have been busy on this route and it is thought by some to be the intention not to rebuild even a temporary line through the Clover Valley canyon, but to put the line at once on the new survey. This, it is said, would avoid much expensive tunnel work.

Henry Ingram, the Caliente attorney, registered at the Hotel Nevada Saturday last.

Luke McNamee, son of Attorney F. R. McNamee of Caliente, was in Vegas Saturday last on his way home from Los Angeles.

DOUBLE FORCE

Reconstruction of Railroad Accelerated by Order of President W. A. Clark

Order to Double the Force in Canyon Brings Many Men and Much Material to the Work

"Double the force on the work and rush reconstruction" is the substance of orders issued by President William A. Clark, of the San Pedro, Los Angeles and Salt Lake railroad, this week As a result, men and material have been passing through Vegas on the way to the front at a lively rate. Thursday there were two trains run from this city to Moapa, taking 24 cars of material, including a large number of mules and about a hundred men, to the front. Chief Engineer Tilton, accompanied by Superintendent T. P. Cullen, J. J. Twomey and E. M. Jessup, also made a hurried trip to the front to take whatever steps appeared necessary to push the work more rapidly.

As a result of this activity, the work of building the temporary line is progressing much more rapidly than heretofore and the trains are now able to proceed to a point about 35 miles north of Moapa. It is understood that the work is being pushed steadily by large construction crews working both ways from Caliente. South from Caliente, the work has progressed about ten miles. North of Caliente a crew is working up the Clover Valley canyon, while many trainloads of material and several hundred men are working south from Acoma. According to the best estimates, the temporary track will be completed so as to permit the passage of trains at slow speed in June, and many hope to see through traffic resumed June 1st. While the exact date when the road will be open cannot yet be foretold to a certainty, it is a satisfaction to know that everything which men and money can do to bring about an early resumption of traffic is now being done. It may sometimes appear to us, far from the seat of the battle and unfamiliar with the details of the fight being carried on, that slow progress is being made. It should be borne in mind, however, that the loss to the railroad company every day the re-opening of the road is delayed, amounts to thousands of dollars, and that they realize the necessity for speedily re-opening the line far more strongly than we do. Therefore, would it not be well to save our criticism and exercise our patience, while we let the other fellows spend their money and do the worrying necessary to rebuild the road for us?

BUSY TIMES

Salt Lake Road Making Rapid Progress in Reconstruction

As a result of the orders to double the force, received from Senator Clark recently, the Salt Lake road is now working 2,000 men at the south end of the gap on the work of placing a temporary line through Meadow valley wash. This large force is being still further increased at the rate of from 50 to 100 men per day who pass through Vegas on the way to the front. In addition to the increased number of workmen, five pile drivers are busy on bridge and trestle construction and three more are to be placed in commission as soon as they can be secured. It is worthy of note that two of the pile drivers now in the canyon have been brought from the Southern Pacific road in the San Joaquin valley. Five work trains are now employed at this end of the work. A steam shovel is to be placed in the gravel pit at Hoya to furnish gravel for ballasting the track.

A gang of bridge carpenters under Foreman B. T. Townsend of the Santa Fe road left San Bernardino Tuesday night, arriving at the front Wednesday. There are now three bridges under construction back of the track crews and 100 additional bridge carpenters are wanted at the front immediately.

Chief Engineer Tilton is again at the front, having arrived from Los Angeles Tuesday after having made the round trip through the canyon and home via Salt Lake and San Francisco. The headquarters or operating station for the work will be advanced to Vigo, probably by the time this reaches the reader. Vigo is about 50 miles this side of Caliente.

From Caliente the work is reaching south and at the latest date of which we have information the crews are at a point about 15 miles south of Caliente. This leaves a gap of probably 30 or 35 miles to be bridged with temporary track before the road will be in shape to open traffic.

Coming south from the Salt Lake end the track is now within 10 or 12 miles of Caliente. There is some difficult construction between this point and Caliente, but the Utah Construction Company is working both a day and a night force and it is said the track will be open for use into Caliente about May 5th.

All ground for criticism as to the vigor with which the work of reconstruction is being carried on has now been removed. The organization of the working force, in all approximately 3,000 men, including those working at both ends of the break, with the vast amount of material which it has been necessary to assemble from all parts of the country, has been a gigantic task. The men in charge now have the great working machine in perfect order and only the intervention of another destructive catastrophe of nature can prevent the running of trains over the temporary track in June.

As to the Pioche branch, that will receive attention after the completion of the road into Caliente, the junction point, when it will be possible to get the necessary material more easily than at present.

Salt Lake Mining Review (Utah)
April 30, 1910

G. W. Woods, mining engineer for the Wasp Mining company, of Deadwood, South Dakota, has been spending some time at Caliente and DeLamar, Nevada, of late. Mr. Woods has arranged for the purchase of some of the machinery included in the equipment of the mill at DeLamar, and this will be utilized by the Wasp company at its South Dakota property.

Las Vegas Age
May 7, 1910

PIOCHE HOPEFUL

Expects R. R. Communication With Outside World May 15

The Pioche Record is responsible for the statement that the Salt Lake railroad will reach Caliente within a very few days and that the Pioche branch will immediately be repaired and put in operation by the 15th.

The old schedule of a train leaving Caliente late in the afternoon for Pioche, and returning next morning, will be put in effect. The reopening of the road will mean much to the big silver camp, as it will be followed by an immediate resumption of work on many of the properties which were forced to shut down when the railroad was destroyed.

Eureka Reporter (Utah)
May 13, 1910

Will Reopen in June

Open for through traffic not later than June 15 is the slogan that has been adopted by the engineering forces and the construction companies which are rebuilding the Salt Lake route through the Meadow valley wash district The belief that through traffic between Salt Lake and Los Angeles will be resumed by the middle of next month is based on the progress that has been made rebuilding the road There are but two gaps to fill of a total of about thirty seven miles Work is being pushed at the rate of nearly a mile a day Three work trains and crews that are working from Acoma have reached a point fourteen miles west and within eleven miles of Caliente Other crews working from Caliente are now about sixteen miles west Crews east from Moapa have progressed sixteen miles leaving a gap of about twenty nine miles to be closed on the Los Angeles division

CLOSING GAP

Only Sixteen Miles of Building Necessary to Connect Rails

The headquarters for construction in the Meadow Valley wash will be moved early the coming week from Leith to Lyle. The progress the past week has been just as rapid as men and money could make it. The present work from the south end of the gap is very difficult, requiring deep fills and many bridges. The work from Caliente south has been discontinued on account of getting in the necessary material, but the track has been pushed south about twelve miles. This leaves a gap of but sixteen miles to finish to connect the track, so that there is every probability that the promise of the company to have the line in operation on or before June 15th will be fulfilled. The track into Caliente from the north will be open next Monday.

Chief Engineer Tilton was in Vegas Wednesday afternoon on his way from the front to Los Angeles, and expressed himself as greatly pleased with progress made.

F. R. McNamee, of Caliente, passed through Vegas Saturday last on his way to Los Angeles. He will return in a few days and will then spend a few days in Vegas.

Train No. 4, the Los Angeles Limited, which left Vegas at 8:25 p. m. on December 31, 1909, has at last been moved from the point near Eccles station, where it was marooned the morning of January 1st, to Caliente. The "Limited" was famous as one of the great trains in the transcontinental business, and to her other records may now add the distinction of being the latest train on record. Five months on the main line without moving is about the limit.

Las Vegas Age
June 4, 1910

ALMOST COMPLETED

Tremendous Work of Reconstruction in Meadow Valley Almost Completed

Track To Be Connected Monday or Tuesday and Through Trains Will Again Run by June Fifteenth

One of the most stupendous tasks in the history of railroading will be completed when the two ends of the track are connected next Monday or Tuesday, a few miles south of Caliente in the Meadow Valley wash. Since January 1st no train has made the trip over the Salt Lake road through the canyon. For months an army of men,

S. P., L. A. & S. L. R. R. DEPOT AT LAS VEGAS

officered by engineers of the highest skill, have been working under
high pressure, striving to replace as quickly as possible the hundred
miles of road and road bed swept away in the twinkling of an eye by
the rush of angry waters New Year's morning. After an expenditure
of money impossible for the average man to appreciate, and overcom-
ing difficulties in engineering, weather conditions sufficient to appall
any but the stoutest heart, the shining steel is again about to link together the two ends of a great transcontinental railroad.

Sunday night, June 12, at 10 o'clock, the splendid Los Angeles
Limited will start for the first time in five and a half months from the
Northwestern depot in Chicago, to pass over the just completed temporary track, and through Vegas June 15th. The first limited from the
West will leave Los Angeles at 10 a. m. June 14th, passing through
Vegas the same evening. Thus will resume the operation of one of the
best and most popular trains on the continent. Through overland
trains will be put in operation just as soon as possible after the rails
are connected.

The completion of the present line really marks but the beginning
of the great work. A new high line to cost $4,000,000 has been sur-
veyed and will probably be completed within 18 months.

CLIPPINGS

John L. Considine, well known in the political and newspaper field of Nevada, has been visiting in this portion of Nevada the greater portion of the past week, leaving Friday to return to Reno. Ostensibly Mr. Considine is here to attend to his duties as state bullion tax collector and he reports a great increase in that source of the state's revenue. Practically Brother Considine is out with a soft-haired brush and pail of whitewash seeking to cover the acting governor's "trail of mud stained despotism," as Frank Nicholas would say. Personally Mr. Considine is a suave and able politician. A good newspaper man also, with a broad experience in state matters. You can't help but like him and recognize his merit, but he certainly selected a pinto and a "goat" when he picked Dickerson for his string.—[Prospector, Caliente.

Deseret News (Utah)
June 15, 1910

LUND, NEVADA.

WILL BUILD RESERVOIRS TO REDEEM MORE LAND

(Special Correspondence.)

LUND, Nev., June 10.—Some of the farmers have began to cut the first crop of alfalfa. This has been a very dry spring, but the cattle on the range look fairly well considering the dry season.

Bishop Orem H. Snow is preparing to move to Canada to leave here between the 15th and 20th of June.

There is a bright future for Lund. A number of new buildings are being erected and the people also contemplate building a reservoir to hold winter water. Some work has already been done. The water has been filed on, sites for the dams have been surveyed and a commencement has been made on the ditches to lead the water from the springs to the reservoirs. This move will aid young men to procure land and water to build homes upon.

Washington County News (Utah)
June 16, 1910

Pres Ed. H. Snow and son, Karl,
returned Monday from Salt Lake
City and Lund, Nevada At the
latter place the ward was reorgan-
ized with A R Whitehead as bishop and Robert Reid and George C.
Gardner as his counselors.

Deseret News (Utah)
June 17, 1910

LUND, NEVADA.

ADOLPHUS R. WHITEHEAD NEW BISHOP OF LUND

(Special Correspondence.)

LUND, Nev., June 12.—On June 9,
Elder David O. McKay of the council
of the twelve and President Edward
H. Snow of the St. George stake arrived here at Lund and held ward
conference. Bishop Oren H. Snow
was released as bishop, as he is going
to move to Canada. Adolphus R.
Whitehead was sustained as the new
bishop with Robert Reid as first and
Geo. C. Gardner as second counselors.
The Saints enjoyed the addresses of the
visitors.

The speaker at the Sunday service to-
The speaker at the Sunday service
was the Hon. Thomas Judd of St.
George, Utah.

Deseret News (Utah)
June 20, 1910

EARLY MORNING MURDER
IN CALIENTE STREET

(Special to The News.)

Caliente, June 20—Matt Wicks is dead, Walter Murphy with his arm half shot away and the stump in a sling and James B. Murphy in jail is the toll of a gun fight in the main street of this Nevada camp at an early hour Sunday morning. The direct cause is traceable to a protracted spree. The shooting took place on the tracks in front of Billy Noble's saloon in Clover avenue. Nearly one-half the population of the town was on the street at the time the loud quarrel began, but no one interfered. A stranger who started towards the spot where the dead man fell after the shooting was warned away by Murphy with his gun pointing to the spot the stranger occupied.

Deputy Sheriff T. J. Harrington and Dr. W. P. Murray were soon on the ground after the shooting. It was too late to give the victim any medical or surgical attention and the sheriff's deputy soon had Murphy in jail guarded by three stalwart men, for it was feared that an attempt to lynch him would be made. Murphy said that the three men had come here from a bridge camp, and that as soon as they landed in the town they began drinking. The dead man formerly lived in Utah and the Murphy brothers were formerly from Colorado.

Las Vegas Age
June 25, 1910

Robert Graham, the genial editor of the Caliente Prospector, was in Vegas Sunday night, on his way home from Carson City.

Deseret News (Utah)
June 29, 1910

PIOCHE AND CALIENTE
CELEBRATE RAILROAD DAY.

(Special to The News.)

Pioche, Nev., June 29—The railroad day celebration here and at Caliente Monday was a huge success. One hundred and twenty people went from here and Panaca on an excursion to Caliente, returning in the evening with 50 more from Caliente where an elaborate celebration and festivities were carried out. Business was generally suspended during the day. The excursions were arranged by the Pioche Commercial club.

Murder at Caliente

In a drunken row at Caliente on the 19th A. E. Wirt was shot and killed by J. B. Murphy. Walter Murphy, a brother of the slayer, had his arm shattered, probably by one of the shots fired by his brother. The preliminary hearing before Justice Maynard resulted in a charge of murder being placed against J. B. Murphy and he was held without bail to answer before the grand jury.

Will Dobson to Marry

The following item, clipped from the San Bernardino Sun, will be of interest to Vegas people, Mr. Dobson having been a resident of this city for some time. We take pleasure in extending congratulations and best wishes.

"San Bernardino friends have been informed of the approaching marriage of William Dobson, formerly of San Bernardino, now of Caliente, Nevada, to Miss Lena Rives, of Salt Lake City. The date as set is near the end of August, and the wedding will take place at the home of the bride's parents, Mr. and Mrs. R. T. Rives. The groom is now in business in Caliente, with his brother, Harold Dobson."

In defining his position, Editor Graham, of the Caliente Prospector, says: "In its attitude toward the state ticket the paper is republican, for the good and satisfactory reason that the democratic combination now in control have given a most unsatisfactory, unfair and unjustly discriminating mis-administration."

Henry Ingram, the Caliente attorney, was a Vegas visitor Monday.

VETERAN DEAD

Col. "Jim" Brown, Former Vegas Newspaper Man

Col. James Brown, who for several years was identified with newspaper work in Las Vegas, Greenwater and Caliente, died in New York June 23d. He had been in poor health for some time and went to the east in the hope of securing relief, but in vain.

He was well known throughout Nevada and Montana, where he had a wide acquaintance and many friends who regret to hear of his death.

The bond of J. L. Denton as constable of Caliente township was approved.

It was ordered by the board that in the future all bids for medical attention against the county contracted at Caliente must receive the O. K. of Commissioner Banovich and that he must be communicated with in relation to same and his consent obtained before contraction.

A proposition was received from the S. P. L. A. & S. L. R. R. Co., offering to drive the pile and furnish the material for the construction of a bridge over the wash at Caliente at actual cost. It was ordered by the board that said proposition be accepted. It was also ordered that Hans Oleson, J. A. Denton and Geo. C. Fetterman be appointed as a committee to designate the point where said bridge is to be built and the length of same.

Earl Hyde of Elgin has secured a position as chef at the local D. & R. G. hotel.

Las Vegas Age
August 13, 1910

Contract for High Line

The contract for the first 30 miles of the new high line of the Salt Lake road will be let on the 15th. This section of the work will begin on the present line a short distance this side of Modena, running westerly through Miller's pass and joining the line of the Caliente and Pioche branch about eight miles north of Caliente.

Deseret News (Utah)
August 26, 1910

LUND, NEVADA.

OLD FOLKS ARE ROYALLY ENTERTAINED

(Special Correspondence.)

LUND, Nevada, Aug 25—On Aug 14. the old folks were royally entertained at the meetinghouse, where a program and banquet were greatly enjoyed by the veterans. A ball in the evening gave the finishing touches to the happy day. The following compose the committee on entertainment: Wm. A. Terry, Geo. C. Gardner, B. H. Ashby, Ruth B. Gardner, Mary Sinfield and Maggie Reid.

The second crop of alfalfa is being cut, a good crop as a rule; the grain crop is also being harvested.

CALIENTE ACTIVE

Great Work of Building High Line Actually Under Way

[Special Correspondence]

Caliente, Sept. 8, 1910.

Ground has been broken for the new high line through the Meadow valley wash, for which the contracts were let some weeks ago. At the present time this is the most extensive railroad work being carried on in the west, as it involves an expenditure of over six million dollars for contract work alone, not including the heavy cost of surveys and preliminary work. What is known as the Brown outfit, part of the Utah Construction company, have established their camp at Aetna, some four miles below Caliente, and active work was begun on Thursday.

A number of sub-contracts have been let by the Utah Construction Co. for a part of their work and these smaller contractors are now establishing camps and will be in full operation the coming week. Twenty-five carloads of equipment, including horses, scrapers, steam shovels and camp equipment, have arrived during the past few days for the Utah Con. Co., and laborers, quarrymen and rockmen are arriving daily. A special passenger coach is being run daily from Salt Lake to bring in workmen, and it is expected that another car will soon be put on from Los Angeles to this point. In extensive work of this kind considerable time is necessary to establish camps, particularly in a country as rugged as the Meadow valley. These camps, however, are now being laid out and workmen are being rushed to the different points.

Within the next 30 days from 1,500 to 2,000 men will be employed at this end. A very large force of miners will be necessary, as the work is principally through rock, and a number of tunnels varying from 200 to 1,100 feet in length will be necessary. At the present time Caliente is one of the boom towns of the state and will continue to be so for months to come.

Not in years has such general activity been shown as at the present time. With the incoming rush of miners and laborers for the new high line of the Salt Lake route it has created a demand for houses and accommodations such as has but once before been known in the history of the town. This extensive work will naturally bring in many permanent residents, in addition to a large

(Continued on Page 5)

CALIENTE ACTIVE

(Continued from Page 1)

floating population, and as a result our storekeepers are putting in heavy stocks and anticipate an unusually good winter's trade. There is also considerable talk of the resumption of mining activity in this section. The closing down of the Salt Lake road during the reconstruction period occasioned by the washouts was a hard blow to a number of shipping mines. These mines so affected can now receive shipments, and it is understood that advantage will be taken of the improved conditions.

The Utah Construction Co., which has the contract for the upper half of the new high line, has established headquarters here and will soon erect a large commissary for supplying its various camps, as fully 2,000 men will be employed when the various camps are in full operation, and as all these workmen will report to the headquarters here and be assigned to the different divisions it naturally follows that this in itself will prove a large source of income to all lines of trade.

The ideal climate of this section will also prove an incentive to many to locate here and establish occupations and lines of business which will be of lasting benefit to the community. On the whole the future is exceedingly encouraging and the general opinion is that Caliente will again resume her position as one of the most progressive and enterprising towns of the state.

F. D. Sturgis, of Caliente, was in Vegas Thursday.

RUSHING WORK

Two Thousand Men Now On New High Line

[Special Correspondence]

Caliente, Sept. 16.—During the past week several trainloads of construction material have arrived for the contractors and subcontractors for the new high line through the Meadow valley wash, and a number of new camps have been established along the line. At Aetna the Brown outfit is making rapid progress both in the cuts and with the scraper gangs, which are rapidly filling in the open grades between the two cuts.

On the western end two large camps have been established above Moapa, while some ten miles to the eastward another camp has been laid out. In these different camps some 2,000 men are now employed and daily additions are being made to the working forces. During the coming week a number of new camps will be established at Elgin, Carp and other way stations and ground will be broken for at least two if not three of the tunnels along the line.

The contractors are still running special cars, both from Salt Lake and Los Angeles, and new workmen are added at the rate of about 100 daily. Another week will see all of the heavy work under full swing, as the new outfits will then be on the ground and the camps established.

The Utah Construction Co. has established a daily supply train which leaves here every morning, carrying material and employees to the various points on the line. The newly arrived workmen are by this means enabled to reach their camps without delay.

As a result of the influx of strangers for this railroad work our merchants report a largely increased business, while the hotels and lodging houses are nightly turning away guests, as the accommodations are overcrowded and inadequate for the increased demand. Not in years has this locality shown the activity of the present season, and our citizens all welcome it as an indication of the return of prosperous times.

NEW HIGH LINE

Work Progressing Rapidly--1100 Ft. Tunnel Being Cut

[Special Correspondence]

Elgin, Nev., Sept. 26.—For the next eight months this point is destined to be one of the most important stations on the new high line of the Salt Lake road. Five contractors have their camps within a few miles and in a few weeks it is safe to predict that at least 1,000 men will be at work in this immediate vicinity; for three miles one of the heaviest fills on the line will be made through here, with heavy rock cuts at each end of the canyon, while above the Box canyon where the old Elgin station stood before the washout a tunnel will be driven, and three miles below a smaller tunnel will be run and heavy rock cuts made between that point and Leith.

Scattered along at various points between Caliente and Moapa are 20 camps, comprising scraper outfits, tunnel and bench camps. At many points ground has already been broken and considerable progress is being made, but it will require a month at least before the full force is at work.

At Leith the Utah Construction Co. is driving the 1,100-foot tunnel, the longest on the line, and will use at this point a battery of air drills to facilitate rapid work. At other points and with the smaller tunnels hand work will be used almost exclusively. This will give employment to many miners, and large numbers are daily arriving from Utah, Colorado and California. As a result of this large employment of skilled labor nearly all the towns within a radius of 100 miles will receive some benefit, as constant changes will be taking place in the forces engaged.

Several extra construction trains have recently been added from the Caliente end to furnish the numerous camps with material, food supplies and men, while the large quantity of machinery equipment and lumber usually requires one or two extras in each direction daily. This is a welcome addition to the railroad men, as it requires more train crews, and many trainmen are now back on their old runs, from which they were temporarily laid off during the reconstruction of the washed-out line. Thus far there has been no interruption to through traffic, but undoubtedly some slight delays will occur later when the full construction force is at work.

The heavy rains of some ten days ago caused no perceptible damage to the temporary pile bridges or new embankments, although for two days the river rose rapidly and for a time looked threatening. Unusual precautions are taken at all points to prevent any serious washouts which could in any manner cause delay.

Las Vegas Age
October 22, 1910

Caliente Notes

John Davis, of Caliente, took carbolic acid in that city Thursday at noon. He suffered terrible agony for a time, when he died. He left letters and papers which indicate he came from New Mexico.

At noon, Monday, while the proprietor was at lunch, the butcher shop was entered by burglars. They took the cleaver and proceeded to smash the cash register, securing the sum of $40 in money

Three men who stole the trunks last Sunday night, were caught and sent to the county jail at Pioche.

Las Vegas Age
October 29, 1910

Mrs. A. L. Murphy left Thursday to join Mr. Murphy in Caliente.

Mrs. G. F. Ferris has returned from a stay of five weeks at Caliente.

Mr. F. R. McNamee, of Caliente, was in Vegas Friday on court business.

Las Vegas Age
November 12, 1910

F. R. McNamee, of Caliente, was in the city attending court the latter part of the week.

DAMAGE SUIT

Case of Est. C. Bailey vs. Salt Lake RR. Lasts a Week

The damage suit of Roy Foster, special administrator of the estate of C. Bailey, deceased vs. the San Pedro, Salt Lake and Los Angeles railroad company to recover $84,000 damages has occupied the entire time of the district court this week.

The plaintiff is represented in court by attorneys Leon French, of Searchlight, and Chas. L. Allison and Robert McHargue, of San Bernardino, Calif. The defense is conducted by Frank R. McNamee, of Caliente.

The plaintiff has brought in numerous witnesses by whom it is sought to show that Claude Bailey met his death in a boiler explosion due to the negligence of defendant. The facts, briefly stated, are that Engineer Bailey, making his run in August, 1907, was killed when the boiler of his locomotive exploded near Arden station. Considerable stress is laid by the prosecution on the record made by engineers in charge of the engine immediately preceding that date, of certain repairs which the engine needed, and the failure to make which plaintiff alleges resulted in the explosion.

On the other hand, the defendant has put expert witnesses on the stand by whom it seeks to show that the explosion was due directly to the negligence of Engineer Bailey in allowing the water to get too low in the boiler. The case is being contested stubbornly, and will probably not be finished before the early portion of next week.

The jurors in the case are being carefully guarded under direction of the court, and will doubtless feel great relief when their monotonous duties are completed. Those composing the jury are C. E. Burdick, J. G. Laravey, W. W. Perkins, Willard L. Jones, S. A. Angell, Geo. L. Whitney, B. F Bonelli, Edw. I. Cox, Edw. Bunker, Jr., Benj. Bunker, Chas. M. Hardy and A. N. Woodberry.

TO VEGAS

Train Despatchers Now Make Vegas Headquarters

Las Vegas, beginning with Wednesday last, is the headquarters for the train despatchers of the Salt Lake road. Chief despatcher, J. A. Jones, formerly of Los Angeles, has been promoted to the position of trainmaster, with his office in this city. He has charge of the division from Otis to Caliente. Under him are three despatchers on duty eight hours each. Messrs. J. P. Fay, W. M. Dickinson and F. F. Small, occupying the positions. Mr. Small is chief despatcher.

J. J. Toomey has been transferred to the Los Angeles division and will have charge of the train service between Otis and the coast.

Las Vegas Age
December 31, 1910

Hetry Ingram the Caliente attorney, was in Vegas to attend court Mondoy.

Las Vegas Age
January 6, 1911

Mrs. Walter Reeder of Caliente spent the week in Vegas visiting friends.

Las Vegas Age
January 28, 1911

Harold Dobson, formerly of Vegas, but now a resident of Caliente, with his father, Wm. Dobson and his sister Miss Dobson, who have been visiting in San Bernardino are in town. They will return to their home in Caliente as soon as train service is resumed.

Frank R. McNamee, of Caliente, was in Vegas Wednesday, looking after the details of the sale of the property of the Moapa Valley Fruit and Produce Co. under foreclosure proceedings.

WISER RANCH

Sold by Sheriff Gay Under Foreclosure for $37,000

The famous and beautiful Wiser ranch in the Moapa valley, closed another chapter in an eventful history Wednesday, when sheriff Sam Gay offered for sale and sold the property of the Moapa Valley Fruit and Produce Co., under foreclosure to Frank Knox, president of the National Bank of the Republic in Salt Lake city. Mr. Knox was represented in the matter of the bidding by Fred Falkner of Salt Lake City. The interests of the plaintiffs in the case were cared for by attorney Frank R. McNamee, of Caliente.

The ranch property comprises 520 acres of the best land in the famous Moapa valley, with the valuable primary water right in the Muddy river attached. There are now 300 acres under cultivation, the land being in the heart of the cantaloupe belt. It is in close proximity to Moapa station on the Salt Lake road, and with proper development will be worth many times the price paid.

This ranch was originally taken up by Jack Longstreet, who shot and killed Alexander Dry in the late seventies, when the latter attempted to jump the claim of Longstreet. The water right is the first water right secured on the Muddy river subsequent to the Mormon settlement at St. Thomas, which was afterward abandoned, leaving this the primary water right in the valley.

Word has been received that A. H. Norris who was severely injured near Caliente last week and who has been in a very critical condition at the L. D. S. hospital in Salt Lake is improving.

Las Vegas Age
March 11, 1911

ABANDONS TRIP TO VEGAS

The Salt Lake railroad's agricultural train, which has been traveling over that company's lines for the past few weeks giving demonstrations in scientific farming, has returned to Salt Lake city and disbanded, according to information received yesterday by T. C. Peck, general passenger agent of the road. The trip extended as far west as Caliente, Nev., travelling 4000 miles, made 150 stops and lectures were given before 40,000 people.—Salt Lake Tribune.

It is to be regretted that owing to the recent wash out, the trip to Vegas had to be abandoned, and the people here, many of whom had looked forward to a scientific demonstration of practical farming, were perforce unable to take advantage of these valuable lectures, given by men who know conditions of soil and climate and needs of the community, and it is to be hoped this good work is only deferred not altogether abandoned.

Las Vegas Age
March 18, 1911

AGAIN TIED UP

Salt Lake to Run Trains Over High Line Track Soon

Snowstorms, rainstorms and washouts have played havoc with the railroads in Nevada and California the past week. The road between Las Vegas and Salt Lake through the Meadow Valley Wash is again out of commission and rumor has it that the old road will be abandoned and work on the high line rushed to completion. It is thought that the new line can be made ready by the 1st of April. There was a little trouble at Afton but not serious enough to cause much delay. At present there are only three trains a week on the L. V. & T.

An examination of the damage caused by last week's flood showed that from Caliente to Boyd, a distance of 14 miles, it will be fully as easy to complete the new high line and connect it with the old track as it would be to make temporary repairs on the old line over those 14 miles.

There is already from 15 to 20 miles of the new high line in use further south, so that when the road is open again much of it through the Meadow Valley region will be well up above the danger line.

Connecting through from Salt Lake City to Caliente will be established tonight, and it will doubtless bring rejoicing to about 60 people who have been marooned at Caliente since March 8. On that date overland train No. 1 bound for Los Angeles, was caught at Caliente by a downpour. It could not proceed through the meadow Valley wash, and before it could go back the tracks had been taken out to the east.

Lloyd Denton, of Caliente, was in Vegas last week.

BIG EXPENDITURE

Double tracks are to be laid by the Central Pacific and the Union Pacific over the whole distance to the Pacific coast, making the fast trans-continental double-track line. Seventy-five million dollars will be spent on the work. So timid were the builders of the first single track road that the government had to give large grants of land to them to induce them to undertake the work. But that was in the days when the maps showed the Great American Desert, and not many years after camels were imported for transportation across the New World Sahara.

A. H. Norris who was severely injured some weeks ago has so far recovered as to be brought home to Caliente from the hospital in Salt Lake.

Mrs. A. L. Murphy came down from Caliente Tuesday, remaining until Thursday evening when she left for Los Angeles to join Mr. Murphy. They will spend the summer in California returning to Vegas in the fall.

Robert Graham, editor of the Caliente Prospector, was in Vegas several days early in the week.

Las Vegas Age
April 29, 1911

VALLEY IMPROVES

Railroad Assured from Logan to St. Thomas

Mr. E. J. Robertson of the Moapa valley, favored the Age with an interesting interview on the Moapa valley country Thursday. Mr. Robertson was in Vegas by appointment with Senator Wm. A. Clark to discuss the railroad question as pertains to the valley.

Mr. Robertson said:

"The conditions in the valley are more prosperous than ever before. The value of combined effort has been demonstrated by the success of the movement to secure the extension of the railroad to St. Thomas. By co-operation of the people of the valley and the formation of the Chambers of Commerce at Overton and St. Thomas, the railroad company has been induced to to extend the road through to St. Thomas instead of stopping at Logan as at first proposed. This will make the branch 26 miles in length instead of 12 miles. The advantage to the valley by this move is apparent in view of the fact that eight tenths of the cultivatable area lies south east of Logan and the valuable kaolin deposits and mountains of salt will be opened up by railroad transportation.

"When the real facts were brought before Senator Clark he lost no time in authorizing the construction of the line on from Logan, and a spirt of enterprise has thereby been awakened in the people.

"The area of cantaloupes planted this year will exceed three times the total area ever before planted. The Moapa Fruit Land Co. and the Irrigation & Development Co, now have 140 acres up and are planting 60 acres additional. This will mean the shipment of at least 200 cars from the lower portion of the valley and should bring the total, including the upper valley to 350 cars for the season.

"In addition to the above, vastly increased shipments of asparagus and early vegetables will be made. The raising of hogs is also rapidly becoming a very important industry, the markets of Caliente, Las Vegas and Goldfield being now supplied with pork from the valley.

VISITS SCHOOLS

State Supt. Bray Makes First Visit Here

State Supt. Bray accompanied by Deputy Superintendent McKay has been visiting the larger schools of Clark and Lincoln counties last week, taking in particularly Las Vegas, Caliente, Panaca and Pioche.

This is Supt. Bray's first visit to this section of Nevada, and he reports school conditions and sentiment much better than he had expected to find them. He saw good school buildings and good school interest everywhere, and was pleased to find in these counties the business, farming and mining outlook in so healthy condition. He thinks that Las Vegas in particular has a great future.

The good people of Panaca turned out to listen to an evening address by Supt. Bray, and manifested strong interest in his suggestions for school improvement throughout the state. Friday afternoon at 2.30 he addressed the Las Vegas teachers on "Nevada School Problems."

Mr. Bray will visit all the counties of the state each year to advise with superintendents and teachers, to address the people on educational topics and to keep in direct touch with the educational work of the state.

BASE BALL LOOKING UP

Local Teams Are Preparing for Active Campaign During the Summer.

The Vegas Ball teams are preparing to make things hum from now on. To compensate for the shiftless game of last Sunday, when the ball loving public deserted the field after two innings of horse play, there will be two games tomorrow, both free and everybody invited.

In the morning the shop boys will play the clerks and in the afternoon the old reliable Vegas team will play a picked nine to be composed of the best players it is possible to get together here.

Wednesday the Vegas bunch is planing to visit Caliente to measure up with the Caliente team, and in all probability a return match will be arranged for the near future.

Vegas will visit Needles May 30th and give that jolly bunch a chance to get even on the game of two weeks ago. After having played one excellent game it is believed that both teams will do their very best work with interesting results. As many citizens as possible should accompany the team and enjoy a pleasant outing.

A game with either Needles or Caliente should be arranged for the Fourth of July. It is probable that Vegas will be well filled with visitors on that occasion and a live game would be a very satisfactory entertaigment.

Luke J. McNamee of Caliente has been in Vegas for several days.

Frank R. McNamee of Caliente is attending the session of the district court.

The Big Feed.

Conductor Geo. A. Goodwin was a guest of the Caliente lodge T. F. B. Tuesday evening, and reports a very enjoyable time. The feature of the evening was a tasty supper given by President J. W. Evans of the Caliente lodge to about a dozen members and guests.

VEGAS WINS.

Hot Game Of Ball at Caliente Results 8 -- 7 in Our Favor.

The Vegas ball team went to Caliente according to program Wednesday morning on No. 4. They were met by Manager Leo McNamee who took them in charge and showed them every courtesy and hospitality.

The game was called about 2:30. Vegas jumped to the fore at once securing two runs in the first and maintaining the lead until the end. In the ninth inning however, the Caliente rooters succeeded in infusing courage into their players and inspiring terror in ours so that the game came near to being another story. In that inning Caliente aided by two punk plays by the Vegas bunch, piled five good ones across the plate, leaving the score when the side was retired 8 to 7 in Vegas favor.

The Caliente people turned out en masse to support their team, and are an enthusiastic, good natured, enjoyable bunch of rooters. A game without the real old businesslike brand of rooting is of no interest to anyone anyhow.

The Caliente team has arranged to meet Vegas here on Sunday, the 28th, and it is hoped that Vegas may properly repay the hospitality she has enjoyed at our northern neighbors.

Las Vegas Age
May 27, 1911

Mrs. Talbert Mitchum and little son, Jesse, of Caliente were here a few days this week on a visit with Mrs. J. C. Gregory.

Las Vegas Age
June 17, 1911

Busy Bob.

Robert Graham, editor and proprietor of the Caliente Prospector, don't let a little thing like a newspaper interfere with his business.

He has taken the agency of the Continental Casualty Co. for Nevada and Utah and is issuing many polices, spending a portion of his time each week on the road. Now the question is, has brother Graham arrived at such a state of affluence through his newspaper business that he can afford to travel about in style writing insurance policies, or is the insurance business so chock full of ready money that he can afford to support a newspaper as a side line?

Richfield Reaper (Utah)
June 27, 1911

Mrs Sidney Pace and her sister, Miss Maud Frickson, left Friday morning for Alamo, Nevada, the home of Mrs Pace. Miss Erickson will spend th summer there

Salt Lake Mining Review (Utah)
June 30, 1911

Joseph McCuffie, of DeLamar, Nevada, one of the veteran stock raisers and mining men of Lincoln county, was in Salt Lake, last week, accompanied by Mrs. McGuffie. Mr. McGuffie is interested in a most promising mining proposition on Papoose mountain, 125 miles west of DeLamar. This is an isolated region, but rich in its mineralization; so rich, in fact, that some day there will be a rush there, and some way will be devised by which the great orebodies of that section can be successfully and profitably worked. On his Papoose mountain property Mr. McGuffie has developed a ledge that is twenty feet in width, that carries average values of $100 silver and gold to the ton. This is a contact vein between quartzite and porphyry, which can be traced on the surface for a distance of 7,500 feet. Mr. McGuffie will devote the summer in the development of this property. Mrs. McGuffie may remain in Salt Lake for two or three months.

CALIENTE KILLING

Three Cornered Affray in Which Mexican Loses Life and Ikey is Badly Cut

At Caliente on the evening of the Fourth of July, trouble occurred between a Mexican armed with a double edged knife with a blade about a foot long, and an individual commonly known as "Ikey" who was armed with a revolver.

The Mexican inflicted several serious wounds, piercing the intestines and lungs of his opponent and inflicting other severe cuts. Ikey in the meantime had drawn his revolver and shot the Mexican twice, one shot entering the head near the eye and the other the body but without stopping the knife play. In spite of his wounds the Mexican still slashed the white man and would have cut him to pieces had not a bystander stepped up, wrested the revolver from Ikey's hand and shot the Mexican through the heart killing him instantly.

Numerous bystanders saw the closing acts of the play but none it is said will identify the man who interfered and killed the Mexican.

"Ikey" is in a very precarious condition and there is considerable doubt as to whether he will survive.

Dr. H. L. Hewetson made a trip up the canyon the Fourth, going as far as Caliente. He reports that the son of fireman Ryan died in the hospital at Salt Lake City of typhoid fever. Also that Jack Overholt, foreman of the steel gang was taken seriously ill with appendicitis and was sent to Los Angeles on number 7 Thursday to be operated on.

Las Vegas Age
July 22, 1911

Old Style

The Wing Trust has purchased the Grand Restaurant, and now Ong Loy will return to the old country and go to wearing his shirt outside his pants again. —[Prospector, Caliente.

Las Vegas Age
July 29, 1911

A. S. McElhinney, formerly of the Caliente Prospector, passed through Las Vegas Wednesday enroute to the east. He intends visiting relatives in Texas and Oklahoma, and will then proceed to Florida where he will look after the land interests of himself and associates, in the reclamation districts of the Everglades.

Emery County News (Utah)
August 5, 1911

From Orangeville Section

Thos. Humphrey and Mrs. Eva Curtis were married here Wednesday afternoon and they gave their wedding ball in the evening. Their well wishers are legion.

Las Vegas Age
September 16, 1911

Frank R. McNamee, of Caliente, associate counsel of the Salt Lake railroad was in this city Tuesday.

Las Vegas Age
September 23, 1911

Engineer Lytle has purchased the Watson house on Fifth Street and will bring his family here from Caliente to reside.

Las Vegas Age
October 7, 1911

Frank R. McNamee, of Caliente, was in Vegas Monday on business before the county commisioners.

Salt Lake Mining Review
October 15, 1911

Engineers and Millmen

Edward Nissen of Salt Lake recently made patent surveys for the Bush mines, near Hiko, Nevada.

R. C. Gemmell of Salt Lake, general superintendent for the Utah Copper company, is in the east on a vacation.

H. F. Widdecome of Salt Lake has been appointed superintendent of the Day Mine at Jackrabbit, a few miles north of Pioche, Nevada.

PROSPECTOR INDICTED

Editor of Caliente's Newspaper Accused by Grand Jury of Criminal Libel

A report made by the Grand Jury of Lincoln County at Pioche returned nine indictments, two of which are against Robert Graham, editor of the Caliente Prospector, for Criminal Libel.

One of said indictments is on charges brought by Dr. W. P. Murray, of Caliente, and the other by W. H. Beason, editor of the Pioche Record.

Of the nine indictments returned, five were kept secret, the names of the parties against whom they were drought not being divulged. According to rumors, there will be something of a sensation when the parties accused are arrested and brought into court.

Las Vegas Age
November 18, 1911

Robert Graham Free

Robert Graham, the editor of the Caliente Prospector, who was recently indicted by the Lincoln County Grand Jury has passed through the ordeal of trial and the result may be called a draw. In the case in which Dr. W. P. Murray was complaining witness the defendant was acquitted. In the other case wherein the charge of libel was brought by Mr. Beason, editor of the Pioche Record, Mr. Graham was convicted but the court granted extreme leniency, imposing a fine of $50 only.

Las Vegas Age
December 2, 1911

F. R. McNamee of Caliente, the attorney for the S. P., L. A. & S. L. road, registered at Hotel Nevada Wednesday last.

Las Vegas Age
December 23, 1911

Rev. Paul B. James will spend the coming week in Caliente and Pioche. He will assist Mr. Dickle with his Christmas exercises on Wednesday evening.

Davis County Clipper (Utah)
January, 26, 1912

From the Layton Section

E. E. Judy and wife, who had been running the railroad boarding house here, left last week, it is believed, for Caliente, Nev.

Las Vegas Age
January 27, 1912

Rev. E. A. Palmer has been holding services in Caliente and Pioche the past week.

Las Vegas Age
February 3, 1912

They Pass

Deputy Superintevdent B. G. Bleasdale reports that the following young ladies who took the teacher's examinations it this city recently have passed and been granted the coveted certificates to teach; Carrie M. Richards, Hannah Crosby, Mesquite; Mrs. Jessie F. Fowler, Caliente; Florence Gilmore, Las Vegas; and Josephine Sanberg, Sunnyside, Nye County.

Las Vegas Age
February 10, 1912

Rev. E. A. Palmer passed through Vegas Thursday evening on his way from Caliente to Los Angeles where he went for the purpose of hearing the famous evangelist, Gypsy Smith.

Las Vegas Age
February 24, 1912

Mrs. Norris of Caliente is visiting her sisters, Mrs. Ronnow and Mrs. Henderson.

Conductor Potts, of Caliente, has brought his family here to reside, and will occupy the house recently vacated by the Crombies, corner 4th and Bridger.

Las Vegas Age
March 3, 1912

When Rev. E. A. Palmer returned from his trip to Caliente and Pioche Friday evening he found a telegram awaiting him telling of the serious illness of an uncle who recently came to Santa Ana in search of health. Mr. Palmer immediately left for California.

Rev. E. A. Palmer left Tuesday morning for Caliente and Pioche where he will hold services during the week.

Salt Lake Mining Review (Utah)
March 15, 1912

The tailings dump of the old Bamberger & DeLamar mine, at DeLamar, Nevada, has been purchased by a Los Angeles syndicate, and a mill is being built for their treatment.

Las Vegas Age
May 4, 1912

Cross Hot Sands

Las Vegas has furnished a liberal number of candidates to take the Shrine in Los Angeles the past week. Nearly all have walked the hot sands and returned unscathed. Among those who took the degrees are the following:

Sam Blount, Caliente; A. G. Sherman, Clyde McLeod, Arden; W. E. Hawkins F. A. Buol, B. W. Hawn, W. R. Bracken, W. B. Mundy, Harry Strong, B. F. Boggs, Moyd T. Thomas, Ed Von Tobel C. A. Dupuis, E. W. Griffith, C. E. Beall, J. E. Frazine, Burt Froman, Roy W. Martin, W. R. Thomas.

Evening Standard (Utah)
March 29, 1912

CALIENTE BOOSTERS ORGANIZE

Caliente, Nev., March 27.—The new Caliente club has been organized to promote civic improvement. Forty-six citizens attended the first meeting. The organization of a band was perfected, and sufficient money was raised by subscription to give it a good start. The temporary officers are: J. W. Evans, chairman; Leo McNamee, secretary; Dr. Marco and Frank Galloway, financial committee.

Las Vegas Age
May 11, 1912

Caliente Commercial

The Caliente Commercial Club is doing a good work in the matter of cementing the interests of the town into a live energy for the welfare of all. In addition to that it is catering to the social side of its business men by providing comforts, amusements and pleasant surroundings for its members.

Its quarters consist of three rooms. In the front room are a piano, a victrola, writing desk, easy chairs etc., with the current numbers of the magazines and daily papers. The middle room contains a pool table and five card tables. The rear room is fitted as a gymnasium with two punching bags, boxing gloves, medicine ball, dumb bells, Indian clubs, etc.

The little city is to be congratulated upon its enterprise. It is an example which Vegas might well follow.

LINCOLN SHERIFF UNDER ARREST

O. H. Smith Admits Shortage In Accounts With the State

A special to the Carson City News, dated Caliente, May 11, is as follows:

Bullion and License Tax Collector Adamson who has been in this city for a few days on his regular inspection of the books of the county, today announced that Sheriff O. H. Smith was a defaulter in a large amount of money and immediately swore out a warrant for his arrest.

Upon being arrested Sheriff Smith admitted he was short in a large amount.

Advices received here today from Carson are to the effect that the Attorney General's office has instructed District Attorney McNamee to at once commence proceedings against him.

Sheriff Smith has many friends in both Clark and Lincoln counties who will regret that he has met with this misfortune. In answer to a telegram to Caliente asking for particulars of the matter, the AGE has received the following:

"Sheriff Smith was arrested on a charge of embezzlement, but it was and is a case of being lenient with many who paid their county dues through him. Not having the money at the time Sheriff Smith carried them, and when the time came for them to pay they failed him and his accounts were checked up short. It is not really a case of embezzlement but a breach of trust I figure it, simply, and so do others. He came out like a man and acknowledged the shortage and immediately made good."

Married

PITCHFORD—LYREMAN: In this city Wednesday May 22, 1912, at 8 p. m., Joseph W. Pitchford, of Las Vegas, to Anna Lyremann, of Caliente. The ceremony was quietly performed at the Methdist parsonage, Rev. E. A. Palmer officiating.

The bride has been a successful teacher in the Caliente schools the past year and the groom is in the train service of the Salt Lake road. After spending a few days in Southern California, Mr. and Mrs. Pitchford will be at home in their apartment at the Palace Hotel.

Iron County News (Utah)
June 28, 1912

Miss Agnes Cosslett made a trip to Caliente during the early days of the week, accompanied by little Nora Palmer, a niece. Mrs. Palmer met them at Caliente and will take the little girl to Goldfield, where Mr. Palmer is recovering from injuries recently received in a mine accident.

Davis County Clipper (Utah)
August 16, 1912

Mrs. Edwin Davis and son, Cyril, left for Caliente, Nevada, last week. Mrs. Davis did not know how long she would be gone.

Davis County Clipper (Utah)
September 13, 1912

From Kaysville Kink

Mrs. Edwin Davis, who recently went to Caliente, Nevada, expecting to make her home there, has located at Hiko, same state.

Washington County News (Utah)
September 26, 1912

M W Harrison left Wednesday for his home at Lund Nevada after having brought his daughter here to attend the State Academy

Evening Standard (Utah)
October 11, 1912

LUCKY BOY-ALAMO DEAL IS CLOSED

A mining deal of more than usual interest and importance was consummated in this city Wednesday, whereby the Lucky Boy and Alamo properties of the Lucky Boy, Nevada, district, fell into the control of the Jesse Knight Investment company of Utah and the Charles E. Knox interests of Tonopah, Nev. Mr. Knox was a visitor in Salt Lake for the past two or three days, and he succeeded in leaving for the east yesterday noon without the newspaper men finding him to get the details of this deal, but enough was learned from an authentic source to show that everything had been closed up successfully, and the ownership of these properties has changed.

Mr. Knox is the president of the Montana-Tonopah company, a director of the Nevada Hills and several other organizations of Nevada, having recently acquired for himself and associates the control of the Prince Consolidated company of the Pioche section. The Knight Investment company of Provo is too well known in Utah to require any extended description of its activities in the mines of this and other states, among its propositions being the Iron Blossom, Colorado, Black Jack, Beck Tunnel, Dragon Consolidated and several others of the Tintic camp, and the Rico-Wellington company of Rico, Colo.

New Company Forming.

Mr. Knox and associates have held a bond and lease on the Lucky Boy properties above mentioned from the former owner, J. H. Miller, and Mr. Miller will be associated with the Knight-Knox interests in the formation of a new company to take over

the same for development. These properties are located in Esmeralda county, about seven miles from the town of Hawthorne, and there is more than a passing romantic interest attaching to this section.

The properties are located by the side of the famous Overland trail leading from Bodie. Following the Goldfield and Tonopah boom several years ago the Southern Pacific company removed its tracks from Hawthorne to the new town of Thorne, thereby shortening its route to the south, but placing the old town of Hawthorne far from railroad connections, and many were the stories printed of the railroad-deserted little village that long had been noted as an oasis of attractive green to the travelers over the desert.

It was shortly after the removal of the railroad tracks that discoveries of rich silver and lead ore began to be made in the Lucky Boy section, and Hawthorne came back to public notice despite the lack of a railroad. Among the history makers of the Lucky Boy camp were the two mines which provide the subject of the deal closed in this city Wednesday, and a production of over $1,000,000 worth shaft struck water, and it became a very expensive proposition to handle the resources showing in splendid quantity at depth.

Plan of New Owners.

It is the plan of the new owners of these properties to drive a tunnel for a distance of between 5000 and 6000 feet to tap the resources, the tunnel to be started directly upon the vein, and when the ores are opened at a depth in excess of any so far reached, the mangement will have the advantage of perfect drainage and no hoisting. This work will be started without delay, and the new company will be organized as quickly as possible, all the details being practically arranged.

Some of the ore from the Lucky Boy has been extremely high grade, and this character of ore with depth from the water zone is anticipated, but should the work open a sufficient tonnage of milling grade rock as well a plant doubtless will be installed at the logical hour for its treatment. It is certain that some of the strongest and most efficient capitalists connected with the western mining fields will give the Lucky Boy camp a thorough campaign of development, and no one doubts but what the strong veins of that section will respond in a gratifying and permanent manner with depth.

USEFUL LIFE COMES TO END

Mrs. Catherine Blackburn Passes to Beyond

At 8 o'clock Monday morning at the home of Henry Robinson, Catherine Foy Blackburn passed from this field of action at the age of 64 years She was born in Iowa on the 18th of March 1848 is one of a family of 19 children, and a daughter of Thomas Burk Foy and Catherine Finn When 3 years of age her parents came to Utah, where she has since resided She married Jehu Blackburn in Minersville, Beaver county, and lived there until 1879 when she moved with her husband and family to Wayne county After residing in Wayne for many years she went to live with her children in Eastern Utah

Mrs Blackburn is the mother of nine sons and two daughters and has 18 living grand children The names of her children living are Jehu Thomas, Chas T. and Leslie, all of Wellington, Utah, Ephraim, Richfield, Frederick in Idaho, Manasseh J., Huntington, Mrs. Katharine J Liddell, Wellington, Mrs. Nellie E Robinson, Richfield Deceased also leaves two brothers, Frederick Foy of Slaterville, Utah, and Wm B. Foy, Delorus, Colorado, and a sister, Mrs Mary Richards, Hiko, Nevada. One deceased sister is Judge J. F. Chidester's mother. A large number of relatives aside from the above mentioned mourn her departure.

The body was shipped to Wellington Tuesday where interment will take place.

The Reaper feels to extend sympathy to the relatives in this their affliction and hopes that the sterling qualities of "Grandma" Blackburn will be transmitted to all her future ancestors

Mr. and Mrs Sidney Pace, of Alamo, Nevada are spending a month in Richfield Mrs Pace was formerly Miss Maggie Erickson, and is well known in this city.

Las Vegas Age
January 4, 1913

John T. Hays, the veteran miner and prospector of this section and chief owner of the famous Cherokee-Nevada property near Caliente, is in Vegas intending to remain several months. He reports that the Cherokee-Nevada is in a very prosperous condition and shipping ore steadily at a good profit. While here he will attend to the annual assessment work on his claims in Railroad Pass adjoining the Alunite property.

Las Vegas Age
February 1, 1913

Leave Caliente.

Former District Attorney Leo A. McNamee has decided to follow his father Hon. F. R. McNamee, and leave Lincoln County to locate permanently at Las Vegas. The father and son have entered a law partnership under the firm name of McNamee & McNamee, with offices in Las Vegas and Los Angeles. The Record extends best wishes.—Pioche Record.

Las Vegas Age
February 8, 1913

Suit for Divorce.

J. O. McIntosh, a former well known Caliente citizen has filed a suit for divorce in the district court against Lula J. McIntosh on the grounds of desertion.—Pioche Record.

Las Vegas Age
February 15, 1913

Mrs. F. P. Thompson and Master Frederick Thompson, Mrs. C. A. Thompson and Mrs. D. P. Sullivan, all of Caliente, were registered at the New Overland Thursday.

Dr. Chas. L. Thompson, the optometrist, has returned from a trip to Pioche, Caliente and the Moapa Valley, and opened his permanent office in the Mesquite building, where he will be pleased to meet all those having eye trouble.

Iron County Record (Utah)
February 21, 1913

Among the new out-of-town subscriptions received during the week, the following are some of the names added: H. W. Esplin, Orderville, Utah; Milton Poulton, Richfield, Utah; and Isaac Higbee, Alamo, Nevada.

Washington County News (Utah)
March 6, 1913

County Clerk Woodbury issued marriage licenses, March 4th, as follows: Winslow R Walker of Delta and Josephine Bunker of St George; A. Angus Moss of St George and Viola Jones of Enterprise, John M. Hunt of Enterprise and Annie Bauer of Cedar City, Marion L Terry of Lund, Nevada, and Sophia Langston of Hurricane, Utah.

Davis County Clipper (Utah)
March 7, 1913

From Bountiful Briefs

Mrs. Vera Scott, a former resident of this place, was among those who were caught in the train wreck on the San Pedro recently, while on her way from Salt Lake City to Caliente, Nev. Mrs. Scott was quite sick when she left Salt Lake to go down where her son is, but was fortunate in not being injured in the wreck.

Washington County News (Utah)
March 20, 1913

Mr. and Mrs. Marion Terry left
Wednesday night for Lund, Nevada,
where they will make their home.

Evening Standard (Utah)
April 18, 1913

CHINAMAN IS A WHITE SLAVER

The trial of the United States
against Charles Wing of Caliente,
Nev., charged with violating the federal "white slave" law, was begun in
the United States district court yesterday. Wing is alleged to have taken
women from Ogden to Caliente for
immoral purposes.

The grand jury which was impan-
eled Monday is still in session and
will probably not make a report until
tomorrow.

Votes for Women.

Miss Anne H. Martin of Reno, president of the Nevada Equal Franchise Society, arrived in Las Vegas Thursday evening on her way home from the suffrage convention of the Mississippi Valley states at St. Louis.

During the early portion of the week Miss Martin held meetings in Pioche, Panaca and Caliente, where there are flourishing branches of the society.

On account of the rain only a small audience attended the meeting held by Miss Martin in the Methodist Church. Those who were fortunate enough to be present heard a very pleasing and convincing talk, and at the conclusion of the address a committee consisting of Mesdames Geo. H. French, O. J. Enking and J. F. Lause was appointed to perfect the Clark County branch of the Nevada Equal Franchise Society.

Miss Martin left for Goldfield, Tonopah and Reno Friday morning.

Rev. E. A. Palmer returned last night from Pioche, where he delivered lectures on Wednesday and Thursday evenings. He preached in Caliente Tuesday evening.

McIntosh Divorce.

J. O. McIntosh, late of Caliente, but now engaged in business at Milford, Utah, was given a decree of separation from his wife, Lulu James McIntosh, in accordance with a contract previously entered into between McIntosh and his wife, who is now a resident of Los Angeles. The property of McIntosh was appraised at $11,651, of which Mrs. McIntosh is to have one-half, the husband giving his note to the wife for the sum of $5825.50, which is to be paid within twelve months after its execution. The note is made a part of the contract. Pioche Record.

Dr. J. West Smith of Caliente was a Vegas visitor Friday. He left with the about-to-be-antlered herd for Goldfield this morning.

Will Dodson, formerly of Vegas, but for the last three years a successful Caliente merchant, has been in this city a few days during the week.

Las Vegas Age
July 5, 1913

Killed at Caliente

William Robinson, Philip Dubois and Joseph Myers were murdered in the Elk's saloon in Caliente at 2 o'clock the morning of the 30th. The three men are said to have been shot by George Harper aged 20, who is a pumpman.

Duchesne County Newspapers (Utah)
July 11, 1913

PUMPMAN SHOOTS THREE.

Kills One Man and Wounds Two Others as Result of Quarrel.

Caliente, Nevada.—William Robinson was instantly killed and Phillip Dubois and Joseph Meyers were fatally injured in a row which occurred in the Elks' saloon here at 2 o'clock Monday morning. The three men are said to have been shot by George Harper, aged 20, who is a pumpman. Dubois is 38 years of age, Meyers is 30, and Robinson was 28. Harper has made his escape.

Las Vegas Age
July 26, 1913

Agent Cogswell of the American Express Co., who cared for the business Vegas office during the absence of Agent Young, has returned to his station at Caliente.

Las Vegas Age
August 2, 1913

Will Dodson of Caliente, formerly of Vegas, was a visitor in this city during the week.

Eureka Reporter (Utah)
August 8, 1913

✦

John T Hayes who followed the mining game in Tintic for many years and who was one of the successful lessees at the Mammoth mine is back in the state again after spending some time at his mining property in Nevada He has been in Salt Lake this week but will probadly be in Tintic for a short visit before returning to his present home near Caliente Mr Hayes is well pleased with the showing at the Cherokee Nevada property in which a number of local people are interested In an interview with the mining editor of the Herald Republican Mr Hayes states that a Colorado syndicate has just taken over the Little Chief mine which is located about eight miles to the west of Caliente A force of fifteen men are now employed and at the present time the property contains a good showing of ore that will run well in lead silver and gold Machinery from the old camp of Delamar has been moved to the Little Chief ground and a motor truck will be used in hauling supplies and ore to and from the mine

Duchesene County Newspapers
August 15, 1913

Suspected of being George Arthur Harper, wanted in Caliente, Nev., for shooting to death two men and wounding a third in a saloon row on the night of June 30, R. F. Spencer has been arrested in Ogden.

Caliente Killing.

Another murder of a Mexican by a bartender occurred in Caliente this week. The affair occurred in the East Side Bar. The circumstances are related as follows:

Two Mexicans indulged in a drunken brawl when "Babe" Denton, the bartender, interfered, beating one of them over the head with a gun, inflicting severe injuries. A short time thereafter another Mexican went to the bar where Denton was and asked him why he beat the other Mexican with the gun. He replied that one of the Mexicans fighting had a knife in his hand. The Mexican replied that it was none of Denton's business if he did have a knife. At this moment another Mexican, a shop man named Corona, who had had no part in the trouble up to this time, approached. Denton assuming, it appears, that Corona was about to assault him, fired at Corona, the bullet taking effect in the thigh, severing the main arteries and causing him to bleed to death.

An inquest was had before Judge Maynard, justice of the peace, and a verdict returned exonerating Denton. It is said that this verdict is by no means the conclusion of the matter, but that the grand jury to be convened this fall will probably investigate the killing carefully.

Las Vegas Age
November 8, 1913

Murderer Captured

Juan Domingo, an Indian, who murdered his squaw on Tuesday, October 28th, at Caliente, was captured in this city by Sheriff Sam Gay Sunday last.

The sheriff had received word of the killing and was on the lookout for suspicious characters. The strange Indian arrived in town and was soon recognized through the description received from the Caliente officers. Sheriff Gay thereupon arrested the suspect, who submitted peacefully, although armed with the same gun with which he had shot his squaw. Deputy Sheriff C. P. Christensen of Caliente was notified and arrived Sunday night. He identified the prisoner and returned to Lincoln county with him Monday morning.

The prisoner, on being charged with the crime upon his arrest, admitted the killing to Sheriff Gay, saying that he had shot his wife because she thought more of a Mexican than of him.

Get a Postoffice

The postoffice department has arranged a series of examinations for the position of postmaster at fourth class postoffices. Those of interest to this section will be held at Goldfield and Tonopah Feb. 7; Caliente, Feb. 14; Moapa, Feb. 16; Las Vegas, Feb. 17; Rhyolite, Feb. 19; Mina, Feb. 21.

Among the postmasters to be appointed from those taking the examinations are those at Alamo, Arden, Beatty, Blair, Bonnie Clare, Bunkerville, Goodsprings, Johnnie, Mary Mine, Millers, Mina, Moapa, Nelson, Overton, Rhyolite, St. Thomas, Tecoma;

Any person may be examined at any of the examinations held, but an applicant for a postoffice must reside within the territory supplied by that office.

Mr. and Mrs. L. L. Burt of Caliente came down to attend the New Year's Ball of the B. of R. T., returning home New Year's day.

Davis County Clipper (Utah)
January 30, 1914

From Bounty Briefs

Frank Jardine left for Caliente, Nev., last week. He expected to stop over at Pioche, on his way ouf, to examine some mining property.

Las Vegas Age
February 14, 1914

MARRIED

DUFFIN — RIDING: In Caliente, Nevada, Monday, Feb. 2, 1914, L. B. Duffin of Las Vegas to Miss Juie Riding of Caliente, Judge Maynard officiating.

The young people returned to Vegas Tuesday after a ten day's honeymoon in Salt City and will make this their home. Mr. Duffin is well known here being in the employ of the grocery house of Dobson Bros. The bride has a host of friends in Caliente who join in best wishes. We extend congratulations.

Las Vegas Age
February 28, 1914

Mrs. A. H. Norris of Caliente has been spending the week in Vegas a guest at the homes of her sisters, Mesdames A. S. Henderson and C. C. Ronnow.

MODENA.

Modena, Feb. 25, 1914.

Rail Road Company Becomes Host.

As a result of the washing out of the rail road between Modena and Caliente, the S .P. L. A. & S. L. R. R. Co. gave free, to the fifty eight passengers of train No. 7, bound Westward, two meals while they were delayed in Modena. No 7 had decided to turn round and go to California on the Southern Pacific, while turning on the "Y" at Modena three cars were derailed. This caused a delay of about eight hours during which the passengers were fed by the Company.

They not only fed the fifty eight at Modena but they fed another train load that were marooned at Calente for three or four days. This came about by the wreckage of No. 2 between Caliente and Modena. A flood had washed the dirt from under the track in such a way that the washout was not noticable. The train was late and as in consequenc it had ___ on an extra Locomotive in order to make up the lost time. The following account of the wreck was told by one of the pasengers:

"The Conductor had just entered the car taking up the tickets and had just stoped in front of me to take my ticket when Crash! and he came plunging head foremost into my stomach, he had just regained his upright position again when another crash came which sent him head long over my seat to inflict a similar undeserved punishment on a young man who sat just behind me. "Good Lord" he cried as he regained his feet the second time, "What's happening," and then he made a very rapid exit, I suppose, because he didn't care to have his cranium investigate the depths of any other fellow's stomach."

But this is the ludicrous side of the matter. The facts are that there was nobody injured and no damage done except to the track. Two cars, the baggage car and the mail car, were tipped over and two Locomotives derailed but not upset.

The wrecker with a crew of about 25 men has been down there since Saturday and they expect to have everything in running order by Thursday night.

* * *

"HELLO, PIOCHE," SAYS CALIENTE

Pioche and Caliente are now connected by telephone. The first "hello" from the railroad town was heard by Postmaster Carman yesterday morning when he conversed with Dr. J. West Smith, O. K. Adcock, Hans Olson and other leading citizens of Caliente.

The line has been built by the Utah-Idaho-Nevada Telephone company under the direction of Hugh Thomas, manager of the Nevada lines of the company.

The Caliente central station has been located in the Caliente Drug Co. store.

The Record is informed by Mr. Thomas that energy will next be bent on extending the line between Caliente and Delamar to Alamo and other points in the Pahranagat valley. When the Pahranagat line is finished the next move will be the extension of the Pioche system to the Mendha mine and this will possibly be followed by the construction of another line to Atlanta. The extension of the telephone lines in the county will prove to be of great convenience in more ways than one.—Pioche Record.

Mr. Bray Here

State Superintendent of Public Instruction, John Edwards Bray, arrived in Vegas Tuesday accompanied by Deputy Superintendent B. G. Bleasdale. They have just visited the schools in Panaca, Pioche and Caliente, in Lincoln county and Bunkerville, Mesquite, St. Thomas, Kaolin, Overton, Logan and Moapa in this county. They report the schools generally in a very satisfactory condition.

Mr. Bray left Thursday morning for the north over the L. V. & T. road. Mr. Bleasdale left by auto Thursday afternoon for Goodsprings, Beatty, Rhyolite and various schools in Nye and Esmeralda counties. He expects to be gone a month or more and travels in his Ford.

Modena, April 22, 1914.—Sheriff Froyd was in town Sunday night searching for the two Mexicans who made their escape from Cedar City a short time since. He reports their having visited a sheep camp between here and Iron Springs last Friday night. The herder at the camp said they had nothing to shoot with and he (the herder) didn't get out of bed, while the Mexicans were in his wagon getting something to eat at 12 o'clock at night. After they had satisfied their hunger they left him unmolested. The wives of the Mexicans are in Caliente, and Sheriff Froyd thinking his men would be more likely to go there than anywhere else, left here en route to Caliente last Monday morning.

A Long Trip

Deputy Supt. of Public Instruction B. G. Bleasdale returned Tuesday from a trip of nearly 2,000 miles in his Ford machine. He left Vegas April 2d and has visited practically all the schools in Nye and Lincoln counties since that date and is now finishing up with Clark county. Since leaving Vegas he made a mileage of 1880 miles by auto up to the time he reached Caliente.

By reason of the condition of the roads south from Caliente he was forced to ship the Ford from there to Moapa. Aside from this short link the roads were found in passable condition.

Las Vegas Age
May 30, 1914

Ex-Senator J. A. Denton of Caliente was a guest at the Overland Monday. He was on his way to Inyo County, Cal., in pursuance of the duties of the government position to which he was just appointed.

Las Vegas Age
July 4, 1914

ELKS' SPECIAL CARRIED CROWD

One Hundred or More Vegas People Visit Goldfield for Celebration

The Elks' Special carrying a large class for initiation into the Goldfield Elks' lodge, as well as a goodly crowd of those who are not members of that order, left at eleven o'clock yesterday morning. The crowd was jolly and a splendid time is anticipated by all. Many women added their charm to the excursion.

The train is stocked with everything for appeasing the appetites of the travelers, especial attention being paid to luncheon for the ladies. The Vegas band of 16 pieces accompanied the party to add harmony to the occasion.

The train arrived at Goldfield at 6 p. m. last evening. The return trip will be made leaving Goldfield Sunday evening in time to get the tired bunch home by midnight.

The following are the Elks elect, nearly all of whom were able to make the trip:

Las Vegas—F. B. Hurlbut, D. H. Carr, F. J. McDermott, Jas. S. Bennett, V. G. Ham, Wm. H. Jackson, Chas. O. Wood, Robt. H Potts, Jas. Clark, Lee P. Barker, H. L. Hewetson, Geo. Doyle, H. H. Clark, John S. Wisner, Geo. W. Taylor, N. C. Randall, John Hinge, Geo. A. Goodwin, Peter Buol, Sam W. Craner, Orton Hoxsie, Fred C. Knecht, J. B. Robicheau, Geo. Ehret, F. E. Black, F. T. Rives, M. D. Newkirk.

Searchlight—C. E. Burdick.

Goodsprings—Jas. Ashbaugh, J. A. Frederickson, J. A. Eggers, L. C. May.

Moapa—C. E. Brown.

Overton—Joe F. Perkins.

Pioche—C. L. Horsey, Dan J. Ronnow, F. S. Robinson.

Caliente—Geo. Senter, Jas. H. Williamson, Hans Olson.

In addition to the candidates the following made the trip:

Mr. and Mrs. Frank A. Clark
Mr. and Mrs. L. D. Smith
Mr. and Mrs. R. H. Schaeffer
Mr. and Mrs. C. C. Corkhill
Mr. and Mrs. J. W. Horden

Mesdames Roy Taylor, Geo. Goodwin, Henry Jackson, J. D. Richards and Henderson.

Misses Louella Wengert, Edna Craglin, Julia Westlake and Genevieve and Lucile McNamee.

Messrs. Harley A. Harmon, Bert Wynaught, A. Kaufmann, Leo A. McNamee, Frank Black, M. I. Newkirk, M. E. Clancy and Woods.

Ephraim Enterprise (Utah)
July 11, 1914

Niels A. Christensen is home from
Caliente, Nev., where he has been
employed for some time.

Davis County Clipper (Utah)
July 17, 1914

From Bountiful Briefs

Ambrose Call returned home
Saturday from a six months'
business trip to Nevada. While
away he visited Caliente, Las
Vegas, Rhyolite, Goldfield, Tona-
pah, Miller and a number of
other towns. He expects to return about the first of the month.

Box Elder News (Utah)
August 6, 1914

Mrs. D. R. Ivins of Lund. Nevada,
has been visiting Mr. and Mrs. Abel
S. Rich for a week. The ladies are
sisters.

Las Vegas Age
August 8, 1914

Leo A. McNamee came down from
Caliente and Pioche Thursday morning
to spend a few days in Vegas before
proceeding to Los Angeles.

Purchased Hotel

Mrs. Lula Vaughn has purchased the Hotel Nevada in Caliente, and is running it as a first-class hotel. Everything is in apple-pie order and the weary traveler will find the Nevada a pleasant stopping place. Mrs. Vaughn is well known here, having lived in Vegas several years, and many friends wish her success in the enterprise.

Las Vegas Age
September 5, 1914

No Snakes

At the suggestion of Contractor Turner, Father Reynolds has furnished some soil and a piece of turf from the sod of old Ireland, to be placed in the front steps of the new court house which are now being built. The soil and turf were brought from old Ireland some time ago by Mrs. Pat Duffy, of Caliente, who contributed them for this purpose.

No snakes can now enter the court house, at least by the front door, it being asserted that the soil of Ireland is death to snakes.

Las Vegas Age
September 19, 1914

O. W. Skinner and wife of Caliente were guests at the Overland Wednesday.

Las Vegas Age
December 5, 1914

Caliente Safe-Crackers

Thursday night the safe of Hans Olson at Caliente, Lincoln county, was broken open and robbed. There were several watches, five ten-dollar gold pieces set for charms, a diamond stud and diamond ring, six hundred dollars in cash and three checks, one for ten dollars, one for twenty dollars and one for $76.40, the latter being signed by A. H. Norris.

Sheriff Gay is keeping a close watch on all box car tourists and suspicious characters of every kind, but with the army of unemployed passing along the railroad it is not possible to entirely ward off evil doers. However Vegas is especially fortunate up to the present date owing largely to the activity of the officers. It is wise for citizens to take especial care that their property is not left unduly exposed, and to take every precaution against robbers at the present time.

Iron County Record (Utah)
February 19, 1915

NEW TIME TABLE FOR THE SALT LAKE ROUTE

A new time table, No. 46, went into effect at 12:01 a. m., February 7, 1915. Some of the most important changes are enumerated below:

Train No. 2 will leave Caliente at 3:35 p. m., one hour earlier than formerly, reaching Modena at 5:31 p. m., Lund at 6:37 p. m., Milford at 7:50 p. m. The time at all stations intermediate to Caliente and Milford will be approximately one hour earlier. Train 2 will leave Milford at 8:20 p. m., Black Rock at 9:10 p. m., Clear Lake at 10:46 p. m., Lyndyl at 12:01 a. m., Nephi at 2:12 a. m., and Provo at 4:20 a. m., arriving Salt Lake at 6:30 a. m., as formerly.

Las Vegas Age
March 13, 1915

Revenue Man Here

W. A. Kelly, deputy collector of U, S. Internal Revenue, with headquarters at Reno, has been in Vegas for several days looking after the income of Uncle Sam. There are many phases of the recent revenue acts which are not properly understood by those affected and Mr. Kelly is giving all assistance possible in making things clear.

Mr. Kelly is an old resident of Nevada, having been prominent in Tonopah and Goldfield during the early days of those camps. He was afterward for several years lieutenant of the guard at the Nevada prison at Carson City. He left last night for Caliente and other points in Lincoln county and will altogether spend several weeks in this portion of the state.

Iron County Record (Utah)
May 21, 1915

Summit, Utah, May 19, 1915.
Mrs. Ada Naegle and children of
Caliente, Nevada are here visiting
with relatives and friends.

Las Vegas Vegas
September 25, 1915

Miss. Katherine Riley, one of the
Caliente school teachers, is the guest
of Miss. Marjorie Potts.

Las Vegas Age
October 2, 1915

EARTHQUAKE SHAKES NEVADA

Slight Tremors Stir Las Vegas Damage Reported From Northern Points

Shortly after 11 o'clock tonight, (Saturday), a slight shock of earthquake was felt in Las Vegas. It was not strong enough to be generally noticed, but was sufficient to cause the lights to swing gently.

Reports from the north indicate that the shock was severe over much of the state. The mill of the Pittsburgh Silver Peak mining company was demolished.

At Hazen the S. P. water tank was thrown down. Some damage is reported from Tonopah. Only slight damage such as the breaking of dishes, is reported from Goldfield.

The shock reached some degree of violence at Caliente. At Salt Lake the telegraph operators were thrown from their chairs. Nothing has been heard from Reno up to the time of going to press

Beaver County News (Utah)
July 21, 1916

Arthur Wood spent a few days in Caliente, this week, in connection with his duties as an official of the Salt Lake Route.

Beaver County News (Utah)
August 4, 1916

Mrs. Steve Shingleton and son, Harold, of Salt Lake City, also Mrs. C. I. Hainstreet of Caliente, Nevada, are the guests of Mr. and Mrs. Phil Orwin this week.

Beaver County News (Utah)
August 18, 1916

By the breaking of a freight train at Caliente, Monday, Brakeman Philips of the Salt Lake route, was badly injured. When the freight parted, the air was automatically set and the sudden stoppage threw Philips from the top of a box car, violently to the ground, injuring him seriously. The injured man passed through Milford Monday night on No. 2, on his way to Salt Lake for treatment.

Millard County Progress (Utah)
September 1, 1916

From the Black Rock Section

Mr. W. H. Foreman an dson of Elgin, Nevada, spent a couple of days here enroute to Monroe where Mr. Foreman was called by th elllness of a sister who resides there.

Eureka Reporter (Utah)
September 15, 1916

Timothy Mahoney Killed

Timothy Mahoney an employee of the Salt Lake Route who for several months was located at Tintic Junction during which time he was a fireman on the engine which handled the switching from the local mines was shot to death at Caliente Nev on Sunday night Mahoney was an engineer at the time of his death and had a family living at Salt Lake He was shot by C L Dawson who will have a preliminary hearing this week

Beaver County News (Utah)
September 29, 1916

Father Slattery of Caliente, Nev., will celebrate Mass in the I. O. O. F. Hall, Milford, Sunday morning, Oct. 3rd, at 8:30 a. m.

Beaver County News (Utah)
November 24, 1916

WILL CELEBRATE MASS

Father Slattery, of Caliente, who makes periodical trips to Milford as a part of his large parish, will celebrate Mass in I. O. O. F. Hall, this coming Sunday at 9 o'clock a. m.

Conductor Tom Payne, upon his return to his caboose at Caliente, after having spent most of the night at the gambling table, shot himself through the breast, just above the heart. Payne was taken to Los Angeles, where he died the following morning.

F. J. Boudreau, Salt Lake agent at Caliente was temporarilly transferred to Milford during the absence of Agent H. C. Banning who was called to Salt Lake City to attend the funeral of his brother. Mr. Boudreau was the regular agent at Milford in 1912 and enjoyed renewing some old acquaintances. He returned to Caliente Monday.

A rabid coyote made its apperance on the streets of Lund, Nevada, chasing Mrs. J. J. Gubber into her home and making a frantic effort to follow her into the house. Discouraged, it ultimately turned back into the street, where it met its death at the hands of a stout neighbor.

Mr. Dobson came up from Caliente Wednesday night to visit his son Will Dobson and wife.

Mangled by Train

John Mullen, a miner recently employed at the Horn Silver fell underneath a moving freight train Wednesday night at 7 o'clock. The unfortunate man had thrown his roll of blankets on the train and was walking on a car of railroad rails when he tried to jump from one car to another and fell under the wheels. His body was horribly mangled and death was instantaneous. The remains were carried in a basket to the undertaking parlors of E. B. Jorgensen and prepared for burial. The deceased had sent a suit case to Caliente by parcel post and the officers sent to that city to have the case returned here hoping to ascertain something of the man's history and to locate his friends or relatives.

A young man named Pat Connely was with Mullen and both had come down from the Horn Silver only the day before. Connely says he knows nothing of Mullen's affairs nor where any relatives might be located. Mullen had about $42 in money in his pockets when he was killed while trying to steal a ride. The wind was blowing hard and the dust was flying and it is said that Mullen had been drinking heavily during the afternoon.

Train No. 2 Salt Lake Route seems to be a sort of "go as you please" accommodation train. Seldom on time. She was over two hours late Sunday night on account, so one of the crew said, of waiting at Caliente for the arrival of a theatrical troupe. Reminds us of other days in the sunny south, when a passenger train would await the arrival of Colonel or Major so and so, if he happened to be a bit late.

Beaver County News (Utah)
April 13, 1917

William Warner, assistant general freight and passenger agent of the Salt Lake Route and M. O. Culton, general agent for the Erie Railroad company were visitors in Milford the first of the week. They went from here to Caliente on No. 1 and returned to Delta in the evening. They were lining up freight and passenger business for their respective lines.

Las Vegas Age
April 17, 1917

ENGINE PLUNGES DOWN STEEP BANK

Westbound Freight Hits Rock Slide on Curve half Mile East of Stine. Engineer Ed. Long Severely Injured

(Special to the Age)

Extra west No. 3656 in charge of conductor T. F. Hollis and engineer Ed. Long, met with a fatal accident this morning, (Sunday) at 2:50, one half mile east of Stine, near mile post 450. While rounding a curve the engine smashed into a rock slide, throwing the engine and one car down a steep embankment. Engineer long received injuries, to what extent, it is impossible at this time to state, although from the fact that a train was sent out from Caliente to take the injured man to that city to await the arrival of No. 7 and then be rushed to Los Angeles, it is feared that his injuries are severe.

In all probability Mrs. Long, who is in this city will accompany her husband to Los Angeles.

Beaver County News (Utah)
May 4, 1917

Mrs. Larue Duffin gave a party in honor of her sister Ida Riding of Caliente Wednesday. The popular game of 500 furnished the pastime for the occasion. Miss Augusta Allen was awarded the ladies' first prize and Harry Robbins won for the gentlemen.

Iron County Record (Utah)
May 4, 1917

Bennie Openshaw, Milton Robb, Marion Daily and William Edwards left Paragonah Wednesday, April 25, for Caliente, where they were they were intending to shear sheep, etc.

FREIGHT WRECK IN DETAIL

Train Wreck Which Resulted in the Death of Ed. Long Told by Crew

The wreck of last Sunday morning, which resulted in the death of Engineer Long, is here related by members of the crew on the fateful trip:

"The crew for an extra west, consisting of Engineer Ed. Long, Fireman Kent, Conductor Hollis and Brakemen Geo. Deverell and E. A. Highwood. were called in Caliente for 2:15 a. m. Sunday. The train was composed of engine 3656, one box car and the caboose. The train was traveling down the grade at a moderate rate of speed and was nearing the station of Stine when the accident occured. About a uarter of a mile to the east of Stine the track goes through a cut, on the west side of which is a fill of possibly 15 feet in height. The track through the cut is on a curve, which makes it impossible to see a very great distance ahead. It was in this cut that the powerful headlight of the engine shown on a great mass of rock which had slid onto the track from the side of the mountain. The speed of the train on the down grade made it impossible for Engineer Long to bring the train to a stop, in fact almost before the brakes could be applied, the engine crashed into the mass of rock. As the engine crashing through the slide neared the opening of the cut and the edge of the fill, is the place where Engineer Long jumped from his seat in the cab. Fireman Kent stayed with the engine until it started down the bank and then jumped to safety.

"The train crew who escaped uninjured, at once rushed to where the body of Engineer Long was lying, in an unconscious condition, and rendered what aid they could. A message was phoned into Caliente and a relief engine was dispatched at once to the scene of the accident with the doctor from that point. Long was taken back to Caliente and given all medical aid possible and put on train No. 7 to be rushed to Los Angeles."

It was several hours later before the wreck could be cleared from the track to allow No. 7 to pass. Mrs. Long, assisted by Mrs. Sheppard, met the train here and accompanied her husband to Los Angeles.

Engineer Long never regained consciousness from the time of the accident until his death on the train.

Mrs. Ed. Marksheffle and Mrs. Fred Jefferson entertained Wednesday at the home of Mrs. Marksheffle complimentary to her mother, Mrs. D. D. McDonald, of Caliente. 500 was the diversion of the afternoon. For the luncheon which followed the games the table was beautifully decorated with pink and white carnations. Beside the honor guest those present were: Mesdames George Jefferson, James Glenn, Thos Banning, Bert Moore, Harry Ward and Miller. The favors were awarded Mrs. McDonald, Mrs. Miller ad Mrs. Jefferson.

Mrs. McDonald, of Caliente, has been the guest of her daughter, Mrs. Ed Marksheffle.

E. J. Denkle of Caliente, Nev., has filed suit against former Sheriff Ronnow, District Attorney Orr and Justice of the Peace Frank Palmer of Caliente at Pioche, in which he seeks to recover $10,000 damages for alleged false imprisonment. The case grows out of Denkle's arrest some time ago when he felled two trees located on railroad property, but which obscured full view of his sign.

George C. Stowell of Alamo, a prominent rancher was killed by lightning in the south end of Coal valley, in Nevada, while out on a cattle roundup. Merl Schofield and John W. Wedge, who were with him, were seriously affected by the bolt.

EXCELLENT BASEBALL

The game of ball last Sunday between Lyndyll and Milford was a corker for sure. The baseball events of this season up to that time have been discouraging—mostly on account of the weather—but Sunday's game was big league ball. The visitors brought a strong team and put up a hard fight. Milford is getting her stride and the balance of the season will see some rare sport on the local diamond. The score was 4 to 5 in favor of the home team.

On July 4th there will be a game between Milford and the Caliente team which gave the Bees such a close call at the opening of the season. They say the Caliente team has an Irish pitcher who has played in the Coast League and who not only pitches but plays all over the lot and at the same time runs his team like a general. This big game will be the sport feature of Milford's Fourth of July celebration.

Beaver County News (Utah)
June 29, 1917

The only thing that has been mentioned to the News as a sure attraction for July 4th in Milford is the ball game scheduled between the home team and Caliente. The Caliente team made the Salt Lake Bees hustle to win at the opening of the season. That is good as far as it goes, what else?

Beaver County News (Utah)
July 27, 1917

Albert Thomas is now time clerk for the Houghton Construction Company, having resigned his position with the Salt Lake Route some three weeks since. The Houghton Construction Company has several crews of builders at work along the Salt Lake Route south of the northern terminal. At Provo the company is erecting a large roundhouse. Forty miles this side of Caliente there is a crew of thirty men at work on a bridge. The same company is also constructing the big bridge near Delta and has other big jobs in progress. Milford is the headquarters of the company for all this work, being very centrally and conveniently located. Superintendent Pope is in charge.

Beaver County News
August 24, 1917

Mrs. Ida McCann and Mrs. I Himstreet of Caliente, Nevada, spent Thursday with friends.

Las Vegas Age
September 22, 1917

VEGAS PEOPLE ATTEND THE FAIR AT CALIENTE

In addition to the Las Vegas Grammar School Boy's Band, the following Las Vegas People visited Caliente to attend the Lincoln County Fair:

Miss Adelaide Phillips representing the University of Nevada Extension Work, Mesdames Wm. Jones, Keyes, Renner, Nungesser, McNeil, Silk, Liday, Draper, Ronnow, Henderson, Crow, Cazel, Squires, Bloedel and Goodwin. They had a very enjoyable time, thanks to the hospitality of the good people of Caliente.

Mrs. Robert Potts left Wednesday evening to visit her married daughter in Colorado. She stopped over a day in Caliente to enjoy the fair, and also a day in Milford, Utah on the way.

Beaver County News (Utah)
September 28, 1917

Bulletin No. 350

There is a vacancy for a conductor and four brakemen in through freight service between Salt Lake and Lynndyl.

There is a vacancy for one brakeman on trains 93 and 94, between Salt Lake City and Provo.

There are vacancies for three brakemen on trains 1, 2, 7, 8, 19, 20.

There is a vacancy for one brakeman on trains 83 and 84, between Salt Lake City and Tintic.

There are vacancies for two conductors and five brakemen in through freight service between Milford and Caliente.

There is a vacancy for one brakeman in local freight service between Lynndyl and Milford.

There is a vacancy for one brakeman in through freight service between Lynndyl and Milford.

Bids will close October 4, 1917.

Traveling Engineer Runswick left Milford on 1st 81 Thursday morning for Caliente.

Beaver County News (Utah)
October 12, 1917

Sheriff Hedges returned from Caliente with company Monday morning.

Train Master W. F. Farrier accompanied one of the soldier trains through Milford to Caliente Thursday. He returned on No. 20 Friday morning.

Beaver County News (Utah)
October 26, 1917

Father Slattery of Caliente officiated at mass for the Catholic organization of Milford last Sunday.

It is reported that master mechanics at Caliente and Lynndyl have both resigned the service.

SEVERAL BOOZE CASES IN COURT

For some reason or other there was unusual activity in the police court this week. It seemed a little like old times.

Two Mexicans who have been employed on the railroad cashed their checks last Saturday. In California that is a sign of trouble. It proved to be the same here, though the trouble seemed to be, as in California, reserved for the said Mexicans. Vicente Melgogo and Jesus Duran sounds some like the names given by the gentlemen from our neighbor republic of tumult and too much. They were found by Justice Nichols to have been under the influence of a jag apiece and were therefore given the same sentence of $56.50 or a like number of days in jail, the $5.60 in each case representing costs in the matter in addition to the minimum fine in such cases provided. They declared that they secured the booze in Caliente and brought it to Milford.

J. J. Booth was before Judge Ingols on a charge of being intoxicated and was fined $175, which he paid. Mr. Booth says he found the booze in a room in the lodging house where he had been stopping and took a drink of it which immediately "went to his head." After being allowed to go on his own recognizance he departed in his auto for Baker, Nevada, where the Sheriff found him and brought him back.

The case of Parkinson came before Judge Ingols Tuesday, Sam Cline appearing with the accused as attorney. Parkinson plead "not guilty" and put up a certified check for $100 for bond. Mr. Cline asked for a continuance for one week as he had to be absent from this city for a few days and the delay was granted. A jury trial is demanded.

Beaver County News (Utah)
November 2, 1917

Conductor Martin, Engineer Davis, Fireman Kerr, Engine 3631, with soldier train out of Milford Sunday morning for Caliente. Nebraska troops.

Beaver County News (Utah)
November 9, 1917

A. R. White, supervisor of block signals, was at Caliente last Thursday where he held a class of instruction covering block signal work.

Beaver County News (Utah)
November 9, 1917

Bulletin No. 355
Conductor J. C. Stoyell, Brake- J. Snyder, W. F. Shields and R. L. Adams are assigned to freight service between Milford and Caliente.

Beaver County News (Utah)
November 16, 1917

It is now understood that Second Trick Operator H. M. Hearn of Caliente is to make that his future home.
Yard Master Mace of Caliente is laying off a few days account sickness. This night stuff is sure tough.

Conductor Sam Blunt was deadheaded to Caliente to relieve Conductor O'Rourke, who will relieve Conductor Smith of the Pioche run.

Big Slim Meeks, night yard clerk and train caller at Caliente, says that some of these confounded brakemen never sleep in the same place twice.

Beaver County News (Utah)
November 30, 1917

DIED—W. J. Smith died at the Holy Cross hospital in Salt Lake last Saturday. Mr. Smith had been in the service of the Salt Lake Route as a trainman since November 29th, 1903.. Up, to the time Mr. Smith was taken ill he was performing the duties of a conductor on the Pioche branch out of Caliente, where his family reside. Mr. Smith and family lived in Milford at one time, his run being out of this place. Many friends will regret to learn of his death.

Mr. Smith's daughters, one from Montana and the other of Colorado, did not arrive in Salt Lake until after their father's death.

Joseph Lawrence, who is working with the Houghton Construction Co. near Caliente, came home the first of the week to spend the holidays with his family.

Beaver County News (Utah)
December 7, 1917

A German Jew representing himself to be a window washer looking for work was given his breakfast at several back doors in west Milford Tuesday morning. Later in the day he was looking for Mayor Pitchforth to buy him a ticket to Caliente. The fellow slept in the local jail the previous night and he is a suspicious character. He refused to try any jobs other than window washing.

CALIENTE RED CROSS HAS ENTERTAINMENT

The Caliente Chapter of the Red Cross had a dance and entertainment on Friday evening of last week. The affair was largely attended and a considerable sum of money raised for the Red Cross.

Rt. Rev. George C. Hunting, Episcopal Bishop of Nevada, was present and delivered an address.

H. C. King of Caliente, formerly of Milford, came up from the Nevada Mecca today to meet Mrs. King, who has just returned from an extended Eastern trip and who stopped off here to visit her many friends in Milford.

1000 NEW COAL CARS

The Salt Lake Route has purchased 1,000 new steel coal cars, with collapsible floors for dumping, at a coat of $2,000 each. This expenditure is part of a general plan to expedite transportation of fuel and to relieve the coal shortage in various localities along the company's line. A modern concrete coal terminal, costing $250,000 and electrically operated, has been installed at Provo, to be used jointly by the Salt Lake Route and the new Utah Coal Route. It includes storehouse, roundhouse, shop, water tanks, chutes, trestle, etc. An engine coaling station, costing $20,000 and with a capacity of 200 tons, has been established at Caliente, Nevada, on the main line of the Salt Lake Route to California.—Mining Review.

Ex-aviator Walter Ernst, former yard clerk of Milford, later yard clerk in Caliente, has severed his connection with the Salt Lake Route.

The nerve of some people. A party at Caliente wired us to send him some calf brains, and he knowing how bad our yard clerks need them. Can you beat it?

H. C. King of Caliente spent a day in Milford on business this week.

Beaver County News (Utah)
February 22, 1918

Caliente Station Force
Agent, F. J. Baudreau; Cashier, Arthur L. Tinsley; Clerk, Mrs. Bertha Galnouer; Night Ticket Agent, John A. Zumstien; Baggageman, Dale Edwards; Day Yard Clerk, Carl Stewart; Night Yard Clerk, Frank Taylor.

Iron County Record (Utah)
March 22, 1918

Mrs. J. P. Fuller returned last Tuesday from her trip to southern California, after an absence of about three weeks. On her way home she stopped off at Alamo, Nev., and visited relatives for several days. Mrs. L. A. Watson accompanied Mrs. Fuller on the trip, but did not stay in Nevada, and arrived home a few days ahead of Mrs. Fuller. Of course they had a fine trip.

Beaver County News (Utah)
April 20, 1918

The Caliente shops, which are under the supervision of Master Mechanic A. P. Neff, went 100 per cent for Liberty Bonds. We say there is some class to this kind of work.

Beaver County News (Utah)
May 17, 1918

A BIG FIRE AT CALIENTE

Fire broke out early Thursday evening in a pool hall, spreading rapidly over the main portion of the business center of Caliente. The following places of business were totally destroyed:

Red Cross building, postoffice, two drug stores, two grocery stores, two saloons, the Caliente Mercantile Co., one shooting gallery, Iris Cafe, one pool hall, one moving picture show, with a number of smaller places. Goods carried out of the burning buildings were placed in the street, but not far enough away, so that they caught fire and burned up.

The Salt Lake Route reports all their property safe. The local fire department was assisted by the Salt Lake Route fire department, and the fire was reported to be under control at an early hour Friday morning. It is estimated that the loss will reach two hundred thousand dollars. Very few of the burned business houses carried any insurance.

Beaver County News (Utah)
May 24, 1918

Bulletin No. 379.

There is a vacancy for one brakeman in through freight service between Milford and Caliente. Bids will close May 30.

The Alamo a silver-lead and gold mine 75 miles west of Pioche, is ready to produce.

CALIENTE SUFFERS A DESTRUCTIVE FIRE

Business Section is Practically Wiped Out.—Loss Estimated at $150,000

Thursday evening, about 6:30, the explosion of a gasoline tank used for a lighting system, started a fire in the rear of Mrs. Buck's billiard and pool room in the business section of Caliente. The flames spread rapidly in both directions, and the entire block was wiped out in a few hours.

A desparate fight to save the town was made by the people, but a scarcity of water and poor pressure, with the entire lack of any organized fire department, placed the workers at a disadvantage.

The postoffice was destroyed with all mail. Among the other losses are the following:

John Shire's drug store and Denton's confectionery store, loss $8,000,

People's Cash Store, Geo. Jess, loss more than $5,000.

East Side Bar, estimated, $10,000.

Alamo Saloon and Cafe, $7,000.

Rex motion picture theatre, $6,000.

Dr. J. West Smith's drug store, $10,000.

Clemm's barber shop and poolroom, $4,000.

Red Cross Headquarters building, loss to the organization considerable.

Mrs. Buck's poolroom.

Caliente Mercantile Company, Wm. Pace, manager, $35,000.

Caliente Mercantile Company's warehouse.

Office of Judge Palmer, justice of the peace.

Norris Opera House and store.

The Caliente Mercantile Co. carried insurance to the amount of $10,000. Mr. Norris' loss is also partially covered by insurance. So far as known none of the other losers were insured. There is but one store, the Blue Front general merchandise store, left, and it is probable that there will be a shortage of provisions to supply the immediate needs of the people.

The Red Cross had made all the arrangements for a Red Cross Circus in the Norris opera house, and had gone to considerable expense to fix up booths, etc. This was also a total loss.

Gunnison Gazette (Utah)
Mary 31, 1918

Fire in a pool hall resulted in the almost total destruction of Caliente, Nev. Practically the entire business section was destroyed, with losses estimated at $150,000.

Beaver County News (Utah)
May 31, 1918

CALIENTE RED CROSS WORK.

When the Lincoln county chapter, with headquarters at Caliente, Nev., was assigned its quota of $2500 for the second war fund drive, the Camp Fire Girls set their quota at $50. The girls not only raised the quota, but went over the top by singing war songs at the passenger trains during Red Cross week. Carrying the emblem of the Red Cross, and wearing the veil and badge of membership, their sweet voices attracted the attention of the travelers, who were pleasantly entertained during their stay in Caliente. Carmen Amante in the "La Dorado" costume danced Mexican dances for the benefit of the Red Cross on Liberty Day.

These girls should have much credit for their enthusiasm and the funds they raised. In the recent fire at Caliente the Red Cross headquarters were burned, but they immediately opened again in the railroad company house No. 3.

CHANGE OF TIME TABLE
EFFECTIVE JUNE 2, 1918

Trains Nos. 7, 8, 19, and 20 will be discontinued.

On and after the date mentioned we will have two daily through trains between Los Angeles and Salt Lake City in each direction, known as 1 and 2, 3 and 4. Trains 1 and 2, which will operate via Tintic, will handle standard and tourist sleeping car equipment only. Trains 3 and 4, operated via Provo, will handle standard and tourist sleeping cars, chair cars and coaches.

The condensed schedule of these trains will be as follows:

No. 4	No. 2	STATIONS		No. 1	No. 3
6:20 P. M.	8:23 A. M.	Lv Long Beach	Ar		5:23 P. M.
6:30 P. M.	8:35 A. M.	Lv Pasadena	Ar 6:05 P. M.		
10:00 P. M.	9:30 A. M.	Lv Los Angeles	Ar 5:30 P. M.		4:15 P. M.
11:55 P. M.	11:15 A. M.	Lv Riverside	Ar 3:45 P. M.		2:20 P. M.
12:35 A. M.	11:50 A. M.	Lv San Bernardin(	Ar 3:10 P. M.		1:40 P. M.
10:30 A. M.	9:10 P. M.	Lv Las Vegas	Ar 5:55 A. M.		3:23 A. M.
4:55 P. M.	3:05 A. M.	Lv Caliente	Ar 3:05 A. M.		11:59 P. M.
9:35 P. M.	6:35 A. M.	Lv MILFORD	Ar 11:25 P. M.		7:50 P. M.
12:42 A. M.	9:02 A. M.	Ar Lynndyl	Lv 9:10 P. M.		5:05 P. M.
	9:02 A. M.	Lv Lynndyl	Ar 9:10 P. M.		
	10:15 A. M.	Lv Tintic	Ar 8:15 P. M.		
	12:45 P. M.	Ar Salt Lake City	Lv 5:30 P. M.		
12:50 A. M.		Lv Lynndyl	Ar		5:00 P. M.
2:31 A. M.		Lv Nephi	Lv		3:25 P. M.
6:30 A. M.		Ar Salt Lake City	Lv		11:55 A. M

All forms of revenue transportation will be accepted on these trains between those stations at which they are scheduled to stop regularly or on signal. Ticket restrictions shown in circular No. 1618 will no longer be regarded.

All trains carry dining cars

Train No. 1 west bound handles U. S. mail.

Train No. 4 east bound handles U. S. mail.

Trains 1 and 2 are all standard equipment; no chair cars or coaches are handled on these trains.

All Pullman car runs terminate and originate at Los Angeles.

Beaver County News (Utah)
July 19, 1918

F. Dewey, roundhouse foreman at Caliente, was transferred to Provo as roundhouse foreman vs. J. J. Blake.

Iron County Record (Utah)
July 19, 1918

Marva Stewart of Alamo Nevada a niece of Mrs. John Fuller is spending a few weeks here. She came before the Fourth and will stay until Mr. Fuller returns.

Beaver County News (Utah)
August 9, 1918

H. C. King of Caliente was in Milford Tuesday visiting friends and made this office a pleasant call. Mr. King made his home in Milford for a number of years.

Beaver County News (Utah)
August 16, 1918

The infant child of Mr. and Mrs. B. R. Eldridge died last Sunday morning. Mr. and Mrs. Eldridge moved here about a month ago from Caliente and have decided to make their home in Milford.

Beaver County News (Utah)
August 30, 1918

John Shier of Caliente, was in Milford this week. Mr. Shier was formerly in the drug business in this city.

Beaver County News (Utah)
September 6, 1918

Bulletin No. 1516

Tonnage of 2500 class Mikado type engines, now used in helper service out of Caliente, will be as follows:

Caliente to Minto—1400 tons

Minto to Islen—700 tons

Islen to Crestline—1100 tons

Beaver County News (Utah)
September 13, 1918

In the case of the State vs. Roy Sterrett last Saturday before Judge Ingols, County Attorney Parsons secured a conviction on a boot-leg charge. The liquor came from Caliente. The Judge sentenced Mr. Sterrett to one hundred days in jail or one hundred dollars fine. The fine was paid.

Beaver County News (Utah)
September 20, 1918

Bulletin No. 394—Vacancy for two conductors on trains 1, 2, 3, 4, between Salt Lake and Caliente. Vacancy for one brakeman on trains 93 and 94 between Salt Lake and Provo. Bids close Sept. 24.

Beaver County News (Utah)
September 27, 1918

Wanted—An experienced clerk for a General Merchandise Store. Must be over draft age, between 45 and 50 years, and capable of taking charge. None other need apply. Good salary. References. Address BLUE FRONT MERCANTILE Co., Caliente, Nevada.   12-tf

Beaver County News (Utah)
October 4, 1918

Bulletin No. 395
Vacancy for a conductor for extra passenger service out of Salt Lake. Vacancy for a brakeman on trains 1, 2, 3 and 4 between Salt Lake and Caliente. Bids will close October 11.

Beaver County News (Utah)
October 11, 1918

Geo. A. Trent, for about two years telegraph operator at the Milford station, and for nearly a year railroad correspondent for the News, will leave tonight for Caliente, where he has accepted a very good position. Mr. Trent also has been conducting a telegraph school in Milford for nearly a year, which has attracted quite a good deal of attention.

Beaver County News (Utah)
December 6, 1918

————— W. S. S.—————
J. W. McCracken, of Caliente, was here for several days recently.

Beaver County News (Utah)
December 27, 1918

Father Slattery of Caliente, has been in town looking over the spiritual interests of the Catholic church and his people.

Beaver County News (Utah)
January 3, 1919

MRS GODEELA HIMSTREET

Godeeta Walker Himstreet, young wife of Thos. Himstreet, passed away Saturday, December 28, 1918, at her home, with pneumonia. She v daughter of Mr. and Mrs. Walker, of Caliente, who were with her at the time of her illness and death, also Mr. and Mrs. Himstreet, her husband' parents. She was born in California, and was a graduate of the University of California. She was a very sweet, capable woman, loved by all who knew her. The funeral was held Mon day at the cemetary, conducted b Father Slattery, of Caliente, who made it very brief owing to the dition of the weather. She was laid to rest beside her baby girl who ; gone beyond just a few days before. Mr. Himstreet returned to Caliente with his parents. We wish to ext our sympathy to the family in th sorrow.

Miss Lulu Bower, waiter at the Railroad lunch counter, left Wednesday night on train No. 1, for Caliente, Nevada, to spend a few days visiting her sister.

Miss Maude Jones of the Mechanical department of Caliente, was a visitor in Milford Friday. Miss Jones left Milford on delayed No. 4 Saturday morning for Salt Lake, where she will visit with friends for several days.

Caliente Day Yard is under the direct management of J. W. Card, assisted by Geo. Vought and Kinney. Kinney has been regularly assigned Night Yard is under the management of W. A. Barr, assisted by Capell and Dickerson.

Mrs. W. C. Ernst of Caliente is up helping in the postoffice while our genial post master is off for a few days vacation. Mrs. Ernst's many friends are glad to see her smiling face at the delivery window once more.

Salt Lake Lineman Tom Neilan of Caliente, contemplates making a trip into Milford. Tom says that he wants to see and converse with some live wires.

Ko. got the R. J. at Caliente when J. returned. Ko is now on third in Salt Lake telegraph office. Some lightning that fellow Ko. Shoves it right along.

Louis, the most popular girl in the Caliente lunch room, is again back to work. Louis has many friends who are all pleased to see her back with the Salt Lake route hotel and lunch room.

Special to Beaver County News—
Caliente. January 31—Yard foreman J. W. Card for the La & S. L. R. R. Co., met with a very painful accident at 5:30 p. m. today while switching the storehouse track. His body was squeezed between the car and the storehouse platform. So far as known there were no bones broken. Injured man was taken to his home.

Engine 3433 on No. 1 out of Milford to Caliente, 34 minutes late with 11 cars. arrived in Caliente 8 minutes late Thursday morning, with a little effort it can be did.

BULLETIN NO. 417

Following assignments have been made.

Patton, conductor through freight service between Salt Lake and Lyndyl.

Dodd, Extra conductor freight service out of Salt Lake City.

Coker, Brakeman Trains 1, 2, 3, and 4.

Markle and Brownson, brakemen through freight service between Milford and Caliente.

BULLETIN NO. 418

There is a vacancy for one conductor in through freight service, between Milford and Caliente.

There is a vacancy for one brakeman on the Warner turn.

There is a vacancy for one brakeman for extra passenger service out of Salt Lake City. Bids close Feb. 22, 1919.

The friends of Mr. C. W. Card are pleased to learn he is improving from his injuries received some days ago, switching in the yards at Caliente. He expects to be back at work in a short time. Hard to keep a good man down and out.

Beaver County News (Utah)
February 19, 1919

Private car 103 H. E. Vanhousen passed through Milford on No. 3 Tuesday evening en route to Caliente.

Train Master W. F. Farrier went to Caliente on No. 3 Tuesday evening.

CALIENTE ITEMS

J. W. Card day yard engine foreman, was slightly injured about a week ago and is being relieved by Switchman Thompson. We expect Jack to be on duty again in a few days.

Following is the line-up of the Caliente telegraph office at present:— B. L. Walker, Manager, 8 a. m. to 4 p. m.; A. J. Locke telegrapher 11 a. m. to 7 p. m.; B. L. Walker Jr. telegrapher 4 p. m. to 12 m; H. C. Anders (Andy) 12 m. to 8 a. m.

Since government supplement No. 13 went into effect, the telegraph forces in all offices along the road have been cut down on Sundays. In Caliente the boys have been alternating, taking Sunday off turn about.

Mr. Wallace, formerly cashier at Delta, assumed the duties of day yard clerk today. He relieved Johnstone who had been on the job for a long time.

We have a new General Manager on the Pioche branch and he is none other than Conductor W. C. Ernst. Conductor Tolbert has been away since about the 18th of January, but his run is in good hands while Conductor Ernst watches over it.

Mrs. Eliza Culverwell, one of Caliente's oldest citizens died last week in Los Angeles. She had been failing in health for some time and the end was not unexpected. The funeral took place in Caliente February 17th, attended by many friends from all parts of the county. The deceased was the mother of Charles, Billy and Amy Culverwell and Mrs. Alice Dixon.

There is a vacancy for a brakeman in through freight service between Milford and Caliente.

The brass checking system has been installed at Milford, Caliente, Provo and Lynndyl in the mechanicla departments.

Caliente reports several new cases of flu.

Mrs. Bowles and Mrs. Anderson of Caliente have rented the former Johnston home and have started a rooming and boarding house. This is a God send for some of the boys of Caliente who have eaten at the Beanery for the past years.

Johnston the day yard clerk at Caliente has resigned and moved to Los Angeles with his family.

CALIENTE

General Foreman Richter is down with an attack of the influenza, which we hope is not serious. He is being relieved by Machinest J. T. Pettee who was general foreman here several years ago.

The paint gang of Wm. Kloos has finished painting the exteriors of the houses on company row, and is now engaged in tinting and painting the interiors. After they are through with company row, the depot is to receive a much needed coat of paint and some minor repairs.

A first class pool table has been installed in the reading room, next to the hotel, and the charge to railroad men is only ten cents per cue per hour.

Engineer Love, of the Pioche branch, has been confined to his home for the past week or ten days, with the flu. He is improving rapidly, and expects to be on his r next Monday the 3rd.

Jack Card, day yard engine foreman, reported for duty March 1st, after an absence of two or three weeks, due to an injury he received while switching. Barnett will return to Milford since Card has come back.

The snow storm last week, accompanied by rain and lightning, played havoc with the automatic block signals and wires between Caliente and Crestline. No less than six track relays were burned out, and the Los Angeles to Salt Lake quad wire No. 2 was grounded for a day.

Mr. Mitchell, formerly manager of the Salt Lake Hotel, is here again, relieving Manager W. P. Corkery, who has gone to Los Angeles on a business trip. Mitchell has been conductor on a diner for some months past.

Walter Ernst, formerly third trick operator at Lynndyl, is visiting with his folks in Caliente. He is on the extra board S. L. division.

CALIENTE ITEMS

The second flu wave which struck Caliente a couple of weeks ago, has aparently blown over, as no new cases have been reported for several days, and all those who were down with it are up and around again.

Effective Sunday, March 16th. Caliente telegraph force was reduced to three straight eight hour tricks. The fourth man, A. J. Locke being the youngest man in point of service was pulled off. He went to Los Angeles, and will probably be placed somewhere on the Los Angeles division.

Spring is here. Manager Welker of the telegraph office has started to dig up the real estate surrounding his company house No. 11, and from present outlooks, a good garden should result, if he would only leave out the inevitable spinich and parsnips.

The paint gang has finished painting the depot with the standard colors—yellow and brown—and we now have the best looking depot on the whole road—that is, if you are on the outside.

The force at the yard office has been increased by the addition of another clerk, making three all told, each of whom works eight hours per day. Raper is on from 8 a. m. to 4 p. m.; Locke 4 p. m. to 12 m.; and Wallace 12N to 8 a. m.

Manager W. P. Corkery of the Salt Lake Hotel, "Beanery," has returned from Los Angeles. Ed Mitchell who relieves him, returns to his run as conductor on one of the diners.

Operator B. L. Welker Jr., went up to Pioche on March 8th, to take the second degree in Masonry. Soon, he will be able to ride the goat with much skill and proficiency.

Miss Edna Himstreet, one of Milford's school teachers, was in Caliente last week to see her folks. She reports that the school building at Milford was about to fall down, so she thought it advisable to get out and give the poor building a chance to be saved from disaster.

Have you paid your income tax yet? Even two of Caliente's operators with honored with the usual slip of paper, saying that they owed said tax. Anders was the hardest hit. His tax was somewhere around thirty dollars, and Welker Jr. had to dig deep down into his jeans and give the collector the sum of 39c (thirty nine) cents. After all, the law compelling us to pay income tax is not such a bad one—providing you have to pay only thirty-nine cents.

H. J. Barton and wife came up from Caliente, Nevada Sunday evening to spend some little time visiting their children, relatives and many friends—also looking after business interests

Beaver County News (Utah)
April 16, 1919

Superintendent H. E. Vanhousen left Milford Saturday morning on Motor car en route to Caliente, making a complete inspection.

Roadmaster Wood of Caliente was in Milford Saturday.

Beaver County News (Utah)
April 23, 1919

T. J. Baudreau of Caliente, but formerly of Milford, was here on Sunday en route to Salt Lake to meet his son-in-law who is returning from the famous 91st.

Mr. and Mrs. Sid Pace and son who had been visiting at the home of their sister, Mrs. J. I. Sanders, left Friday night for their home in Alamo, Nevada.

Effective 4 p. m. Wednesday May 7th, the following hours will prevail in the Caliente and Milford yards— First crew will go on at 4 p. m. and work through until 12 midnight; 2nd crew will go on duty at 12 midnight and work through until 8 a. m. There will be no switch engine working between the hours of 8 a. m. and 4 p. m. The Lynndyl yard will be continuous 7 a. m. to 7 p. m. with three crews.

Mr. and Mrs. James Tanner had as dinner guests Tuesday night, Mrs. E. Tanner and family, Mr. and Mrs. Will Miller. Miss Angie Harmon of Salt Lake and Mrs. Joe Kinney and daughter of Caliente. The dinner was given in honor of Marion Tanner.

Mr. and Mrs. E. Tanner entertained Saturday night, with a family dinner for their son Marion, who has just received his discharge from the army. A feature of the dinner was the Christmas turkey which had been saved for the boy's home-coming. The guests were, besides the immediately family, of Mr. and Tanner, Mr. and Mrs. Wm. Miller Mr. and Mrs James Tanner, Mr. and Mrs. Dave Tanner. Miss Angie Harmon of Salt Lake, Miss Mary Richards of Frisco, Mrs. Joe Kinney and little daughter of Caliente.

Marion Tanner arrived home last Thursday evening, having received his discharge from the army at Ft Russell, Wyo. He was accompanied home by a cousin, Miss Angie Harmon of Salt Lake. His sister, Mrs. Joe Kinney, and little daughter, came up from Caliente, Nev., to spend a week visiting with him and their parents. Mr. and Mrs. E. Tanner.

The Liberty Loan special will leave Caliente 7 a. m., Thursday, .It is to be hoped that each and every one will do their bit by subscribing to the Victory Loan.

Beaver County News (Utah)
May 14, 1919

CALIENTE ITEMS

Operator E. R. Williams, formerly with the Western Union at Los Angeles, relieved Operator B. L. Welker Jr. for a few days last week, while the latter went up to Pioche and took the Master Mason's degree.

The Pioche base ball team came down to Caliente last Sunday and played the Caliente ball team. The final score was 15 to 11 in favor of Pioche. The stars of the game were Cook and Fieldson, who work in the Caliente shops.

Caliente Telegraph went way over the top, in the victory Loan. The force of three operators and one messenger subscribed for a total of $2150.00, or a per centage of ovfier 411 per cent. This does not include the subscription of $700 made by Lineman Neilan.

Tom Neilan, Caliente Lineman, went up against a tough proposition a few days ago, when he went west to look for a ground on No. 51. After traveling back and forth between Caliente and Elgin for four days, he finally located the ground on top of a mounain, and in accomplishing the task, he wore out a pair of perfectly good shoes.

Lincoln county was one of a few counties in Nevada to exceed their quota in the Victory Liberty Loan drive. The quota was $40,000, and the total amount subscribed was over $46,000.

It is reported in Railway circles that there is to be an additional fifty cars of fruit daily.

Beaver County News (Utah)
May 21, 1919

Father Slattery came up from Caliente, to hold services Sunday. The Catholics have moved their church up stairs over the Utah Theatre.

LADIES' AUXILIARY

The Ladies' Auxiliary of the Engineers' Club held an all day session in the Odd Fellow's hall last Thursday. Mrs. Pettis of Grand Junction, Colorado, an appointed Grand officer met with them and inspected the lodge. The ladies held business sessions both morning and afternoon in the hall. In the evening they gave a 6 o'clock luncheon in honor of Mrs. Pettis at the home of Mrs. F. Calloway on North Main. A delicious luncheon was served and the honor guest was presented with a beautiful souvenir spoon. Out of town members present were Mrs. F. C. Sullivan, Lynndyl; Mrs. C. I. Himstreet and Mrs. M. McCans of Caliente; Mrs. S. K. Runswick and Mrs. Russell of Salt Lake.

The other members are Mrs. J. C. Jeffers, President; Mrs. Wm. Sterling, Mrs. G. C. Cuddy, Mrs. John Killam, Mrs. George Ranson, Mrs. F. Calloway, Mrs. Charlie Husbands, Mrs. Elmer Blanpied and Mrs. Wm. Dawson.

J. A. Ingols came down from Salt Lake last Friday on his way to Caliente. He returned Saturday evening and spent Sunday here. Mr. Ingols is now Material clerk for the Salt Lake Route and will make trips to Milford and the other division points frequently. Mrs. Ingols and little daughter will come down from Salt Lake Thursday to visit friends and be here for Decoration Day.

DESERTER FROM THE ARMY IS CAPTURED

Louis Ronco of New York, who enlisted at the recruiting station in Milford last week and who was furnished a number of meals and transportation to Salt Lake, decided that he would take French leave on the blind baggage of train No. 3 Sunday evening. Through the personal efforts of Special Agent A. G. Hedges of the Salt Lake Route and Chief of Police Charles Baxter, the man was apprehended at Caliente by Special Officer Denton. When the officers of the army recruiting station took the matter up with the commanding officer in Salt Lake, they were advised that nothing could be done to the man from the stand point of a deserter. He, however, could have been prosecuted for receiving meals under false pretense but this would involve the county to an unnecessary expense, so the man was ordered turned loose This was done, much to the chagrin of both special officer Hedges and Chief of Police Baxter.

NEGRO BURNED IN ICE HOUSE

Caliente—Fatal accident occurred here Tues. morning when ice house west of town belonging to Less Denton burned to the ground, burning to death, a negro, who must have been asleep in the building when the fire started. It is not known just how the fire started, but before help could reach there the man was dead. A corner's inquest was held before Frank Palmer, and although the remains were so burned that identification was impossible, the jury agreed that the deceased was a negro. A watch and several pieces of silver found in the corner, where a pile of straw had been led them to the conclusion that the man was asleep and that in trying to escape, he had been overcome with the smoke and flames. It is possible that he may have left a lighted cigar or cigarette, as that is about the only way a fire could have started in that remote building.

Howard Tanner returned the first of the week from a visit in Caliente with his sister, Mrs. Joe kinney.

Mrs. J. A. Yoakam of Caliente, was having dental work done here last week.

Mr. Robert Mayer of New York City and Miss Amy Culverwell of Caliente were married Friday night, June 13th in Pioche, at the home of the bride's brother, Charles Culverwell, the ceremony being performed by Judge Wm. E. Orr. The couple returned to Caliente and will remain here a short while, when they will leave for Texas, where they will make their home. The bride is a Caliente girl, and for several years was a teacher in the Caliente public schools. She has a gracious, winning personality, and her jolly disposition and kindness of heart have made a genera favorate of her. Hosts of friends, not only in Lincoln county, but throughout the entire state, will congratulate Mr. Mayer upon his choice. She is a daughter of the late Charles and Eliza Culverwell, and a sister of Sheriff Wm Culverwell, and Charles Culverwell. It was while visiting her sister, Mrs. Geo. Coxe at Hanover, New Mexico that she met Mr. Mayer, who later joined the Canadian Army as a member of the Royal Flying Corps. Upon his discharge, he came to New York City, where he visited relatives, and then came West to claim his bride.

Quite a few of the train and enginemen would like to know why it is that they are run out of Milford to Caliente on short rest and they lay in Caliente from twelve to twenty four hours and even sometimes longer.

Trainmaster W. F. Farrier is covering the line between Salt Lake and Caliente during the absence of Asst. Supt. W. H. Smith who is in Los Angeles.

Beaver County News (Utah)
July 9, 1919

It is more than likely that the third engine in the Caliente and Lynndyl yards will be taken off on account of slack business.

Beaver County News (Utah)
July 16, 1919

Miss Georgia English of Caliente,
is visiting in Milford for a few days
before going on to Idaho

Miss Georgia English of Caliente,
is visiting in Milford for a few days
before going on to Idaho.

Beaver County News (Utah)
July 23, 1919

Mrs. Joe Kinney and two children
came in from Caliente Wednesday
morning to visit her parents, Mr.
and Mrs. E. Tanner.

Beaver County News (Utah)
July 30, 1919

Bert Frasure was sent to Caliente
Sunday night to do some welding at
the shops.

Beaver County News (Utah)
September 3, 1919

Mrs. Joe Kinney and children who
have been visiting her parents, Mr.
and Mrs. Eb. Tanner, returned to
their home in Caliente, Wednesday.

Beaver County News (Utah)
September 10, 1919

Jack Krause went to Caliente on
Tuesday to spend a few days on company business.

Robert Sands came up from Caliente this week again.

MOTOR CAR AND FREIGHT TRAIN COLLIDE

A motor car west bound and an east bound freight train in charge of Conductor D. R. Martin, collided on curve just east of Islen station last Saturday evening about eight o'clock.

The motor car was carrying A. S. Petty, signal maintainer, Reuben Johnson, track walker and Chas. N. Clark, section laborer. Both the motor car and freight train were making about fifteen miles an hour when they collided. A. S. Petty, signal maintainer and Reuben Johnson were killed instantly. Chas. N. Clark jumped from the motor car and sustained several bruises. The dead bodies were taken to Caliente where an inquest was held.

It appears that the men riding the motor car disregarded caution signals and carried no lights on their car at time of accident.

Mrs. Vivian Duffin of Caliente, passed through Milford Tuesday evening en route to Salt Lake to visit relatives.

GRADE SCHOOLS OPEN

The grade school opened Monday with a good enrollment. The following teachers are in charge.

H. Thorpe of Ephriam, 6th grade, and Principal.

Miss Edna Himstreet, Caliente, 5th grade.

Miss Alice Southworth, Garfield, 4th grade.

Mrs. H. Thorpe, Ephriam, 3rd grade.

Miss Tressa Pickering, Payson, 2nd grade.

Miss Carlotta Southworth, Garfield 1st grade.

Mrs. L. G. Clay, Milford, Music.

Prof. Thorpe is organizing the grade school ball teams and reports great interest. The school has new basket ball, a volley ball

Prof. Thorp is organizing the 6th grade boys' basket ball team. Mrs. Clay and Miss Alice Southworth will have charge of the 5th and 6th grade girls' volley ball teams. Prof. Thorp is much pleased with the interest the boys and girls are taking in the games. The new balls andn net cost $16. He told the pupils Tuesday morning that $4. was necessary to finish paying for them and at noon the money was ready.

STRUCK BY TRAIN AND
WAS INSTANTLY KILLED

A man by the name of John Sorg said to be a deaf mute while walking eastward on the railroad tracks two miles east of Caliente, was struck by passenger train No. 4, Tuesday evening at about 720 p. m. Whistle was sounded but without avail. Remains were taken to Caliente and there turned over to the corner.

Beaver County News (Utah)
October 8, 1919

Mr. and Mrs. Press Duffin of Caliente were here the first of the week looking after their property annd are shipping their furniture to Caliente.

Beaver County News (Utah)
October 15, 1919

George Moore went to Caliente Sunday night where he has a run as fireman.

Marion Tanner went to Caliente Monday to work for the Salt Lake Route.

Beaver County News (Utah)
October 29, 1919

Miss Edna Milsap of Caliente, is visiting Milford friends this week.

George Moore came in Tuesday from Caliente where he has been working for the Salt Lake Route.

Beaver County News (Utah)
November 5, 1919

Mrs. W. C. Ernst is up from Caliente, assisting in the post office, while Postmaster Stoker is off deer hunting.

Beaver County News (Utah)
December 17, 1919

A wireless telegram informs us that Engineer C. I. Himstreet of Caliente is laying off on account of a weak ankle and stiff knee. All of these ailments creep upon us when Mr. Age stalks about wanting to shake hands with us.

TRAIN MASTER'S OFFICE

W. F. Farrier, Train Master
Louise Poulton, Chief Clerk

This is one of the most important offices on a line of railroad.

Mr. Farrier covers all territory between Salt Lake and Caliente, which has a main line mileage of 325 miles in addition to the Provo district, which has a mileage of 134 miles and the following districts, Tintic Fairfield, Pioche, Frisco and Delta.

Mr. Farrier has had some thirty five years experience in the railroad game, has been associated with the Salt Lake Route since July, 1903. Just ask any of the boys about Fred they will tell you that he is a square shooter, from start to finish.

Beaver County News (Utah)
December 24, 1919

Mrs. H. J. Barton is here from Caliente to spend a few days with her daughter, Mrs. Alma Jacobsen.

Beaver County News (Utah)
December 31, 1919

Ida Rogers is here from Caliente.

CALIENTE

Mr. and Mrs. W. P. Corkery, Manager and Cashier respectively of the Salt Lake hotel are away in California, taking a vacation. They are being relieved by H. P. Speicher and wife.

Operator H. A. Allred, who relieved Operator Welker Jr. in Caliente telegraph office last month, is now working in Las Vegas telegraph office. Before coming to Salt Lake Rt., he worked for the Western Union in Salt Lake City.

Miss Edna Himstreet, teacher in the Milford Grammar school is visiting her parents during the holiday recess of her school.

Wm. Kloos and his carpenter gang have been busy the past week unloading ice and filling the ice house. They expect to complete the work in a few days.

Brakeman Keeney is working extra on the Pioche branch in place of Brakeman Bodine, who is laying off.

Second trick operator B. L. Welker, Jr. spent Christmas with his mother and sister in San Diego, California. Before going to San Diego he was initiated as a Shriner in Kerak Temple at Reno, Nevada, and reports that he got more than his money's worth at Reno.

P. S. Austin's outfit is still at Delmues, on the Pioche Branch, doing some bridge work near Mile Post 19.

Mrs. Sarah L. Savage, ex-messenger in the telegraph office, is now working in the Royal cafe.

W. E. Ferron, owner of the Caliente Pharmacy, was in town this week from Las Vegas, looking after his business interests here.

Dr. W. W. Stockham passed thro Caliente Saturday en route from Pioche to Los Angeles.

Misses Mildred Wilkes and Bettie Himstreet are home from school in Salt Lake, spending their vacation with their parents.

John Zumistein, night ticket clerk and sister, Mrs. F. J. Boudreau have returned from Colorado, where they spent Christmas with relatives.

George Jeffs is in charge of the Blue Front store during the absence of Mr. and Mrs. C. L. Alquist who are in Salt Lake City.

Mrs. Ida Rogers returned from Milford last Saturday after a visit with her sister, Mrs. LaRue Duffin.

Mrs. Webb, formerly Miss Edna Millsap, has returned to Caliente, after an extended trip.

Westbound freight business is exceptionally heavy at present; and the eastbound tonnage is light, causing a reduction of the helper board to two regular assigned crews, with several extra crews.

Beaver County News (Utah)
January 14, 1920

CALIENTE

The lowest temperature we have had this winter was registered at 8 a. m. Friday when the mercury dropped to 2 degrees below zero.

Sheriff Billy Colverwell has gone out to his ranch in the country for a brief sojourn. He says no town for his vacation. He always takes to the woods for a real good time.

Engineer Fred. W. Cram and family left for California last week for a few week's vacation.

Superintendent W. H. Smith, in company with Merrrs. Strong and Bigelow, in business car 103, came in on No. 3. Friday afternoon. They made an insepction trip over the Pioche branch Saturday, and left for Milford on Extra 3662 East Sunday morning.

Clyde Olson and Miss Mary Rivard were united in marriage last week. It is reported that several other young couples of Caliente are to be married within the next week or two. Wonder if Leap year has anything to do with it?

Attorney Leo A. McNamee was in town from Las Vegas this week on business.

Supt. T. P. Cullen of the Los Angeles division came in from Las Vegas last Tuesday on an extra, and returned on No. 3 that afternoon.

Frank C. Pace made a business trip to Los Angeles and return last week.

Third trick operator at Las Vegas, and pumper operator at Rox are open for bids on the Los Angeles division.

J. M. Anderson's water service outfit is back from Milford, to do some work on the power plant.

The census enumeration in this district is in charge of Mrs. Ella Ernst. The work should be completed by January 31st, and it will then be in order to guess the population of your city, for which no prizes are offered.

Brakeman Bodine has resumed duty on the Pioche branch, displacing Brakeman Keeney, who relieved Switchman Capell in the yards for a few days.

Otto Olson is working on the freight house as warehouseman, while Clair Norris is laying off.

First No. 1, Engine 3701, Conductor Goodwin and Engineer Matthews went into the ditch near Vigo, 46 miles west of Caliente, Tuesday morning. Eight cars and engine were derailed, but no one was injured. The wreckers from Caliente and Las Vegas were called out to the wreck and the main line was cleared at 1 p. m. It is thought that the cause of the derailment was due to the track spreading. 2nd. No. 1 was held at Caliente until 1:15 p. m. awaiting the clearing of the main line, and No. 4 was delayed about 3 hours.

CALIENTE

Thursday night the yards were completely blocked with westbound tonnage; there being about 5500 tons on hand for the west, most of it being empties.

Miss Alice Corkish and Buck Tennille were quietly married on Thursday morning and left for Los Angeles the same day on their honeymoon. A crowd of young couples, friends, were at the depot with the necessary supply of rice to see the newlyweds depart, but when the latter did not show up, it was discovered that they had gone to Etna in an auto, and boarded No. 3 there. Miss Corkish has been clerk in the post office for a long time and Mr. Tennille is a rancher.

There are slow orders out on the third district covering ten different sections of track. There should be no more derailments on this district now.

Switchman W. M. Card has resigned from the night switch crew.

Trainmaster J. T. Wardenberg made his first official visit to Caliente last Friday, coming in from Salt Lake on Second 1 and returning on First 4 Friday night.

Wm. Pitts, Merchant of Pioche, passed through Saturday on his way to Salt Lake City.

Operator Booth, who has been working extra in Salt Lake X office went through on No. 3 Friday en route to Los Angeles, where he will do some more extra work in Los Angeles D office.

Operator C. E. Kendrick has assigned to the job of operator-pumper at Rox on the Los Angeles division. Third trick at Las Vegas has not yet meen assigned, as it was not bulletined over the entire system. It will appear for bids on both divisions on February 1.

Dr. Robert J. Pace, dentist of Los-Angeles, visited with his brother Frank C. Pace, a few days last week.

Arch Swapp Jr. stockman from Utah, was in town last week.

CALIENTE

Extra 3704 West Snyder and Engineer Wengret, with a train of fifty loads, 2223 tons, had one car derailed just west of Kyle, Tuesday evening the 20th. The Caliente wrecking outfit was called out and cleared the main track at about 9:-45 p. m. Supt. W. H. Smith and Trainmaster Wardenburg accompanied the wrecker, and lent their assistance in clearing the track.

First and Second 4 were delayed nearly 8 hours Tuesday night by the derailment at Kyle.

Claim agent F. W. Crisswell was in town Monday. He left Tuesday morning on a motor car, going east.

Attorney Luke J. McNamee of Pioche passed through last Sunday night on his way to Los Angeles.

A bundle shower was given at the home of Mrs. J. Less Denton Saturday night in honor of Mrs. Alice Corkish Tennille.

Joseph Spoots, car repairer, is in the hospital in Los Angeles for needed medical attention. Mr. Spotts is about 75 years old, but for many years past he has been able to be on the job regularly.

Operator H. C. Anders, better known as "Andy", is thinking about buying himself a Ford. Says he thinks it would cost less to run a flivver than to play poker.

One of the most successful dances for a long time was given Friday night in the Rex Theatre building. The music was furnished by a three piece jazz orchestra consisting of Hall Wilks, car foreman, at the piano Lloyd Denton, special agent at the drums; and Lee Welker, telegrapher, on the saxophone. There were about twelve young couples down from Pioche at the dance, besides a good turn out of the Calienta citizens.

Mr. Kloos and his outfit left Thursday morning for Topliff where they expect to be located for a while doing some boiler work at that point.

Night roundhouse foreman, Walter J. Muliken is back on the job after a couple of weeks vacation in Los Angeles. He was relieved by machinist James Pettee.

At 6:08 p.m. Thursday, an earthquake shock was felt at Caliente and as far west as Rox, sixty miles from here. The depot here rocked back and forth for about 15 seconds actingas though it would fall down any minute. In the canyon west of here, there were some rock slides but no damage was reported to the track.

Mr. and Mrs. W. P. Corkeryhave returned from a months vacation in California, and are back at the Salt Lake Hotel.

Traveling Auditors Chernault and Johnson were in town Wednesday and Thursday checking up freight, passenger and telegraph offices.

Chas. Norris, Warehouseman, and wife, retlrned last week from Los angeles where they have been for the past month.

Mr. and Mrs. H. P. Speicher, who were in charge of the Salt Lake Hotel during the absence of the Corkerys, left Friday for Los Angeles, where thew will spend a few days before taking charge of the eating house on the O. S. L. railroad.

CALIENTE

Company Doctor, J. West Smith made a trip to Los Angeles and return last week.

Mr. R. B. Robinson passed through on No. 4 in U. P. car 107 Sunday evening.

No. 2 Friday morning was 3 hrs. and 25 mins. late into Caliente. Engine 3432 bursted a flue at Garnet, and another engine was sent out from Las Vegas to move the train.

The inspection special arrived at 1:30 p. m. Saturday, and went up to Pioche and return, tying up here for the night. It left for Las Vegas Sunday at 7:30 a. m.

The seniority list of the Los Angeles division shows a total of 99 telegraphers and agents on the division. This list, however, does not include supervisory agents. The oldest man on the list is Nels Peterson, Agent at Moapa, whose seniority dates from September 14, 1898.

Several cases of influenza have been reported in this vicinity, but they all seem to be mild in form.

George Himstreet and Miss Blanch Jeffs were married Monday afternoon. In the evening they gave a banquet and dance for their many friends. The music for the dance was furnished by the Denton-Wilkes-Welker Jazz orchestra.

Sunday afternoon we had a light rain that lasted for about half an hour—the first for several months.

Tom Himstreet went to Caliente Monday to attend the wedding of his brother, George.

Some engines certainly have attractive **whistles when** entering t city of Caliente. It becomes interesting too, when the regular man is not with that attractive whistle.

Las Vegas Age
March 20, 1920

W. G. Fulton has returned from a business trip to Pioche. He made the trip by Ford, the running time from Las Vegas to Caliente being nine hours.

Las Vegas Age
May 8, 1920

FIFTY NEW ELKS WILL BE INITIATED HERE

Officers of Goldfield Lodge Will Put Horns On Big Class May 21 and 22

The officers of the Goldfield Lodge of Elks, to which most of the local Elks belong, will browse their way into Vegas for a little round-up May 21 and 22.

There are about fifty candidates waiting for the privilege of wearing an Elk's tooth on their watch chain, in this section, including several from Pioche, and Caliente. The local members of the herd are making great preparations for doing the thing up just right. The local committee of arrangements is composed of Harley A. Harmon, F. A. Stevens, C. E. Pembroke, M. M. Riley and Leo A. McNamee.

Elks' Initiation and Round-Up Proves a Happy and Successful Event

HELLO BILL!!!!

LAS VEGAS CAPTURED BY THE HERD OF GOOD FELLOWS. EVERYBODY HAS A GOOD TIME, BUT FORTY-FIVE CANDIDATES SUFFER FOR THEIR SINS

Las Vegas is captured, subdued, subjugated and held helpless by the Antlered Herd which gathered here to browse with their fellows yesterday and today—but Vegas is still happy—as happy as the coy maid who has just said "yes" to the bold and dashing lover.

For days past there have been mysterious gatherings and schemings and wise nods passed between the stray Elks of Vegas, and the result is a happy program of entertainment and pleasure for the visitors.

The following is a brief synopsis of the

PROGRAM

FRIDAY MORNING, MAY 21

Greetings to Candidates and Visiting Elks.

Music .... Grammar School Band

FRIDAY EVENING, BEGINNING AT 8:30

Initiation of Candidates at New Fraternal Hall

Banquet.

SATURDAY AFTERNOON

1:30—Kangaroo Court at First and Fremont; open to the public.

4:30—Parade of Elks in Uniform to LADD'S RESORT, where there will be Boxing Contests, Swimming, Sports and the BIG FEED.

SATURDAY EVENING
Elks Ball

GRAND MARCH .... 9:00 O'Clock Sharp

The following are the local committees in charge of the festivities:

COMMITTEES

PROGRAM COMMITTEE—Jack Price, chairman; Lester Corbett, Harry Bennett.

EXECUTIVE COMMITTEE—M. M. Riley, Chas. S. Sprague, C. E. Pembroke, Frank A. Stevens, Harley A. Harmon.

TOASTMASTER—H. M. Lillis.

ELEVEN O'CLOCK TOAST—Chas. S. Sprague.

REFRESHMENTS—C. E. Pembroke, chairman.

DECORATION—Harley A. Harmon, Munro S. Brown, C. F. Semple, Howard Conklin.

MUSIC AND DANCE—Walter E. Seare, E. H. Hunting.

LAW AND ORDER—Sam Gay.

PROGRAM OF THE DAY—Jack Price.

INITIATION—Munro S. Brown.

RECEPTION—R. F. O'Brien, Leo A. McNamee.

LADIES—Mrs. C. E. Pembroke, chairman; Mrs. Harley A. Harmon, Mrs. Chas. S. Sprague, Mrs. Jack Price, Mrs. R. F. O'Brien, Mrs. M. M. Riley, Mrs. W. E. Seare, Mrs. Howard Conklin.

IN CHARGE OF HERD—Harley A. Harmon.

The whole affair was in charge of Goldfield lodge B. P. O. E., 1072, who came in force to hold a session of the Lodge here for convenience in initiating a class of forty-five candidates from various portions of southern Nevada.

The officers who served in the Lodge sessions are the following:

F. J. Somers, Jr., Exalted Ruler; G. E. McKenna, Leading Knight; L. L. Dellinger, Loyal Knight; J. J. Jordan, Lecturing Knight; D. L. Ward, Secretary; Roger Foley, Esquire; E. C. Edwards, Inner Guard; C. E. Mills, Tiler; J. T. Murphey, Chaplain; Jack Price of Redlands Lodge, acted as Organist.

Among the visitors from Goldfield were the following:

GOLDFIELD VISITORS

A. B. Parker, H. C. Oakley, Dr. Geo. P. DeVine, Louie Polin, Wm. J. Tobin, Dave Ashland, Monro Brown, Chas. S. Sprague, George Greenwood, Pete Bleed, L. L. Dellinger, J. J. Jordan, Thos. F. Dunn, E. C. Edwards, C. E. Mills, D. L. Ward, F. J. Somers, Jr., Judge J. E. Welsh, G. B. Hartley, Thos. Keane, Elmer Burt, W. P. Phillips, M. J. Sullivan, G. E. McKenna, D. D. Findley, Chas.

Buzzard, H. A. McQuarrie, Roger Foley, John J. Murphy, Dave Patterson, Bob Dobro, Gordon Bettles.

The initiation was held Friday evening at New Fraternal Hall where the Lodge was opened in due form. There were 13 candidates from Caliente, four from Pioche, one from Moapa, four from Goodsprings and 23 from Las Vegas.

As far as an outsider can tell, judging from the cries and groans of the victims, the angry altercations and the sound of small artillery issuing from the lodge room, the initiation was a huge success and the candidates received everything there was on the program and then some more for good measure. Ask them.

The following were the

CANDIDATES

CALIENTE—C. L. Alquist, Lester Burt, W. P. Corkery, Wm. Culverwell, Lloyd Denton, Less Denton, P. W. Duffin, A. H. Millsap, Elmer Mitchell, F. C. Pace, James T. Pelter, Ralph Salt, E. W. Underhill.

PIOCHE—L. J. McNamee, J. D. Van Vleet, Hugh Love, R. P. Jones.

MOAPA—J. H. McHugh.

GOODSPRINGS—W. E. Allen, P. H. Springer, W. E. Shostedt, R. W. Leeper.

LAS VEGAS—Harry Blanding, Arthur Busch, J. J. Cannon, C. L. Clemm, F. L. Frazier, J. T. Fleming, A. W. Ham, G. E. Ketchum, W. F. Merry, H. P. Mitchell, Clarence Stocker, Lester Stocker, F. A. Walt, M. E. Ward, T. B. Allen, H. E. Anderson, Joe E. Keate, Harry Coffee, Frank DeVinney, M. J. Sullivan, E. W. Cragin, W. H. Pike, W. E. Arnold.

An important part in the initiation of the candidates was performed by the Grand Lodge of Jolly Corks (?) which exemplified the work of the second degree, under the direction of Supreme Exalted Jolly Cork, Munro S. Brown. Harley A. Harmon was Supreme Esquire Jolly Cork and Leo A. McNamee, Harry Bennett, Les Corbett, Dr. R. F. O'Brien, Dr. E. B. Gratto and Thos. Linehan were assistants to the Supreme Ruler of the Jolly Corks.

The reception to the candidates arriving by train was warm in the extreme, notwithstanding the coolness of the atmosphere. A message was produced charging the bunch with a violation of the Volstead Act. The sheriff of Lincoln county was handcuffed and chained as the ring leader, following which the whole bunch was rounded up, hand-cuffed, roped and otherwise rendered helpless. Then surrounded by the armed guard of Elks they were marched ignominiously to the county jail where they were incarcerated while their luggage was searched for incriminating evidence. It is believed that the evidence found is sufficient to convict the entire bunch, but those in charge of the search refuse to disclose the nature of their plunder and it is doubtful if the "evidence" will be in shape to be produced in court when the cases are brought to trial.

This afternoon order is being restored by placing the most nortorious criminals in town in the temporary Elks' jail at the corner of First and Fremont streets. The officers are doing their full duty and full justice and then some is being meted out by the Kangaroo Court, presided over by Judge Buol. "Let no guilty man escape" is the axiom of the court.

The parade of Elks to Ladd's Resort was escorted by the Las Vegas Grammar School Band, who made a handsome showing in their new white uniforms decorated with the Elks' colors.

At Ladd's Resort there is fun galore, supplemented by a "Big Feed." Those of the bunch who are still able to be up and about will close their round of festivities tonight with a grand ball at which the beauty of Southern Nevada will bow before the manly strength and vigor of the Antlered Herd.

This is the first occasion in Nevada where the Elks have been permitted to open Lodge for the initiation of candidates at any place away from their home town. Through the efforts of Thos. F. Dunn, deputy grand exalted ruler for the State of Nevada, a dispensation for this purpose was secured for the Goldfield Lodge. It speaks well for the loyalty of its members that there were 116 members present in Vegas to take part in the exemplification of the degrees.

FIRST BAD TRAIN WRECK IN COUNTY

Engineer and Fireman Meet Death When Engine and Cars Part in Half Open Switch.

ENGINE AND FOUR CARS COMPLETELY DEMOLISHED

Accident Overtakes Local No. 3 Sunday Morning at Latimer Siding—Passengers Escape Almost Uninjured—Property Loss Great

Engineer Thorpe Waddingham, 55 years of age, 350 West Fifth North Street, Salt Lake, and Fireman Edwin L. Miller, Caliente, Nev., were killed at 10 o'clock yesterday morning when the west-bound Los Angeles & S. L. passenger train No. 3 which left Salt Lake at 12:30 o'clock Sunday morning was derailed at Latimer about twenty-seven miles west of Milford, Utah, and nine miles east of Lund. Waddingham and Miller had taken charge of the train at Milford.

The accident was caused by an open switch. The engine and four baggage cars were overturned, the cars being completely demolished. The day coach next behind the baggage coaches left the track but was not overturned. The two victims were pinned under the engine.

The train was in charge of Conductor John B. Milligan 560 N. Second West street, Salt Lake, and was composed of an engine, four baggage cars, a day coach, a chair car, a tourist car and three Pullman cars.

Baggagemen Believed Safe.

No report of the injury of Frank Houghtaling of Los Angeles, baggageman on the train, had been received late last night by the Salt Lake office of the railroad company and it is thought he escaped death when the four baggage cars were smashed. Two of the baggage cars contained the scenery of the show "Mis' Nelly of N' Orleans," featuring Mrs. Minnie Maddern Fiske, which completed a three-day engagement Saturday night at the Salt Lake theatre.

Passenger train No. 4, eastbound due in Salt Lake at 6 o'clock this morning, will be ten hours late as a result of the wreck, and the wrecked train, No. 3, due in Los Angeles at 8:08 o'clock this morning will be fourteen hours late. Wrecking trains and crews have been sent from Lynndyl, Utah and Caliente, Nev., to clear away the wreckage and repair the track. At a late hour last night reports from the wreck were that the track, which was torn up for 300 feet, was repaired at 12:05 o'clock this morning.

4- trackaway. morn- Lll due-cmmm

Wreck at Siding.

The accident occurred at a siding. As trains had passed over the track only a few hours before the derailment, railroad officials are inclined to believe the switch may have been tampered with, causing the cars to leave the main track. W. H. Schmidt general superintendent of the railroad left yesterday afternoon for the scene of the accident to investigate.

Mr. Waddingham was born in Lincolnshire, England and came to the United States thirty years ago. He was a locomotive fireman and engineer in England and continued the work for ten years at Forsythe, Mont. before coming to Salt Lake twenty years ago. He had been an engineer on the Los Angeles and Salt Lake route for the last fifteen years.

Surviving him are his wife, Mrs. Phyllis Waddingham, a son, Lindsay B., and two daughters, Lillian Waddingham and Mrs. H. C. Barning, 352 West Fifth North street, all of Salt Lake. The body will be brought to Salt Lake for funeral services and interment.

Beaver County News (Utah)
June 2, 1920

NOTICE FOR PUBLICATION

Department of the Interior, U. S.
Land Office, Salt Lake
City, Utah

May 29, 1920

Notice is hereby given that Thomas W. Neely, of Lund, Utah, who on February 14, 1916, made Homestead Entry, No. 016520, for E 1-2, Section 25, Township 31 South, Range 14 West, Salt Lake Meridian, has filed notice of intention to make 3-year Proof, to establish claim to the land above described, before Herbert Nichols, U. S. Commissioner, at Milford, Utah, on the 6th day of July, 1920.

Claimant names as witnesses:
Melvin Casneau, Mary J. Cazneau, Colin Grant, all of Milford, Utah, and Bertha Holcom of Caliente, Nevada.

GOULD B. BLAKELY, Register.
First Publication, June 2, 1920.
Last Publication, June 30, 1920.

Las Vegas Age
June 5, 1920

CALIENTE HAS NEW NEWSPAPER

The first issue of the Caliente News made its appearance in Pioche today, bearing date of Thursday, May 27. The newcomer is composed of eight pages and the general appearance of the new paper is striking and judging from its initial effort should be a successful venture. The Record extends the fraternal hand of welcome and wishes for the unvarying success of the News, which will be published weekly, according to the present plans of the management. —Pioche Record.

Yesterday afternoon, a jolly party went up to the hot springs north of Honeyville and spent a few hours splashing in the warm water, visiting together and partaking of a sumptuous luncheon. Those who made up the party were Mr. and Mrs. W. H. Shurtliff, Mr. and Mrs. W. H. Ivins of Lund, Nevada; Mrs. Abel S. Rich and children; Mesdames Ellen Dryner and O. H. Snow of Raymond, Canada; Mrs. Thomas Adams of Parowan and Mrs. J. Redd of Provo.

Mrs. Abel S. Rich has had for her guests this week, four of her sisters, one of whom was acompanied by her husband. The visitors are Mr. and Mrs. W. H. Ivins of Lund, Nevada; Mrs. Ellen Dryner and Mrs. O. H. Snow of Raymond, Canada and Mrs. Thomas Adams of Parowan, Utah.

BASE BALL IN MILFORD

When the dust cleared away at the ball park Sunday, we learned that the Caliente bunch was to lucky for us.

When Barton hit the first ball over the pan for a home run, it seemed to put a chill in the local team, that they couldn't get over. But you know it is almost impossible to win them all. This is our first game with Caliente this year, so look out for the game that is played with them next time.

Steve did good rooting Sunday

Barney couldn't see them Sunday.

SOME BALL GAME ANYHOW

Those fellows play ball, and if you don't think so, you ought to see them play once. This is what seems to be on the tongue of every one since seeing the ball game between Monroe and our local team here on Tuesday, and I call it some ball game

The Monroe team are the champions of the three following counties, Sanpete, Sevier and Millard, so you see we were up against a real ball team.

Oh, yes, they also beat the Army team three straight games. They thought they had easy picking dur-

Asleep at 3rd. base in the 6th—Barton or Bell? Which.

ing the first seven innings, which we will admit they did, but when we brought the score up to 3 to 4, they found out they were up against it.

If the errors that were pulled by Kinney, Fotheringham and Barton could have been avoided, the game would have been 4 to 2 in favor of the local team. But at that, you know you can't win them all, boys, so try and do better next time.

FOR STATE ASSEMBLY WOMAN

Mrs. W. C. Ernst, who is now visiting in Detroit, will return to Caliente about August 20. As announced in a previous issue, Mrs. Ernst is a candidate for the state assembly and her card will found with the others in the political column. A great many are in favor of a lady in the lower house of the legislature and there are a number of reforms of vital importance to women and girls that need attention from the lawgivers and besides, Mrs. Ernst has in mind a number of improvements that will benefit the towns in Lincoln county.

Mrs. Ernst has been an ambitious worker in community and commercial affairs for many years. Her experience has brought her in touch with the public and her pleasing manner supplemented by an attractive personality would give her a big advantage as a public official. She has held important offices in the Rebekah lodge as well as Eastern Star, and was retained for years by the members in important posts because of her accuracy and efficiency.
—Caliente News

Mrs. Ernst was formerly a resident of Milford.

BOULDER CANYOU PROJECT INTERESTING TO CALIENTE

There is an item of more than usual importance published in the News this week, relative to the construction of the big power dam in Boulder Canyon on the Colorado river. This is but the upshot of recent legislation regarding the development of power sites in the west, enacted by the last congress, after many years of dillydallying over a question that means much to the west.

Still the evils that existed have been their own remedies. With so much well paying freight to be hauled, railroad companies have been compelled to pass up this lucrative business while they diverted thousands of cars to the hauling of coal necessary for motive power and for use in the numerous repair shops along the right of way.

This is being done while millions of horse power are going to waste down the rivers. So the big interests of the country are waking up. They are the ones who brought the proper pressure to bear with the result that all sections are going to profit by the movement.

The proposed power site on the Colorado river will furnish abundant energy for every purpose. It will propell the trains, light the towns along the route with electricity, replace fuel for heating purposes, furnish power to the housewife for household appliances and best of all, will make possible pumping plants for lifting water onto land that cannot at present be irrigated.

Near at hand is the time when electric trains will be gliding noiselessly up the canyon and the Salt Lake route is due for a heavy traffic because the cheap motive power will cause much freight and passenger traffic to be routed through here.—Caliente News.

CANDIDATE FOR OFFICE

Mrs. W. C. Ernst who for sometime was assistant in the post office here, but for some time a resident of Caliente Nevada, is a candidate for the office of representative to the Nevada legislature.

Mrs. Ernst is well and favorably known here and her many friends wish her success. She is a lady who is well qualified for the position which she seeks, and would be a credit to her constituents, should she be elected.

Blames Utah For It.

"That illicit liquor has been manufactured in and near Caliente by a quartet of Utah offenders who came to Lincoln county for that purpose has been proven beyond a shadow of doubt and the fact that there has been a temporary miscarriage of justice is no fault of the peace officers of this county. In justice to Caliente and Lincoln county it may be said that none of those implicaed in the operation and transportation of this illegal plant are Nevada residents, all having come here from Utah, the western home of the moonshiner, less than six months ago.

There is an undercurrent of opinion prevailing throughout the country that the aid of the federal government will be requested in order to deal with this and other flagrant abuses of the national liquor laws.

"The charge against W. Kaulbaugh of Caliente of having an illicit still in his possession was dismissed last Tuesday by Justice of the Peace Frank Palmer on the ground of insufficient evidence to convict in the higher court. Attorney Luke J. McNamee for the defense and Prosecuting Attorney A. L. Scott went down from Pioche to attend the trial.

"Mr. Scott first called Sheriff William Culverwell and Deputies J. L. Denton and L. C. Denton, who made the arrest, to the witness stand, all of whom related the same story with reference to the search at Klondike Well, and each corroborated the other's story in regard to the capture of the still in Kaulbaugh's residence in Caliente. According to officials, the still was practically complete, there being offered in evidence one five-gallon copper kettle and worm, one brass tube connection, one rubber hose connection one specific gravity testing instrument which is used to ascertain the alcohol content and three vessels containing one-half gallon each of liquor.

Caliente Justice Shows Bias.
"When the parts of the still and the

(Continued on next page)

SOURCE OF "WHITE MULE" DISCLOSED

(Continued from first page.)

liquor were offered in evidence by the district attorney Attorney McNamee for the defense objected on the ground that a man had the right to have a reasonable quantity of liquor in his own home and on the further ground that the still as offered in evidence was incomplete. This objection was sustained by Justice Palmer and the district attorney was forced to continue the fight without the vital evidence of the still parts and the liquor.

"Attorney Scott has informed the Record that Justice Palmer remarked during the trial that 'this man is not going to be bound over anyway unless you prove to my absolute satisfaction that he is guilty.'" This attitude is amusing when it is considered that the laws of the state of Nevada plainly say that a defendant shall be bound over to the district court if there is probable cause for guilt shown.

Caliente Druggist Implicated

"W. A. Theyson, manager of the Caliente Pharmacy was called to the witness stand and testified that on July 12 Kaulbaugh came to him and asked to borrow his Overland car, but that as the machine was not working well he (Theyson) was not over-anxious to allow it to go out, but he agreed to accompany the machine and do the hauling himself. Theyson was certain that he did not know where they were going when they left Caliente, but said that after some little time driving they landed at Klondike Wells, where they found Waddell, Kaulbaugh's partner, and the other member of the alleged gang of moonshiners, who, according to Theyson, mixed up a batch of gems, which were baked and eaten with molasses, the latter being taken from the contents of a barrel on the place. After the 'meal' was finished, Theyson testified the other members of the party rolled up some bedding and also loaded a large box into the automobile. Theyson being told, he said that the box contained cooking utensils. Theyson was so certain that it was not a still that he hauled it to town on this occasion. He testified that he was surprised to find Waddell at the Klondike Wells, as he had believed him to be in Salt Lake.

"E. B. Waddell, Kaulbaugh's partner for whom a warrant was also issued, has not been found and it is believed that he has left the state. He will be arrested as soon as apprehended.

"Incidents relating to the search of the Klondike Wells haunts of the men who were under surveillance by the officers are indeed interesting to the casual reader and are here outlined as related to a representative of the Record by Sheriff William Culverwell when he was in Pioche Monday afternoon.

Sheriff Gets Wise to Facts.

"According to the sheriff, he had reason to believe, without conclusive evidence, however, to prove his opinion, that a still was being operated in Caliente, and that the product therefrom was being peddled in the vicinity. He believed that he had enough evidence to warrant a search being made of the Waddell and Kaulbaugh pool hall, and if necessary the residence of the pair in Caliente. When he visited Pioche at the time of the meeting of the county commissioners June 6 the sheriff confided his belief to District Attorney A. L. Scott and a warrant in blank was issued, to be placed in operation by Mr. Culverwle when he deemed the action most advisable.

"An ever-watchful eye was kept on the comings and goings of the alleged still operators and moonshine whisky peddlers for a period of over thirty days, and the trap was sprung on the night of June 17, when a search was made of Klondike Wells, located four miles south of Bennett Springs, 12 miles from Caliente and at the northern end of Chief mountain. The birds had flown from there, however, but there was evidence to the effect that an effort had been made to destroy the former presence of a still there. A large quantity of prunes and barley around on the ground, three fifty-gallon barrels, three ten-gallon kegs and

"They left camp for Caliente, Theyson said, about 8:30 p. m. but broke down on the road in and were rescued by a sheepman, who took the load on into town, arriving there at 2:30 a. m. on July 13. Theyson admitted that he drove through the back alley to the rear of Kaulbaugh's and Waddell's home, where the load was taken from the machine.

Theyson's Lame Story.

"Theyson said he never saw Waddell again, and that it never occurred to him (Theyson) to ask an explanation for the curious manner in which the load was handled and the fact that they reached the house thru a back alley, etc. He said it was none of his business, although he received no pay for making the trip to Klondike Wells. He further said that it was not at all unusual for him to leave his business in Caliente and embark upon pilgrimages into the country for which he received no pay.

"At the conclusion of the evidence for the state the defendant, W. Kaulbaugh offered no evidence whatever and Justice of the Peace Palmer immediately ruled that there was not enough evidence to warrant the defendant being held for the district court and he was accordingly discharged.

one five-gallon keg were found in the water tank, where they had probobly been placed to keep well soaked up. The officers making the search were Shariff William Culverwell and Deputies J. Less Denton and Lloyd Denton.

Still and Whiskey Located.

"The next day, July 18, a search of the pool hall operated by Waddell & Kaulbaugh in Caliente was conducted, to which Manager Kaulbaugh readily consented, but nothing stronger than soda water was found. At the completion of the search Sheriff Culverwell remarked that "we will now go to your house and see what we can find there." This remark caused a look of consternation to pass over the face of Kaulbaugh and he requested of the sheriff permission to again look at the warrant. This was assented to by the sheriff and as the warant also called for a search of the home further objection upon the part of Kaulbaugh was useless. Sheriff Culverwell requested that Kaulbaugh go with him to the home, but the latter said he was too busy and could not get away, at which the sheriff changed request to a demand and took the pool hall man with him and made a thorough search of his residence.

"One and a half gals. of moonshine liquor was found, together with the still in which it was supposed to have been manufactured. Here once more Kaulbaugh asked a favor of the sheriff and requested a drink of the stuff. saying that it was his own private stock and that his system required a certain amount of the beverage. To this the sheriff consented, but instead of taking a drink, Kaulbaugh is said to have filled a flask, a part of which he drank.

At Least 100 Gallons Output.

"Sheriff Culverwell informed the reporter that in his opinion there had been at least one hundred gallons of moonshine manufactured through the medium of the still and the alleged operators, judging from the amount of refuse discovered at Klondike Well. He said he also believed it was peddled by the gallon and in lesser quantities in the immediate vicinity of Caliente and that some of it was probably taken to Salt Lake where it doubtless could have been easily disposed of.

"According to the sheriff there was a fourth party connected with the operations of the alleged law-breakers in the person of a man said to have hailed from Salt Lake, whose name was never learned and whose identity is unknown. It is known, however, that this man put in his time for about five weeks at Klondike Wells where the still is supposed to have been in operation, and it is believed by those on the inside that he was the "expert" in manufacturing the booze. He is known to have departed for Salt Lake a day or two previous to the search and arrest of Kaulbaugh. As he had several trunks shipped to the Utah city it is also believed that a quantity of booze was transported to Salt Lake in that manner. Sheriff Culverwell notified Salt Lake officials as soon as this information was learned and requested that a lookout be kept for the alleged offender, but to date no information has come to the sheriff's office to the effect that he has been taken into custody.

Paper's Publicity Strikes Home.

"Last week's issue of the Record contained the news of the raid on the home of E. B. Waddell and W. Kaulbaugh, in Caliente, where a still which had been used in the manufacture of "moonshine" liquor was confiscated, in the transportation, at least, Druggist Theyson was implicated.

"Attorney McNamee, who represented Defendant Kaulbaugh, last Tuesday informed the manager of the Record that he had been instructed by Mr. Kaulbaugh to have his subscription to the Record discontinued.

"Two days later, Thursday, a postcard was received from Druggist Theyson instructing the Record to discontinue the four copies being mailed to the news department of the Caliente Pharmacy.

"The Record gladly complies with the requests of these gentlemen, as it desires not to handle any of their ill-gotten gains."

CALIENTE VS. MILFORD

They can't hit 'em, when they can't see 'em, can they Art?

At least that is the way it looked at Caliente last Sunday when Milford took Caliente to a regular annual cleaning, the score being 8 to 1.

There were times during the game that the umpire called time to investigate the possibility of being gently placed on the end of a rope and suspended from the grounds indefinitely. The grandstand fans were sure up in arms at times. You know it pays to carry weight, on such an occasion. This is the information we get from Hickman, and we guess he should know.

The little South Paw let 'em down with three hits and not an earned run. The run was made through an error on Theissen at first. The Milford boys proceeded to extract the Caliente pitcher from the game as soon as the umpire called, "play ball" and they completed the extraction in about the sixth when he was removed by the captain and replaced by a big huskey who they thot would strike out the visitors with ease, but you know there is such a thing as getting disappointed, because the visitors had no trouble in locating the pill.

Don't miss seeing the game between the Soldiers and our boys on Thursday, August 12.

NEVADA BOOSE

A still which has undoubtedly been the source of much "white mule" which has been supplied throughout Nevada and Southwestern Utah was discovered July 17 by Caliente officers. The still was located at what is known as Klondike Well, near Caliente.

W. Kaulbaugh of Caliente was arrested and held for trial, but his case was dismissed by Justice of the Peace, Frank Palmer, on the ground of insufficient evidence. A warrant is also out for E. B. Waddell, Kaulbaugh's partner in the Waddell and Kaulbaugh pool hall at Caliente, but he has not been found and the officers believe he has gone to Salt Lake City.

Four men are supposed to have been implicated in the production of the liquor, and according to the Pioche Record, they are all Utah men.

The Iron County Record prints a full account of the arrest and trial as given in the Pioche Record, which says in part:

"That illicit liquor has been manufactured in and near Caliente by a quartet of Utah offenders who came to Lincoln county for that purpose has been proven beyond the shadow of doubt and the fact that there has been a temporary miscarriage of justice is no fault of the peace officers of this county. In justice to Caliente and Lincoln county it may be said that none of those implicated in the operation and transportation of this illegal plant are Nevada residents, all having come here from Utah, the western home of the moonshiner, less than six months ago.

"There is an undercurrent of opinion prevailing throughout the country that the aid of the federal government will be requested in order to deal with this and other flagrant abuses of the national liquor laws."

While the Pioche Record gives Utah and Utah men the blame in this case, it would seem that someone in Caliente is interested, as this same article states that some prominent business men there have stopped their subscription to the Record since the publication of a similar article the week before.

Box Elder News (Utah)
August 13, 1920

Mr. Lorin Ivins of Lund, Nevada, has been visiting his aunt and uncle, Mr. and Mrs. Abel S. Rich. Mr. Ivins is a young man a member of the Service and has been made a member of the faculty of the Industrial School in Elko, Nevada. Lowell Rich accompanied his cousin to Nevada where he will remain a month.

Beaver County News (Utah)
September 15, 1920

Mrs. Jos. Matthews left Tuesday morning for Caliente to visit her sister, Mrs. H. J. Barton.

Beaver County News (Utah)
September 22, 1920

The Milford ball team went down to Caliente last week to play against the Pioche team, but it is evident that Pioche included part of California, a fact which the Milford boys overlooked. The score stood two to eight against us.

Beaver County News (Utah)
September 29, 1920

Miss Evelyn Williams left on Sunday for Caliente, where she has obtained a position as stenographer for the Salt Lake railroad.

LANDIS BUILDING PLANT TO MANUFACTURE CHINA

Empire China Company Buys a Site of Thirty-Five Acres for Factory

The immediate construction of the first unit of the Empire China Company's plant at Burbank was announced yesterday when the company completed the purchase of thirty-five acres of land in the city limits between the main line of the Southern Pacific railroad and San Fernando boulevard, about a quarter of a mile west of the business district of Burbank. The company plans to erect on this property a factory to cost about $250,000, and the construction of the first unit, which will represent an expenditure of $100,000, will be started at once. According to present plans, the plant will be under operation about January 1 of next year.

The first building to be erected on the site will be an administration and factory building two stories in height, and covering a ground area of 140 by 350 feet. Following this, a grinding, sagger and mould-making building 50 by 200 ft., one story high, will be constructed. Other units will be erected as the need for them arises, the site being ample to provide for a large future expansion. The property is readily accessible to electric power lines and natural gas mains, as well as railroad facilities and paved highways.

The preliminary plans for the group have been prepared by Richard D. King, architect. The buildings, to be of attractive design and appearance, will be of concrete and brick construction throughout. A large amount of glass will be used in the walls and roof, assuring the best possible lighting and ventilation.

Every provision will be made for the comfort of the employees. A large space will be set aside for recreation grounds, on which will be laid out tennis courts and a baseball diamond. Plans also include a clubhouse containing showers and locker rooms. The grounds along the boulevard side will be attractively gardened.

The plant will open with a force of about 150 employees. All of the products used by the company in the manufacture of china tableware are located in Nevada and Southern California and are controlled by this company. John Rowe, who has spent thirty years in the manufacture of china porcelain ware and other clay products will be the superintendent of the new factory. I. Rohrer Landis is the general manager of the company.—Los Angeles Times.

(Ed. Note.—The plant described above is for the purpose of using the material from the property purchased from N. E. Williams and T. J. Parker early in July. The property is located on the line of the Salt Lake railroad this side of Caliente. General Manager Landis has many friends in Vegas who wish him the greatest success in his enterprise.)

Las Vegas Age
October 16, 1920

ODDIE AND ARENTZ ARE STRONG IN THE VALLEY

Meeting at Overton Tuesday Evening Rouses Enthusiasm For Republicans

CALIENTE, Nev., Oct. 13.—Campaigning is slow work in Clark, Lincoln and White Pine counties. After energetic eneavors in southern Clark, Candidates Oddie and Arentz left Las Vegas shortly afternoon Tuesday. Five hours of strenuous driving were required to reach St. Thomas, a distance of 58 miles. Here a few calls were made and arrangements completed whereby some private rigs and the school 'bus transported a majority of citizens to Overton, eight miles further north, for an evening meeting.

The speechmaking was done in the auditorium of the fine district school house at Overton. President W. L. Jones, of the Mormon stake, introduced the Republican candidates. Patriotic music was furnished. President Jones told the audience that a grave responsibility rests upon the voters of Nevada this fall in selecting men to represent the state at the national capital. He commended the candidacy of Tasker L. Oddie for U. S. Senator, and said the people of Clark county, together with those of other sections of the state, had reason to know that Sam S. Arentz would make a capable Representative in Congress.

The Overton audience was a most attentive one and spontaneous applause greeted the speakers as they made their telling points in condemnation of the Wilson administration. Mr. Oddie said the Democratic candidates in Nevada are divided in their campaigning methods and are promising all things to all people in different sections of the state. He condemned this method of striving for votes, and told how he and Captain Arentz are sticking to straight Republican principles.

Sam Arentz was particularly interesting to Clark county voters, wherever he spoke, for the reason that he was the engineer appointed by Gov. Boyle to represent Nevada at the meeting last April of the League of the Southwest. This meeting was to further plans for a reclamation project in southern Nevada, Utah, and Arizona, by means of impounding works in the Colorado river near Las Vegas, probably in Boulder Canyon. Engineers of the Reclamation Service are now at work taking soundings for available foundations for a huge dam. Their supplies come by railroad to St. Thomas. Mr. Arentz has told several of his audiences that he would, if elected to Congress, be particularly interested in furthering legislation which will hasten this great work which promises so much for southern Nevada.

Henry M. Lillis, justice of the peace at Las Vegas, a well known and respected man of Clark county, who had accompanied the candidates on their rocky ride from the county seat, was invited to speak after the candidates. In a pointed talk he told the assemblage that the election of a Republican President of the United States this fall is "as sure as that the sun will rise tomorrow," and he advised all people to elect the Republican candidates for Senator and Representative if they really want results for Nevada. He said voting for a Republican President and a Democratic Senator or Representative would be "arrant nonsense."

Because of impossible trails north from Overton, the campaigning automobile was turned back to Las Vegas. It will take the valley road north from Indian Springs and meet the candidates tomorrow either at this place or Pioche. All members of the party are enjoying the strenuous trip. Many voters are met en route. Representative men are continually being encountered who say they have been consistent Democratic voters in the past, but have become disgusted with the incompetence shown by the present administration, and will vote the Republican ticket this time. Candidates Oddie and Arentz are becoming more forceful in each succeeding speech. They "take" with audiences. Indications are splendid for an increased Republican vote.

At Overton the interesting fact was mentioned that ex-Governor Oddie brought the first automobile into the valley when he was campaigning with Senator Nixon ten years ago. He told an amusing story of the engine stopping in the middle of the river one night, and how he endeavored to avoid getting wet by standing on the springs while he cranked the machine. Naturally enough he fell into the cold water. The machine was of the old chain drive type, and when a start was attempted the chain fell off and a long time was spent hunting for it in the waist dee pwater. Then a link was lost from the chain and an hour or more was spent in making grab samples of the bottom of the river to recover it. The party was exhausted when daylight came, but they had to go on to keep from freezing. As is usual with a real Western man, Mr. Oddie enjoys telling the hard luck story better than describing the success which attended the campaign.

Sam Arentz tells the people he wants to represent the state because he believes he can impress upon Congress the real importance of Nevada and the West, from a practical standpoint. One of his favorite remarks is:

"I believe in and have always practiced, the strenuous life. You get out of life just about what you put into it; and you will get out of Congress just what you put into it."

BANDITS LOOT UTAH BANK.

Rifle Deposit Boxes of Bank at St. George, Taking $5000.

St. George, Utah.—Sometime Saturday night burglars entered the Bank of St. George, opened safety deposit boxes and tried to force the vault and escaped with Liberty bonds and securities estimated hastily, it is said, at $5000.

Entrance was gained by cutting wire from a rear screen and jumping through a transom.

Some residents of the city, aroused during the night, have reported to the authorities that they saw two men leave the bank premises and go west in a Ford touring car at an early hour Sunday morning.

Further west on the road which goes to Callente others reported that the car contained but one man. Searchers who, who out for some distance along the road in an automobile found papers and non-negotiable securities, which had apparently been thrown from the fleeing car.

Charles Doyle, better known as "Biddle", arrived in Callente a few days ago on his way from Columbus, Ohio, and Huntington, W. Va., where he has been spending a several weeks' vacation. Mr. Doyle is employed on the L. A. and S. L. between Los Angeles and Las Vegas.—Callente News.

CALIENTE NEWS

Mrs. George Trent, city treasurer of Islen, is spending the city revenue in Los Angeles.

Tom Himstreet passed through Caliente Monday on his way to Tiajuana, Mexico. where he is going to view the big motor races that are to be pulled off there. Hhe was met at the train by his mother, relatives and friends.

W. C. Ernst and wife returned the past week from Los Angeles, where Mr. Ernst was a patient in the Good Samaritan hospital. The report that Mr. Ernst has been suffering with typhoid seems to have been erroneous as he was afflicted with an ailment that the doctors had difficulty in diagnosing. Mr. Ernst has been very sick and his many friends are glad to have him back again as is Mrs. Ernst welcomed back once more. Mr. Ernst took up his duties again as a conductor on the Pioche branch Wednesday morning.

CALIENTE NOTES

Josh McKosh

Editor Caliente News—will you enlighten me as to why the Salt Lake route issues green tinted checks?—Subscriber.

Subscriber—Anyone but a squarehead would know that the Irish built the Salt Lake road, that is why the pay checks are green. Editor.

Some people are ordering goat glands from Sears Sawbuck Co. in Chicago. Certainly no need of this in a town like Caliente.

Some of the merchants will get their head cut in and make arrangements for a representative from the bank at Pioche to come to Caliente on pay days to handle the railroad checks. Wonder who it will be. Or perhaps the merchants of Caliente will arrange for a clearing house on pay day to handle all checks, which shall it be gentlemen?

L. C. Dutro is filling the position of third trick telegrapher at the union station. Mr. Dutro was formerly located at Milford after his release from overseas duty as a wireless telegrapher.

Some one reports that the forty carloads of giraffes which were sent to Los Angeles to pick oranges could not be used for that purpose until their teeth had been extracted and rubber ones installed as the orange growers complained that the giraffes bruised the oranges with their natural teeth.

A wireless message advises us that former manager Jas. A. McKay, of the Western Union telegraph office of Milford is now located at Garfield, Utah. That he and Supt. Haymond of the B. and G. road are installing a complete sending wireless outfit in order that they may be in close touch with far distant wireless stations.

Beaver County News (Utah)
December 8, 1920

CALIENTE NOTES

Josh McKosh

Editor Caliente News—will you enlighten me as to why the Salt Lake route issues green tinted checks?—Subscriber.

Subscriber—Anyone but a square-head would know that the Irish built the Salt Lake road, that is why the pay checks are green. Editor.

Some people are ordering goat glands from Sears Sawbuck Co. in Chicago. Certainly no need of this in a town like Caliente.

Some of the merchants will get their head cut in and make arrangements for a representative from the bank at Pioche to come to Caliente on pay days to handle the railroad checks. Wonder who it will be. Or perhaps the merchants of Caliente will arrange for a clearing house on pay day to handle all checks, which shall it be gentlemen?

L. C. Dutro is filling the position of third trick telegrapher at the union station. Mr. Dutro was formerly located at Milford after his release from overseas duty as a wireless telegrapher.

Some one reports that the forty carloads of giraffes which were sent to Los Angeles to pick oranges could not be used for that purpose until their teeth had been extracted and rubber ones installed as the orange growers complained that the giraffes bruised the oranges with their natural teeth.

A wireless message advises us that former manager Jas. A. McKay, of the Western Union telegraph office of Milford is now located at Garfield, Utah. That he and Supt. Haymond of the B. and G. road are installing a complete sending wireless outfit in order that they may be in close touch with far distant wireless stations.

Beaver County News (Utah)
December 22, 1920

The Silver Prince Consolidated Mining & Smelting company, owners of the Mount Irish mines in the Pahranagat lake mining district, near Hiko, Lincoln county, Nevada, are developing a large tonnage of silver-lead copper ore on their property and expect to erect a mill at Hiko in the near future.

Salt Lake Mining Review (Utah)
December 30, 1920

History of Hiko District And the Pahranagat Valley

Pahrangat district lies in the southeastern part of Nevada, near the 38th parallel of latitude, and about 115 degrees west from Greenwich. Its distance from Pioche, Nevada, is estimated at about seventy-five miles. The mines were first discovered in March, 1865, by T. C. W. Sayles, John H. Ely, David Sanderson, Samuel S. Strut, William McKlusky and Ira Hatch, Indian interpreter. These parties were from Utah and were guided to the locality by an Indian. A district was formed and many ledges were located. The name given it was the name borne by the Indians living in an extensive valley lying at the foot of the mountain bearing the mineral; the word "pah" meaning water, and "ranagat" any vegetable as melon, squash or pumpkin growing on vines. It is indicative of the agricultural value of this section.

District Named Hiko.

The mountain bearing the mineral was named Mount Irish, in honor of Mr. Irish, the United States Indian agent for the territory of Utah. The place where the discoverers were encamped being at a spring of water in the valley was called by the Indians Hiko, meaning white man, and the village now at that place and formerly county seat of Lincoln county, bears that name.

The chief physical features of the district are Mount Irish, a lofty peak attaining an elevation of 11,000 feet above the sea, with other hills and peaks constituting a range of mountains; the Pahranagat valley, are experienced in winter and frosts are not severe.

Springs and streams afford water for irrigating a large area, which, with the good soil and mild climate, will enable it to furnish such products of the farm, garden and field as the population may require. The springs, of which there are three, Hiko, Crystal and Ash, are natural curiosities, from the amounts of water they pour forth, being 1,000 to 2,000 inches, and the peculiarity of their high temperature, which is from 65 degrees to 75 degrees Fahernheit.

Mountain of Chemically Pure Salt.

A remarkable deposit of salt exists about seventy miles south of Mt. Irish. It is reported to be about five miles in length and 600 feet in height. The body of salt is of unknown depth. It is chemically pure and crystalline, and does not deliquesce on exposure to the atmosphere. Like rock, it requires blasting from the mine, whence it is taken in large blocks as transparent as glass. This would afford an abundant supply to the world, could it be cheaply mined and transported, but it now stands in the wilderness, an object for the admiration of the curious and the inspection of the scientific.

The Early-Day Mines.

The most important mines in 1865 were the Illinois, the Indiana, the Webster and the Alameda. The Illinois lode is situated high up on the eastern slope of Mt. Irish, of some thirty miles in length and twelve in width, a portion of which is agricultural land; and its large and singular springs.

Formation of Porphyry and Lime.

The mountain, as described by Mr. R. H. Stretch, the state mineralogist of Nevada, "is a mass of white porphyritic rock, the flanks consisting of a blackish limestone overlying slates and capped with a heavy body of quartzite. On Silver hill and Sanderson mountain, the outcroppings of the lodes are in limestone. On the western slope of the range crystalline eruptive rocks are abundant." The trend of the mountain range is north and south, and the strike of the vein is generally northeast and southwest with a slight dip to the southeast, or stand nearly vertical. There have been upwards of one thousand locations made, the principal of which are the Illinois, List, Crescent, Bay State, New Hampshire, Eclipse, Utah, Ulric Dahlgren, and Victoria. Many others are worthy of mention, but their developments are slight and the catalogue would be useless.

Rich Valley Close to District.

The valley of Pahranagat lies at an elevation estimated at from 6000 to 7000 feet above the sea but for so great an altitude the climate is warm and pleasant. This is accounted for by its being in a measure open to the valley of the Colorado and the warm region of the south. Very slight snowstorms

and is cut through by a deep canyon giving an opportunity to examine the vein, and to open it by tunnels at a great depth. It crops out boldly, showing an apparent width of from fifteen to twenty feet. The vein has been opened up at several places, and found to be valuable.

The Indiana, on Peter's mountain, has been tapped by a tunnel of 125 feet, at a depth of 120 feet below the croppings, showing a pay streak of six feet in a vein of ten feet between the walls.

The Webster, on Raymond mountain, has been struck by a vertical shaft 100 feet below the croppings, with a pay streak of ten feet in width.

The Alameda made several shipments of high grade ore to Austin for reduction and produced profits of $100.00 per ton; more ore was worked at the Crescent mill, near the vein, yielding $80.00 per ton. The mine development consisted in 1865 of an incline shaft twenty-three feet in depth and a shaft fifty feet deep, from the bottom of which a tunnel has been run to cut the vein.

The early promise of the Pahranagat valley has been more than fulfilled, as is evidenced by the prosperity of both Alamo and Hiko, in its agricultural developments, and it now seems likely that modern methods of transportation and improved milling practice will again give this district the prominence it once had as a producer of mineral wealth.

Beaver County News (Utah)
January 26, 1921

Mr. and Mrs. George A. Trent returned to Islen Sunday, after about thirty days spent on the coast durin gthe holidays. They report a very good time while away but are glad to get back on the works again for the balance of the winter.—Caliente News.

Marion Tanner spent last week in Caliente visiting friends.

Beaver County News (Utah)
February 26, 1921

TRENT HAS A DREAM

Last Friday afternoon, as a signal maintainer, Howard Kanagy, was traveling south on his motor car, making inspection of block signals, he came upon a full grown bob cat, crouched behind a small bush along the side of the railroad track, ready to spring upon him as soon as he came opposite. Fortunately Mr. Kanagy had a shot gun with him which he grabbed at first sight of the cat, and firĕd, sprinkling the cat in the side and near the heart.

After being satisfied that the cat was beyond all danger of attacking him, Mr. Kanagy brought the animal to Islen.

The cat weighed forty pounds and was in splendid condition considering the vast amount of snowfall in the hills.

The mayor of Islen has a house cat of the yellow variety, so in order to see just how yellow the house cat was, it was carried out and placed along side of the bob cat. The house cat took one big whif of the bob cat and just then the tail of the house cat became as large as a barrel and with one mighty big spring. He started toward Caliente making sixty-three miles per hour.

Bob Sands, road master, made a strong protest against such high speed down the canyon, claiming that the sharp curves would not stand under such a strain.

MAKING A MINE AT HIKO, NEVADA.

Last fall Emanuel Decker, of Hiko, Nevada, located a group of six claims for himself and assoicates, including Dr. F. B. Ladd of Fort Wayne, Ind., and others, on the west side of Irish mountain, in the Hiko or Pahranagat district, Lincoln county, Nevada. The Lost Treasure Mines Company was organized to operate the property and Mr. Decker was made the manager. Rich silver-gold-copper ore was quickly uncovered and when the year closed several carloads of ore had been mined and was awaiting transportation facilities to get it to market.

Sample assays of the two carloads or more of ore on the dump gave returns of silver 134 ozs., gold 3.8 ozs., and copper, 11.3 per cent. During the latter part of January Manager Decker came to Salt Lake and purchased trucks with which to transport the ore to Caliente, the nearest railroad station, a distance of fifty-five miles. Mr. Decker landed at the foot of Mt. Irish with his trucks on the 5th of this month. There he encountered two feet of snow and the coldest weather ever known in that region.

The property is located twelve miles west of Hiko and, being unable to reach the ground with the trucks, there was nothing to do but lay off until spring, or until the roads are again in shape for heavy hauling.

It is reported that the property gives every evidence of opening up into a real bonanza mine and the owners are naturally anxious to 'get busy" again. It is declared that when shipping becomes possible much ore of the grade mentioned can be mined and sent to market. As a matter of fact is is stated that selected samples of the ore carries 600 ounces and up of silver, with proportionate higher values in both gold and copper.

Las Vegas Age
April 30, 1921

CALIENTE NEWS EDITOR TAKES BRIDE IN VEGAS

Mr. C. G. Campbell, editor of the Caliente news, and Miss Minda Hogseth, of Chippawa Falls, Wis., met by appointment in Las Vegas Thursday and were united in marriage, Rev. Leo C. Kline officiating.

Mr. Campbell is quite well known in this portion of Nevada through his activity as a newspaper man. Prior to coming to Nevada, he was a resident of Lloyd, Pa.

The bride, who claims Chippawa Falls as her home town, has for several years been dietician of the government public health service, having been stationed at Fox Hills, N. Y., Norfolk, Va. and Fort Bayard, N. M.

The Age, in common with many other friends, is pleased to extend hearty congratulations to Mr. and Mrs. Campbell in their happy venture.

Beaver County News (Utah)
May 4, 1921

Milford Takes Two Games From Beaver

There might have been a baseball game in Beaver Saturday and one in Milford Sunday if it had not been for two minor drawbacks. In Beaver the worse-than-plowed field gave all eighteen players a grouch and it took the entire nine innings for the said grouch to work off. In Milford, the gentle zephyrs which come often enough to cool an otherwise torrid climate, and make our town so much desired when all other towns in the state are suffering with the heat, developed an unusual case of nerves or "suthin" and actually became strong enough to blow a little dust across the diamond.

As stated before, excepting for these two small minor causes, there might have been two good games of baseball. As it was, an attempt was made by both teams to play ball and in a measure success attended their efforts. In Beaver, Bell and Hermansen engaged in a fairly good pitcher's battle, and with any kind of diamond but the type played on, the score would have been 1 to 1 in the ninth instead of 5 to 3 in favor of Milford. For Milford, Barton had the old club working and succeeded in getting three hits—all good ones. Lynch caught the kind of game needed to win, and helped materially in the success of our players. Hermansen, of Beaver struck out 16 of our players—'nuff said.

In Milford, the score was 9 to 6 in favor of Milford, and that is about all that can be said on the subject. We don't know who has control of the weather in Milford, but whoever he is he must have been to the dance the night before and forgot to operate the switches, so that our usual refreshing, cool breeze would come at 5 o'clock rather than at 3. Really at times the breeze was so stiff that several players were compelled to pull their caps down a little tighter in order to stay with them. You could not expect men to play ball under such unheard-of conditions. Anyway Milford won both games and that's that.

Next week the league games begin. Caliente, Provo, Milford, Deseret, and Delta are the five teams comprising the league.

A regular schedule has been adopted and an organization effected which will give us the best baseball ever had in town.

Below is the official schedule adopted by the League. The season will be opened here on May 8, Provo being the team opposing our boys.

	CALIENTE	MILFORD	DESERET-OASIS	DELTA	PROVO	RUSTLE
CALIENTE	DON'T	JULY 10 SEPT. 18	SEPT. 4 SEPT. 5	MAY 29 AUGUST 7	MAY 15 AUGUST 28	MAY 8 AUGUST 21
MILFORD	JUNE 5th AUGUST 14th	FAIL	JULY 3 JULY 4 SEPT. 11	MAY 15 JULY 24 JULY 25	JUNE 12 AUGUST 21	JUNE 26 JULY 31
DESERET-OASIS	MAY 22 JUNE 26 JULY 31	MAY 29 AUGUST 7	TO	JUNE 12 AUGUST 21	JULY 10 JULY 24 JULY 25 SEPT. 18	MAY 15 AUGUST 28
DELTA	JULY 3 JULY 4 SEPT. 11	JUNE 19 AUGUST 28	MAY 8 JULY 17	SUPPORT	MAY 22 JULY 31	JUNE 5 AUGUST 14
PROVO	JUNE 19	MAY 8 JULY 17	JUNE 5 AUGUST 14	JUNE 26 SEPT. 4 SEPT. 5	THESE	MAY 29 SEPT. 11
RUSTLE	JUNE 12 JULY 17 JULY 24 JULY 25	MAY 22 SEPT. 4 SEPT. 5	JUNE 19	JULY 10 SEPT. 18	JULY 3 JULY 4 AUGUST 7	GAMES

Las Vegas Age
May 7, 1921

REDUCE FREIGHT SERVICE TO CALIENTE AND PIOCHE

The public service commission has denied the application of the Los Angeles & Salt Lake line for permission to reduce the daily passenger and express service from Caliente to Pioche, but has permitted the company to run freight trains to Pioche three times a week instead of daily as at present.—Carson City News.

STRAY ELKS PLAN FOR CALIENTE BIG DOINGS

Sixty Candidates From Over Lincoln County To Join With the Herd

Caliente has wired a special invitation to all of the stray Elks of Las Vegas to attend the big initiation at that town on the 19th, 20th and 21st, which will be held under the auspices of Goldfield Lodge No. 1072, B. P. O. E.

A class of sixty candidates, coming from all parts of Lincoln county, will be put through, Friday the 20th.

Arrangements have been made to show the visitors the whole of Lincoln county, Thursday the 19th. Machines will be pprovided, and the bunch will visit Panaca, Pioche and probably the new boom camp of Silverhorn, as well as several of the Valley Towns.

After the initiation, the candidates will be turned over to the Exalted Order of the Golden Buck and the Third Degree will be exemplified by a team furnished from Las Vegas.

The Stray Elks of Las Vegas will hold a meeting Monday evening at 7:30 o'clock in Judge Lillis' office, to arrange the final details of the trip and to ascertain the number that will attend from Las Vegas, and to arrange for railroad rates.

Goldfield will send about thirty, and it is expected that about sixty members will go from Las Vegas.

Dr. Geo. P. DeVine of Goldfield has been delegated by the Goldfield Lodge to make arrangements, and he has been on the job in and around Caliente for the past six weeks getting the class lined upp.

Beaver County News (Utah)
May 11, 1921

One of those nice even rains fell in the canyon which was badly needed on the dry farms between Crestline and Caliente. The rye fields are in splendid condition at this time.

Assistant Foreman Fisher of the tunnel gang, tells this on himself: "The other day I went into the Beanery at Caliente and the waitress in an undertone asked me if I would like a little "white mule" I said "yes." She handed me a card with a little white mule on it.

MILFORD WINS GAME EASY

First League Game Taken from Provo Boys--14 to 8

The Arrowhead league opened the season Sunday with games at Delta and Milford.

Both towns were out in force, giving the league the necessary good start needed to make a successful season.

Our opening game was with Provo and despite the fact that the Provo team were late in arriving, was a good game from every angle.

Pitchers for both teams were hit fiercely, and on one or two occasions the support given was ragged. However, Milford came out on the long end of a 14 to 8 score, so that all errors on our side are easily overlooked.

A crowd of 300 saw the game.

Innings	1	2	3	4	5	6	7	8	9	R	H	E
Provo	0	0	0	1	2	5	0	0	0	8	12	6
Milford	1	0	2	0	5	0	6	0	x	14	16	3

Delta, May 10—In the opening game of the season the Delta club defeated Deseret on the local diamond by a score of 9 to 6. A crowd of about 400 attended the game.

Arrowhead League

Delta	1	0	1,000
Milford	1	0	1,000
Provo	0	1	1,000
Provo	0	1	.000
Deseret	0	1	.000
Caliente	0	0	.000
Lynndyl	0	0	.000

Caliente and Lynndyl no game.

Milford won a so-called game of ball from Beaver yesterday. For perhaps half an inning it looked like a regular affair, but after that—Salt Lake playing in the Coast league, has nothing on Beaver. Score 12 to 6.

Beaver County News (Utah)
May 18, 1921

14 Chalked For Milford Delta Gets 5

Milford Lands on Delta's Bush League Pitcher Unmercifully

The game at the San Pedro park grounds between Milford and Delta, was the best and most interesting game ever seen here.

It was much better than the score would indicate.

Delta went to bat first with Bell in the mound and Lynch behind the bat

Leia the first man at bat swatted the first ball thrown for a little infield hit, which was poorly fielded. Batter easily reached second only to die by a brilliant out at third. Lynch to Ogden.

In Milford's half of the first with fly over first base. It sure was a pippin.

Still another feature of the game was the fact that neither pitcher gave a man a base on balls.

The game was late getting started and was further delayed in the fifth by a passing shower.

Umpires—Hickman and Smith

Score

Innings	1	2	3	4	5	6	7	8	9	R	H	E
Delta	0	0	0	2	0	0	0	1	2	5	16	5
Milford	0	1	4	0	3	1	5	0	x	14	21	3

Batting averages of Milford players for first two League games:

two men on bases and two out. Bell batted out of turn—knocked what would have been a two-bagger, and was declared out retiring the side.

Thebald was in the box for Del-ta, and Cox behind the bat. In the second Lynch knocked the longest fly ever seen on the home grounds—way out over center field. For this he was given an ovation by his many admirers, as he came galloping home with the first run of the game.

Thebald was replaced by Delta's new crack pitcher, Green, but the Milford sluggers recognized only his name and not his pitching ability, and to prove it they made four runs in the next inning.

Among the features of the game, some of the most striking were:

The brilliant catch by Coon in deep center field of what surely looked like a home run batted by Reid Del-ta's chack batter. Reid was so sure of a home run that it was with diffi-culty that he was convinced by his own coachers that he had been rob-bed.

Home runs by Lynch and Coon.

The out Bell to Hickman of Toxer at second, was a pretty piece of work.

Perhaps the most brilliant play of the game was Aller's catch of Bell's

Players	AB	H	R	Av
Ogden	10	6	3	600
Coon H.	9	5	4	555
Astler	10	5	4	500
Bell	8	4	1	500
Winn	4	2	3	500
Fotheringham	10	4	3	400
Barton	8	3	4	375
Thiessen	11	4	3	364
Lynch	10	3	3	300
Hickman	5	1	0	200
Duffin	2	0	0	0
Kirk Al	1	0	0	0
	88	37	28	427

Standing of Club:

	Won	Lost	Pc
Milford	2	0	1,000
Deseret	1	1	.500
Delta	1	1	.500
Provo	1	1	.500
Caliente	0	1	.000
Lynndyl	0	1	.000

Sunday games resulted as follows:
At Deseret—Deseret, 8; Caliente, 4
At Milford—Milford 14; Delta 5
At Lynndyl—Provo 7; Lynndyl 6

Schedule for Sunday:
Milford at Caliente.
Provo at Delta.
Lynndyl at Deseret.

Mr. and Mrs. Hugh Barton and Sam Barton, of Caliente, are in Mil-ford for a few days.

Las Vegas Age
May 21, 1921

ODDFELLOWS WILL GO TO CALIENTE NEXT TUESDAY

About twenty-five members includ-ing the degree team, of Artesia Lodge No. 22, I. O. O. F., will go to Caliente Tuesday, May 24.

They expect to confer the degrees of the order on about 50 candidates, and to have a general good time in the meanwhile.

ARROWHEAD LEAGUE
CLUB STANDING

Milford—Won 2, lost 1, per cent .667.

Delta—Won 2, lost 1, per cent .667.

Deseret—Won 2, lost 1, per cent .667.

Caliente—Won 1, lost 1, per cent .500.

Provo—Won 1, lost 2, per cent .333.

Lynndyl—Won 0, lost 2, percent .000.

Miss Ella Johnston returned this week from a trip to Caliente.

WEARING CREPE

It was a sad looking bunch of ball players and rooters that returned Monday noon from Caliente Manager Pratt Root was wearing a big rosette of crepe, presented by Josh Mc-Kosh of Islen, and Barney wanted to borrow 39c with which to get a sandwich and a cup of coffee. Earl hadnt a word to say, and Bell has stopped ringing. Well, Milford can't always win, and Caliente needed a little encouragement.

The game was very interesting to Caliente, and the score close—9 to 10 with Milford on the short en.

Mr. and Mrs. H. T. Hanks and little daughter, Catherine, attended the ball game at Caliente Sunday.

ODD FELLOWS & REBEKAHS HAVE CAPTURED CALIENTE

At the request of the Grand Master of the Grand Lodge of I. O. O. F. of Nevada, the degree team of Artesia Lodge No. 43, of Las Vegas, went to Caliente, and instituted a new lodge, Meadow Valley Lodge No. 46, Tuesday night, May 25.

The degree team which went from this city included Henry M. Lillis, Degree Master; F. A. Stevens, Noble Grand; Wm. E. Orr, Vice-Noble Grand; Arthur R. Anderson, Past Grand; H. J. Woodard, Chaplain; A. S. Henderson, Outside Conductor; E. K. Hull, Conductor; Thomas D. Fanatia, Warden; Lester Stocker, Inside Guardian; W. F. Rector, Right Scene Supporter; Jack Reynolds, Left Scene Supporter; Harley A. Harmon, David; Lee Collins, Outside Guardian; J. G. Bisinger, Right Supporter of Noble Grand.

The members of the degree team were so well trained that the same members of it could put on Initiatory, and each of the other three degrees.

Grand Lodge officers present were George P. Armstrong, Grand Master, A. S. Henderson, D. D. Grand Master and P. C. Christian, Past Grand Master.

The Grand Lodge was opened at 7 p. m., Pacific time, and at 6 a. m., May 25, Meadow Valley Lodge No. 46 with a class of 22 candidates, had been duly installed, all of the degrees conferred, its officers duly elected, appointed and installed, and was open for business.

During the same period, a Rebekah Lodge was instituted. Miriam Rebekah Lodge No. 29, of Pioche came to Caliente with its degree team, and under the supervision and authority of Jennie E. Werner, President of the Rebekah Assembly of I. O. O. F., of Nevada, assisted by Rose F. Armstrong, instituted Wildey Rebekah Lodge No. 38, with a membership of 22, and a waiting list to be installed ater. The instituting of a lodge of Odd Fellows and a Rebekah lodge in 12 hours, when both lodges had to be instituted in the same hall, is a record never before made in Nevada, and shows what can be accomplished where well drilled degree teams are engaged in the work.

Two ladies went from Vegas with the team, Mrs. Jack Reynolds and Mrs. E. K. Hull.

THE ANTLERED HERD ENJOYED CALIENTE

Visiting Elks Given a Big Time Friday and Saturday — 63 Members in the Class

Martial law was declared for Caliente during Friday and Saturday of last week. Business of all kinds was suspended and extra train crews had to be called from Milford and Las Vegas to keep the trains running.

It was only through the severe penalties imposed by Judge Underhill that the town resumed normalcy. The main disturbers were local residents, and after they had been fined for everything they possessed, they faced the problem of returning to work or starving. The Judge was not so severe on the out of town rioters; they were left their clothes and sufficient money to get out of town.

It certainly was worth it and Caliente set an enviable mark as hosts and good fellows. A dance starting early Thursday evening and ending late Friday morning furnished the initial pep, and from then on things began to go. A roulette wheel was set up on the main thoroughfare, and no one had a chance to win except the banker. At the base ball game much money was lost betting that Enterprise would get to first. And then came the initiation.

Sixty-three baby elks became full fledged members of Goldfield Lodge No. 1072 ,B. P. O. E. These came mostly from Caliente, but Pioche sent a dozen candidates, Panaca, Silverhorn, Alamo and even Moapa and Logandale sent their quotas.

During initiation, a midnight lunch was served at Warren hall, where the ladies were entertaining the visiting ladies while their men were being put through. The brothers then returned to the Rex theatre for the final degree and the goat was butting the last candidate as the clock struck thee.

After that a goodly number went to bed, but high-bailiff Wm. Culverwell had them all routed out and before the court by noon the next day. If you refused to get up and dress you were loaded, bedding and all, into the patrol truck and haled before the high Judge to answer for the sins of your past life.

Saturday evening the Elks and their ladies attended a most beautiful banquet prepared by the ladies of Caliente. The tables were loaded with purple and white flowers, and all kinds of good things to eat and drink. There were covers for one hundred only, which necessitated the setting of a second table after the first had finished.

J. L. Denton as toastmaster, called on several for toasts, and appropriate responses were made by the officers of Goldfield Lodge, including the Exhalted Ruler, L. L. Dillinger, State Deputy Dunn, Foley and others.

A dance was in progress when the banquet let out, and at four o'clock Sunday morning the last shimmie was shimmied, the orchestra quit from exhaustion, and thus ended the biggest and happiest event in the history of Caliente.

I. O. O. F. FORMED AT CALIENTE

I. O. O. F and Rebekah lodges were formed at Caliente last week and several former Milford people were elected to prominent positions.

Mrs. W. C. Ernst was elected as Noble Grand of the Rebekah lodge and Mrs. Press Duffin was elected secretary.

Mr. W. C. Ernst was installed in the chair of Junior past grand of the I. O. O. F. by the State Grand Master and was also appointed as deputy grand master and will be delegate to the Grand lodge convening at Reno, June 21.

Larue Duffin, Pratt Root, Mr. and Mrs. H. T. Hanks and A. P. Neff attended the Elk's roundup in Caliente last week.

THREE IN A ROW

Deseret, Delta and Cedar City Teams Fall before Milford Invincibles

Delta and Cedar Shut Out Entirely on Decoration Day

It is seldom that a small town gets as enthusiastic over baseball as Milford is today. And who can blame it. A winning team always makes the fans feel good, but to win such a game as the Delta game Monday, makes the whole town happy, and the loss of the game at Caliente ten days ago is forgiven, but not forgotten.

The league game played last Sunday at Deseret, was won by Milford with a score of 17 to 9, Theissen and Lynch battery. Delta played at Caliente the same day and won 23 to 3.

Milford had arranged a game for Decoration Day with Cedar City, when Delta sent up word from Caliente, that they would like a game here on their way home, and Milford obliged her by saying "come on"

Two games were therefore played here Monday. The first one with Delta team fresh from its victory over Caliente and full of enthusiasm, and money—Caliente's money. And by the way Caliente, we wish to thank you for returning our loan so promptly.

Delta was provided with a dark horse in form of a semi-professional pitcher, who was supposed to be able to shut out the Milford team, but they forgot that Milford had a little semigambian named Kinney, who pitched for us last season—and believe me, he is some twirler.

The game was a real pitcher's battle, with honors very slightly in favor of Kinney. But when it came to support, the Milford team was airtight. The batteries were Kinney and Lynch for Milford and Unknown and Cox for Delta.

Milford made three hits and Delta two. At no time was Delta able to knock the ball out of the infield.

The unknown issued only one base on balls and struck out ten men, while Kinney issued two bases on balls and struck out 15 men. Milford team had only one error charged up against it, and Delta had nine. It was a great game. Score 4 to 0.

The second game was played against Cedar City and was fairly a good game, but following the Delta game it looked rather tame. Milford won with a score of 8 to 0.

NOTES

The crepe which Caliente hung on our manager down in Nevada, May 31st, was passed on to Delta who we understand promptly forwarded it to Caliente as security. Milford extends its heartfelt sympathy to Caliente as we understand that Caliente financed Delta's team while here.

Caliente, we thank you for returning our doll rags—some of them we do not recognize.

Ez Barton is sure playing a pretty game at first.

If any amateur team in Utah has a better catcher than Earl Lynch, we would like to meet the gentleman.

Milford will loc khorns with Caliente on the SanPedro grounds, here, next Sunday. It will be a game for blood. Let everybody turn out and see our boys in action. Hermanson and Lynch will be the battery.

ARROWHEAD LEAGUE
CLUB STANDING

Club	Record	Pct.
Milford, won 3; lost 1		750
Delta, won 3; lost 1		750
Deseret, won 2; lost 2		500
Caliente, won 1; lost 2		333
Provo, won 2; lost 2		500

A MOST PECULIAR LAW

The Anti law which went into effect? this week, has some most peculiar points to it.

A merchant in Utah cannot sell or give away cigarets or the makins, but a merchant in Caliente or Evanston can sell them in Utah. No Utah newspaper can advertise them, but the Saturday Evening Post or Ladies Home Journal can.

It is a crime to sell them in Utah, but no crime to smoke them. It is a big boost for mail order houses, which are the curse of Utah

BASEBALL

Results of last Sunday Games—
At Milford, Milford 12; Caliente, 1.

At Delta, Lynndyl 4; Delta 10.
At Provo, Deseret 3; Provo 5.

Standing of Teams—
Milford—won 4; lost 1; percentage 800.
Delta—won 4; lost 1; per centage 800.
Provo—won 3; lost 2; percentage 600.
Deseret—won 2; lost 3; percentage, 400.
Caliente—won 1; lost 3; percentage 250.

Next Sunday's Games—
Provo at Milford
Delta at Deseret
Lynndyl at Caliente.

CALIENTE FANS THE AIR--CANT HIT HERMANSON

We mean that Milford almost shut Caliente out, but not quite. The score was 12 to 1.

The slaughter was awful. Blood on every sack, but it wasn't Caliente's blood, for no Caliente player occupied 3rd long enough to bleed. In fact only one ever saw third, and he was going so fast that he was never introduced to it.

The batteries were Hermanson and Lynch for Milford, and Delaney Stephenson and Cook for Caliente.

Caliente came to bat first and retired one, two, three. Hermanson fanned ten out of the first twelve men up just to show what he could do. After that he eased up a little and that was the time Fieldson. Caliente's 3rd bagger made the only hit his team got, a long home run dr' to right just over first base. This was the only ball to reach Milford outfield, in fact it was the only ball which has reached the home teams out field and the only run made against the home team the past three games. That is some record.

Ez Barton hit a home run in the third with one on; and Ogden made a homer in the fourth, which was a pippin.

In a game so well played as the game played by Milford, it is hard to pick out the high points, but it is safe to say that Hermanson and Lynch played good ball, but we are inclined to give the cake to Barton at first—five hits, one home run, in five times up, four runs and no errors is about as good a day's record as you could reasonably expect. And by the way, that catch made by Hickman, over second, was no slouch of a play.

Milford pitcher is credited with 18 strikeouts and one base on balls, with only one hit made off his delivery.

Two Caliente pitchers are credited with 8 strikeouts and one base on balls and sixteen hits.

Seventeen Caliente men were put out before one reached first base.

Only three Caliente men reached first base.

Innings	1	2	3	4	5	6	7	8	9	R	H	E
Caliente	0	0	0	0	0	0	1	0	0	1	6	
Milford	1	0	3	1	4	2	0	1	x	12	16	2

Beaver County News (Utah)
June 15, 1921

ARROWHEAD LEAGUE

Standing of the Clubs—

Milford—Won 5; lost 1; .834 per cent.

Delta—Won 5; lost 1; .834 per cent.

Provo—won 1; lost 3; .250 per cent.

Caliente—won 1; lost 3; .250 per cent.

Deseret—won 1; lost 4; .200 per cent.

Sunday Results—

At Milford—Provo. 1; Milford 14

At Deseret—Delta 13. Deseret 4.

Caliente and Lynndyl. no games.

Games Next Sunday—

Milford at Delta

Deseret at Lynndyl

Caliente at Provo.

Beaver County News (Utah)
June 22, 1921

ARROWHEAD LEAGUE

Standing of the Clubs—

Delta—won 5; lost 1; percentage .883.

Milford—won 5; lost 2, percentage, .714.

Provo—won 2 ;lost 3; percentage .400.

Caliente—won 1 ;lost 4 ;percentage .200.

Deseret—won 1; lost 4; percentage .200.

Games Sunday—

At Delta—Milford 2; Delta 3.

At Caliente—Provo 12; Caliente 7.

At Deseret—No game.

Games Next Sunday—

Delta at Provo.

Caliente at Deseret.

Milford—No game.

Box Elder News (Utah)
July 15, 1921

Mrs. D. W. Henderson of Ogden, entertained Wednesday afternoon at Lorin Farr Park in honor of Mrs. Le Roy D. Young and her guest Mrs. Floyd H. Denton of Caliente, Nevada.

Davis County Clipper (Utah)
August 8, 1921

* * *

The Caliente Commercial club, of Nevada, which is fostering the Lincoln county fair, called a meeting for the purpose of getting the fair commission organized for the season of 1921, and selected J. L. Denton, chairman; C. G. Campbell, secretary; C. L. Alquist, treasurer, and Gardner Chism of Alamo as chairman in charge of agricultural exhibits.

* * *

Iron County Record (Utah)
August 12, 1921

Miss Jesma Stewart of Alamo, Nevada, is visiting in Cedar at the home of her aunt, Mrs. John Fuller. Miss Stewart is here under the doctor's care.

CALIENTE SEEKS STATE AID FOR COUNTY FAIR

Plans Making Fair This Fall Bigger and Better Than Any Before Held

Senator E. W. Griffith, of Las Vegas, was in Caliente Monday evening and addressed the Lincoln county fair committe on fairs, farming and legislation.

Mr. Griffith has been senator from Clark county for a number of years and has been active on matters of importance to all parts of Nevada and especilly to this southern section.

At the last session of the legislature Senator Griffith sponsored a bill creating the Southern Nevada Agricultural board to promote the welfare of ranches in our section.

Senator A. L. Scott was also on the job and got a bill through bringing Lincoln county under jurisdiction of the board. From the sum appropriated to the board this county has already benefitted to the extent of $1,000.

The sum is used to help defray the expenses of the county agent. Thus dispensed it is doing a general good that will benefit both now and in the future.

Senator Griffith explained that out of the fund he would try to secure Lincoln county $500 to be used for premiums but could not guarantee the sum owing to opposition of the attorney general who holds that the county fairs do not tend toward better farming.

Senator Griffith is leaving Las Vegas for Carson City Friday and will make a plea before the dispensors of the fund to the end that the fair till is enriched in the sum above named.

The fair secretary has written a letter to Senator Griffith setting forth all the advantages which are accruing to Lincoln county as a result of the fair.

Using this letter as a basis the senator will lay the matter before those thru whom the money comes in a manner which usually gets results.

County Agent Gardner Chism was in attendance at the fair meeting and gave same valuable pointers on fairs and how they should be organized earlier so that ranchers might have more time to place displays.

Mr. Chism in getting around over the county finds considerable interest in the farming communities regarding the fair with large numbers intimating that they will bring in displays this year.

The secretary is in correspondence with a carnival company and if it comes included in the equipment are a ferris wheel, merry-go-round, with a number of side showes and concessions, enough to make a whole fair in itself.

Evxerything points toward a good exhibition this year and the commission is working consistently with that end in view.

Beaver County News (Utah)
August 24, 1921

HOT GAME COMING

The Caliente ball team has issued a challenge to the Milford team to play a ball game next Sunday at Caliente, for a purse of $2,000.

Milford has accepted on condition that the game be played on neutral ground and suggests either Beaver, or Delta as acceptable.

Jack Theissen went to Caliente this morning to see if satisfactory arrangements can be made.

Mrs. H. J. Barton of Caliente was in Milford Friday and Saturday.

Las Vegas Age
September 3, 1921

CALIENTE PERSONALS

(Caliente News.)

Joe Kutcher of the American Clay Co. was unable to attend the big factory warming at Burbank on account of rush of work at the kaolin camp.

Ike Orr of Pioche left last week for Las Vegas to spend a couple of weeks.

W. M. Kessler and wife of Las Vegas arrived in Caliente Tuesday to make their home while Mr. Kessler pursues his work a fireman.

Ira Baxter has now taken an engineer run on the main line since being bumped from the switch engine. —Caliente News.

Beaver County News (Utah)
September 16, 1921

FIRE AT CALIENTE

The Salt Lake hotel caught fire shortly before noon Friday and burned 'till it was a total loss despite the heroic efforts of the fire-fighters to save it.

Hose attached to the switch engine threw water on the flames but before long the pressure gave out and little could be done. Meantime an army of railroad employees and town people were busy removing everything in sight.

All movable effects were gotten out in fairly good shape and the only loss was the building itself. All canned goods were in the cellar and were saved.

From 20 to 30 employees in the hotel here in Caliente, will now be thrown out of employment temporarily. Passengers are served meals at the town cafes. A defective flue is probably the cause of the fire—Caliente News.

Las Vegas Age
September 17, 1921

CALIENTE RAILROAD HOTEL TOTALLY DESTROYED BY FIRE

The Salt Lake hotel caught fire shortly before noon Friday and burned till it was a total loss despite the heroic efforts of the fire fighters to save it.

Hose attached to the switch engine threw water on the flames but before long the pressure gave out and little could be done. Meantime an army of railroad employees and town people were busy removing everything in sight.

All movable effects were gotten out in fairly good shape and the only loss was the building itself. All can goods in the cellar were saved.

From 20 to 30 employees at the hotel here in Caliente will now be thrown out of employment temporarily. Passengers are served meals at the town cafes. A defective flue is probably the cause of the fire.—Caliente News.

Box Elder News (Utah)
September 20, 1921

Mrs. Dan Davic of Caliente, Nevada, and Mrs. Charles Hill of Evanston, Wyo., are visiting friends and relatives here. They came to attend the funeral of their father, Mr. Andrew Stratford, which was held Friday.

Beaver County News (Utah)
September 23, 1921

Mrs. Hugh Barton of Caliente, is spending a few days here looking after her property interests.

Las Vegas Age
October 1, 1921

Dr. and Mrs. Wm. S. Park , Mr. and Mrs. Leo A. McNamee and Mrs. McCrystal motored to Caliente Wednesday to attend the Lincoln county fair.

Dr. and Mrs. E. M. Dobbs are in Lincoln county where they expect to remain for about two weeks. They visited the Lincoln county fair at Caliente during the week.

Beaver County News (Utah)
October 21, 1921

Mr. and Mrs. Paul Roberts, of Caliente, are the proud parents of a nine and a half pound baby boy, born on Tuesday, October 11. Grandpa Kuckenmeister is doing nicely.

Las Vegas Age
November 5, 1921

WHITE CROSS DRUG CO. CHANGES OWNERSHIP

Gratto Sells To Ralph Wilson and Himself Buys Drug Store at Caliente

Mr. Ralph Wilson has purchased the interest of Earl B. Gratto in the White Cross Drug Company and has assumed the management of the business. Mr. Gratto has purchased the drug store at Caliente and will leave shortly to take possession.

Mr. Wilson has been in the employ of the White Cross for some time and has made many friends who will be pleased to hear of his advance in the business world. On the other hand Vegas will greatly miss Mr. and Mrs. Gratto from business and social circles.

Beaver County News (Utah)
November 18, 1921

G. I. A. to B. of L. E.

The ladies of the G. I. A to B of L E. entertained at the home of Mrs. George Ranson Thursday afternoon of last week, with a quilting bee.

Members present were: Mrs. Frizzell Mrs. Killam, Mrs. Jeffers, Mrs. Steenbock.

Invited guests were: Mrs. Delbert Duffin, Mrs. Chas. Newhart and Mrs. Rogers of Caliente.

Dainty refreshments were served.

Beaver County News (Utah)
December 9, 1921

FAREWELL SOCIAL EVENT

Saturday afternoon a farewell social function was given by the members of the Homemakers' club, complimentary to Mrs. C. I. Himstreet and Mrs. W. C. Ernst, who are leaving Caliente soon to take up their residence in Milford, Utah Mrs. Himstreet will be in Milford; likewise Mrs. Ernst.

The party was very well attended and the usual game of Five Hundred was played.

—Caliente News.

MILFORD JEWELERS IN TOWN

C. S. Arnold and E. E. Mueller, jewelers of Milford, were in Caliente the first of the week. They have been appointed railway watch inspectors and also have a fine stock of new jewelry for the holiday and regular trade. Their ad is on an inside page of this issue.—Caliente News.

MAY ESTABLISH AIR DELIVERY SERVICE

Frank Dorbandt of Salt Lake has been in our city this week. Mr. Dorbandt married a Lincoln county girl Miss Mary Ann Price, who is very well known in Caliente and they have been visiting at Mrs. Dorbandts home near Pioche, but at present, Mrs. Dorbandt is calling on friends in Panaca while he went to Las Vegas on business.

Mr. Dorbandt is an aviator of skill and daring and during the summer was chief of the Deseret News airplane squad. He and his flying partner, Rex Smith, gave exhibition flights at many fairs throughout the northwest during the summer and at more than one place were the crowds thrilled by the daring of the two bold aviators.

Exchanges is speaking of the exhibitions staged by the fliers tell how Mr. Dorbandt walks about on the wings of the plane while soaring at an immense height, and at other times he will tempt fate by flying while hanging to the plane by the knees or feet. He has had narrow escapes on a number of occasions.

Mr. Dorbandt says he is planning on opening a transfer airplane line probobly in Utah, and that other parties will extend the system so the line will connect Salt Lake City and Los Angeles whereby mail, express and passengers will be carried by air between the two cities by wayq of Milford and Caliente and Las Vegas.—Caliente News.

Beaver County News (Utah)
December 16, 1921

Mr. and Mrs. Ira Baxter of Caliente, came up to attend the ball given by the Elks Friday night.

J. W. Dinwiddie of Caliente, Nev., made an over Sunday visit with relatives here.

Beaver County News (Utah)
January 13, 1922

John Hansen of American Fork, passed through Milford enroute to Caliente and made a short call at the home of his cousin, Mrs. James Tanner. Mr. Hausen is a carpenter, and was going to help repair and build the bridges which were washed out by the recent storms.

Las Vegas Age
January 21, 1922

CALIENTE WILL HAVE GOOD SCHOOL BUILDING

When completed Caliente will have a splendid school building, a credit and an asset to the town for years to come. It is to be one to which we can point with pride when friends come to visit us .

The building is to be what carpenters call a double-L in shape and roughly 49x90 feet in size. One end will be taken up by an assembly and study room while the opposite end will be devoted to manual training and domestic science rooms while the intervening space is to be used for class rooms.

Arrangements are made for book rooms, closets, lavatories and toilets while there wil be ample play ground for all the students. Work will, no doubt, begin as soon as preliminaries can be arranged and the warm weather opens.—Caliente News.

Beaver County News (Utah)
February 17, 1922

LEAVING FOR CALIFORNIA

Mrs. Addie Toland was given a pleasant surprise by her friends, at her home, No. 7, railroad row, Tuesday night. The evening was spent in playing five hundred with Mrs. Itha Kinney and Mrs. Russell Parsons winning the prizes.

Mrs. Toland was presented with a beautiful hand-painted dish.

At midnight, a delicious luncheon was served by Mesdames Newhart, Cuddy and Jeffers The dining room was decorated with valentine day colors of red and white. The favors and place cards were valentine designs.

Those present were:

Mrs.: Clark Kesler, Mrs. Leslie Clay, Mrs. George Fernley, Mrs. Harry Yeager, Mrs. Russell Parsons, Mrs Enis Jonesfi, Mrs. Lulu Germo, Mrs. George Ranson, Mrs. George Rogers, Mrs. Jo. Kinney, Mrs. Henry Hunter, Mrs. Addie Toland, guest of honor. Miss Martha Walker, Mrs. Charles Newhart, Mrs. C. W. Cuddy, Mrs. J. Jeffers, Mrs. Hortop of Los Angeles.

Mrs. Toland and her daughter are leaving soon to make their home in Caliente. Their many friends and acquaintances regret to have them leave, but wish them success and happiness in their new home.

Beaver County News (Utah)
March 3, 1922

SURPRISE PARTY

A number of friends surprised Mrs Wm. Ernst Wednesday afternoon, at her home. The occasion was her birthday anniversary. The afternoon was spent with cards and social time, after which a dainty luncheon was served to Mrs. Ernst, Mrs. Chas. Himstreet, Mrs. Otto Steenbock, Mrs. Phil Orwin, Mrs. George Himstreet, of Caliente, Mrs. John Hanlon.

Beaver County News (Utah)
March 10, 1922

H. F. Dinwiddie is taking a vacation from his work on the B & B. gang in the canyon near Caliente.

Beaver County News (Utah)
March 17, 1922

Father Slatery of Caliente, spent Sunday, March 5 here among his parishioners. Mass was held at the Armstrong home. A movement is being made to build a chapel and a neat sum has already been raised.

Beaver County News (Utah)
March 24, 1922

Clyde Casterline of Caliente, was the dinner guest at the home of Mrs. Lulu Germo Sunday.

Las Vegas Age
March 25, 1922

Joe Kutcher and I. R. Landis, foreman of the kaolin mine and general superintendent, respectively, of the American Clay company, arrived in Caliente Wednesday from the camp near Elgin. They made the trip by car and they are about the first ones to get through by auto since the big washout of earlier in the year. The roads are mighty rough but they got here, explained Mr. Kutcher. Mr. Landis states that the company at Burbank have shipped two car loads of dishes back east and he therefore is highly elated over the fact especially since the dishes are giving such good satisfaction because of their good quality. The camp at Elgin is supplied now with company made dishes, Mr. Kutcher says.—Caliente News.

Las Vegas Age
April 1, 1922

CALIENTE NOW HAS LIBRARY

The Homemaker's Club in Caliente has opened a public library. Books and magazines are kept at their club rooms and are accessible on Thursday and Sunday afternoons.

Beaver County News (Utah)
April 7, 1922

INITIATION

Victory Rebekah Lodge No. 43, held regular session Wednesday evening, with a large attendance. Initiation was the order of the evening.

The candidates were: Elizabeth Swanson, Theo Kronholm and Jack Sherwood.

Delegates were elected to attend the Rebekah assembly which will be held at Provo, April 18. Those elected were: Frances Jefferson, Lulu Germo and Katherine Cline.

A dance will be given by the lodge in honor of the anniversary of the order, April 26.

At the close of the meeting, delicious ice cream and cake were served by the committee in charge: Lulu Germo, Mrs. Harry Griffiths, Mable Coleman and Hallie Sherwood.

Mr. Carl Fuchs, of Rachel Rebekah Lodge No. 8, Harlowton, Montana; W. W. Smith, Noble Grand of Meadow Valley Lodge No. 48, Caliente, and Mrs. William Ernst, Past Noble Grand of the Meadow Valley Rebekah Lodge were present and gave splendid talks.

G. I. A. ANNUAL DANCE

It has been said by a number that the dance given by the G. I. A. Saturday night, at the opera house, was one of the best ever given here. A large crowd attended and it was a big success, both socially and financially.

Among those from out of town who attended the dance were: Mr. and Mrs. Millsap, of Caliente, who were guests of Mr. and Mrs. Sam Reveal.

Mrs. George Dearing and two daughters, of Salt Lake City.

Mr. and Mrs. Ez. Barton.

Mrs. Dan Williams of Beaver, came from Beaver Monday morning to meet her daughter, Mrs. Evelyn Anders, of Caliente. She was a guest at the home of Mrs. John Williams. They left the same evening for Salt Lake.

Mr. and Mrs. Eugene Hughes and two little girls, people without means landed in vicinity Sunday and applied to the Red Cross for aid. They were fed and sheltered over Sunday and one-half of their car fare paid to Caliente.

W. W. Smith and A. E. Wicks, of Caliente were up to the Safety meeting on Wednesday.

D. V. Harris and J. H. Handley

Beaver County News (Utah)
May 5, 1922

M. B. Mosher, of Inglewood, California, who was shot while rading a house to get a couple of boot-leggers, who had been operating there for some time and proper officials had not tried to enforce the law. It is thought he was a member of the Ku Klux Klan. With him was his son who was severely wounded. Mr. Mosher has visited friends in Nada several years ago. He leaves a wife and two sons who have many friends here.

Mrs. Swartsfinger and daughter returned Wednesday from Caliente, where they have been visiting their son and brother.

Iron County Record (Utah)
May 5, 1922

Marion Millett is in Caliente working at the cement business. His family moved there this week. We understand that Mr. Millett has all the work he can possibly attend to this season, which necessitated his wife going there in order to do the cooking for the men working with him.

* * *

CALIENTE IS FIGHTING
FOR LINCOLN COUNTY SEAT

Lincoln county is facing a county seat fight, Caliente having begun a campaign for removal of the seat of the county government from Pioche to Caliente. There are many arguments advanced for the change, chief of which is the location of Pioche on the branch line of the railroad over thirty miles from the main line.

THE CALIENTE NEWS
CHANGED HANDS LAST WEEK

A deal was consummated last week whereby the ownership of the Caliente News passes into the hands of J. C. McDonald, of Pioche and Ely, a newspaper man of wide western experience.

The Caliente News will be run as an independent weekly paper for the benefit of Caliente and Lincoln county as a whole and every effort will be made to properly serve the best business interests of all the advertisers and subscribers who have, by their support in the past, made the Caliente News an influence for real progress in the Railroad town.

Mr. C. G. Campbell, who has conducted the paper with satisfaction to Caliente and the county for the past two years, expects to leave for Oceanside, California, about May 15th, where he has business interests. Mr. Campbell will leave many friends in Caliente who recognize that he has done much to build up the town and promote progress.

E. C. D. Marriage, who has resided in Lincoln county for the past 18 years has been engaged by Mr. McDonald as associate editor and he will take up his new duties at Caliente about May 15th.—Pioche Record.

Las Vegas Age
May 27, 1922

Caliente has qualified at Washington as being both up-to-date and veracious. An extensive petition regarding the appointment of a postmaster reached Congressman Arentz last week. The paper was unusually complete as such things go, in the matter of careful attention given to stating occupation and residence of the signers. There were "laborers" and "car men" and "engine men" and "merchants" and so on, and many feminine names giving the occupation of "housewife". Beside one pretty little signature the word "flapper" appeared as the occupation of the subscriber.

Beaver County News (Utah)
June 9, 1922

Mrs. Sam Reveal and children returned Saturday evening from a few days visit in Caliente.

NOWERS—CASTERLINE

Miss Ethel Nowers and Mr. Clyde Casterline were united in marriage Sunday evening at 10:30 at the home of Mr. and Mrs. Jack McCann.

The Rev. Zook of the Methodist church performed the ceremony. The bride and groom were attended by their sister and brother, Mrs. Lulu Germo and Mr. Floyd Casterline.

The remainder of the evening was spent with social time and luncheon was served.

The bride is a fine young woman. She was born in Beaver, where she obtained her education, but for several years has worked here as operator on the telephone exchange.

The groom is a well respected young man and has been an employe here of the Union Pacific railroad for some time. After a short honeymoon, the happy couple will be at home to their friends at Caliente, after July 1st.

FALLS FROM GRACE—Clyde Casterline, veteran member of the Batchelor club, a man's man, and an all round good sport, has fallen from grace and his many friends will know him no more. Reliable reports state that he has resigned from the club and while the Ladie's name has not as yet been learned, the gaily decorated trunks which arrived on No. 3 yesterday, indicate a long life of wedded bliss—Caliente News.

Mrs. Clyde Casterline of Caliente, spent several days here with her sister, Mrs. Lulu Germo, last week. She returned home Sunday, accompanied by her nephews, David Engleke and Master Harold Germo.

Ralph Casterline of Caliente, attended the Elks' dance here Saturday night and went on to Salt Lake Sunday morning.

Las Vegas Age
July 29, 1922

INJUNCTION MADE PERMANENT AT VEGAS AND CALIENTE

The application of the Union Pacific for an injunction against strikers in Clark County towns, pendente lite, was granted yesterday by Judge E. S. Farrington of the United States district court after a hearing and consideration of affidavits presented by Attorney Fred Pettit, of Los Angeles. The affidavits were fourteen in number and were in support of the eight contentions set out in the order to show cause issued by Judge Frank S. Dietrich before he left the state after having presided at the Henderson-Journal trial.

Acts of violence on the part of strikers, and beating up the company employees, taking men off a train and deporting them, were some of the alleged unlawful acts charged.

Under yesterday's restraining order, which will remain in force until again considered in court, the strikers are permitted to have two pickets on duty, one at the point of ingress to the railroad property, and one at point of egress. Acts such as charged in application and affidavits are expressly prohibited.—Carson City News of July 23.

Beaver County News (Utah)
August 18, 1922

Mrs. McCann, of Caliente, is here spending a few days with her mother, Mrs. Dan James

Mrs. Wm. Ernst went to Caliente Wednesday morning to enstall the newly elected officers of Caliente Rebekah lodge.

Davis County Clipper (Utah)
August 18, 1922

San Francisco.—The railroad strike situation cleared somewhat in the west with the moving of passengers who had been marooned on desert points at Needles, Calif., and Caliente and Las Vegas, Nev., and an announcement by the Western Pacific Railroad company here that there was a possibility of its renewing operations in California after an enforced suspension.

Las Vegas Age
August 19, 1922

CALIENTE CITIZENS FORM CHAMBER OF COMMERCE

The citizens of Caliente have formed a Chamber of Commerce which is pledged to work for progress of the community. The following gentlemen will serve the organization the coming year: J. Less Denton, President; George Senter, Vice-President; E. C. D. Marriage, Secretary, and L. L. Burt, Treasurer. These officers, together with Press Duffin, Thos. Dixon, A. O. Blad, E. B. Gratto and George Jeff will act as the board of governors. E. B. Gratto, George Senter and the Secretary have been appointed to draft the by-laws.—Caliente News.

MADE QUICK TRIP FROM CALIENTE TO RENO

Making the trip from Caliente to Reno in two days by Ford, Congressman S. S. Arentz reached Reno Tuesday morning last. He was called by a message received in Las Vegas stating that Mrs. Arentz was very ill, but on reaching her bedside found that her condition was somewhat improved.

Sidney McCulla, a Yerington boy, whom Mr. Arentz left in charge of his Ford when he was forced to abandon it at Caliente on his way to Vegas, accompanied Mr. Arentz on the run to Reno.

Congressman Arentz is anticipating a call to Washington, but if this does not come in the course of a few days, he will resume his campaign tour, providing Mrs. Arentz's condition is such as to permit him to leave her.

Washington County News (Utah)
August 24, 1922

Mrs Betsy Hardy returned Thursday from Elgin Nevada where she has been visiting her daughter Mrs Ethel Bradshaw

FLOYD CASTERLINE IS SERIOUSLY INJURED

The many Milford friends of Floyd Casterline will be grieved to learn of a serious accident to him, which happened near Caliente last Friday.

He was out on the line with a motor car, to pay the men, when in traveling from one crew to another, something went wrong with the car, throwing him and another man off.

His head was badly cut, one leg broken and one arm badly injuerd. He was taken to the Good Samaritan hospital in Los Angeles, where he is resting as easily as could be expected.

His brothers Ray, of Lynndyl, and Clyde of Caliente, are with him.

The other man on the car was also badly injuerd and is in the hospital.

Mr. and Mrs. Spencer Schow of Caliente, arrived here Tuesday evening by auto to visit Mr. Schow's parents, Mr. and Mrs. Nels Schow. Spencer returned to Caliente in the morning to prepare his house hold goods for shipment to Salt Lake, where he has been transfered. Mrs. Schow will remain here for a few days.

Mrs. C. L. Alquist, of Caliente, visited with Mrs Ella Ernst Friday on her way home from Salt Lake City.

Mrs. Charles Himstreet returned home Tuesday from a week stay in Caliente with her son and wife, Mr. and Mrs. Geo. Himstreet.

Harry Larson has returned from Caliente where he has been installing a wholesale gasoline station for the Hal Oil company.

Mr. Wm. Faucett expects to go to Caliente on a hunting expedition the last of the week.

Mr. and Mrs. Clyde Casterline, of Caliente, Nevada, were attending the wedding festivities of Mr. and Mrs. Ralph Casterline.

LYNXWILER--- CASTERLINE

The home of Mr. and Mrs. B. P. Stephenson was the scene of a very pretty wedding Saturday evening, October 21, at 8 o'clock, the contracting parties being Miss Myrtle Lynxwiler and Mr. Ralph Casterline.

The wedding ceremony was performed by Rev. Zook. Besides Mr. and Mrs. Stephenson, son and daughter, Mr. and Mrs. R. C. Lemon, and son, Larry, the out of town guests were Mr. and Mrs. C. M. Casterline, of Caliente, and Mr. and Mrs. Celer, of Lund.

A wedding dinner was served, and they received many use and arafaar they received many useful and beautiful presents.

The young couple will make their home in Lund, where Mr. Casterline is cashier for the Union Pacific railroad.

The News joins with their many friends in wishing them all happiness.

LADIES VISIT CALIENTE

The ladies of the G. I. A. to B. of L. E. made a brief trip to Caliente, Nevada, for the purpose of holding lodge and visiting with the members of this division at that place.

After lodge they were taken to the new depot for a delightful supper. That evening a card party was given, 500 being played. Mrs. C. I. Himstreet and Mrs. John Hallon won high score. Mrs. Reveal and Mrs. Killam second, and Mrs. E. A. Olson consolation. Following this, refreshments were served.

Those who were there were: Mrs. C. I. Himstreet, Mrs. Revela, Mrs. Ranson, Mrs. Killam, Mrs. Dawson, Mrs. John Hanlon, Mrs. E. A. Olson, Mrs. Newhart, Mrs. Wm. Sterling, Mrs. Blanpied.

The sisters in Caliente who entertained so royally, were: Mrs. F. Calloway, Mrs. Mitchell, Mrs. McCans, Mrs. Millsap.

The trip, though short, was greatly enjoyed.

The ladies returned Friday.

CALIENTE MEN CHARGED WITH VIOLATING PROHIBITION LAW

Lloyd C. Denton, R. A. Roberts, Hans Olson, E. J. Capell, L. B. Amante, Joe Colombo, Charles W. Raynard and James Decker, all of Caliente, were arrested Oct. 31 on the charge of selling liquor. They were brought to Las Vegas for hearing before U. S. Commissioner A. A. Hinman and, waiving examinations, all were bound over to await trial at the February term of the U. S. District Court at Carson City.

Bail was fixed at $1,500 in each case. All gave bond and were released except Charles W. Raynard and James Decker, who were unable to make the raise and were remanded to the Washoe county jail to await trial.

CALIENTE RAIDED BY PROHIBITION AGENTS

Caliente was an almost deserted village Monday. Its leading citizens were in Las Vegas arranging bonds for their release from bootlegging charges.

A dry squad raided Caliente Sunday and arrested the hotel men, the keeper of the general store, four pool room proprietors and two unclassified citizens, charging all of them with bootlegging. Arraigned at Las Vegas before U. S. commissioner, all pleaded not guilty except C. W. Reynolds, a transient, who was held for sentence in the district court, while his seven companions were freed on bond to await later hearing—Ely Record.

Las Vegas, Nev.—Caliente, a little railroad town near here, was almost a deserted village when its leading citizens were in Las Vegas, arranging bond for release from bootlegging charges.

Beaver County News (Utah)
November 17, 1922

TELEGRAPHER ASSIGNMENTS

The following assignments are made covering Telegrapher's Bulletin of November 1.

Caliente—Third trick, S. D. Forbes.

Caliente—Extra trick, 10 a. m. to 6 p. m., H. A. Dunlap.

Caliente—Extra trick, 7 p. m. to 3 a. m., G. R. Bannister.

Beaver County News (Utah)
November 24, 1922

Mrs. Wilson Moore returned the past week from a trip to Los Angeles. She expects to go to Caliente to make her home.

Las Vegas Age
November 25, 1922

NAVAJO INDIANS STAGE A WAR DANCE AT CALIENTE

A party of 60 full blooded Navajo Indians spent an hour in Caliente last Tuesday (Nov. 14) and a large crowd of Caliente residents gathered to see them. Their chief addressed the crowd and explained that they had just left the Movie Colony near Baker, Nevada, and were on their way to complete their part in the big Nevada picture, "The Covered Wagon," at the Studios at Hollywood.—Caliente News.

CALIENTE STRIKERS FOUND GUILTY OF CONTEMPT

The trial of Walter O'Conner and George Bullerwell, of Caliente, charged with contempt of court by violating a federal strike injunction was brought to a close last Friday in Carson. Attorney E. E. Roberts argued for the defendants, while United States Attorney George Springmeyer presented the case for the government. The two men were charged with having beaten a railroad guard and shop strikebreaker of the Los Angeles & Salt Lake Railroad in the Post Office at Caliente The jury brought in a verdict of Guilty.

The two men were fined $400 each by Judge E. D. Farrington.

LOCAL CLUB WOMEN MAKE "RECIPROCITY DAY" PLANS

The members of the Mesquite Club are busy as bees planning for "Reciprocity Day," when delegates from Panaca, Caliente, Overton and Searchlight will meet with them to discuss various problems of interest to women in this part of the state.

Clark and Lincoln counties form the second district of the Nevada Federation of Women's Clubs and this is the first "get-together meeting" of the women in this district.

The first session will be held Monday evening at the Club Room. It will be a reception to the visiting club women. There will be music and Judge Charles Lee Horsey will speak on "The Status of Women Under Nevada Laws."

Tuesday morning at 10:00 o'clock there will be a business meeting which will be followed by talks on subjects of interest to women who feel themselves a part of the community. A luncheon has been arranged at The Chocolate Shop for Tuesday at 1:30 in honor of the visiting women

There will be an afternoon session and in the evening a theatre party. Wednesday morning the visitors will be given a ride around the city.

Beaver County News (Utah)
December 22, 1922

Mr. and Mrs. Vingard of Caliente, were the guests the first of the week of Mr. and Mrs. Wm. Faucett.

Beaver County News (Utah)
December 29, 1922

Mr. and Mrs. Babe Waddingham, of Caliente, were in Milford the last of the week visiting with relatives

Mr. Dan Davis of Caliente, has purchased the D. O. Fotheringham residence and expects to move here for the coming summed to make his home.

Las Vegas Age
December 30, 1922

RICH STRIKE REPORTED NEAR CALIENTE

The Pioche Record reports a rich strike of ore which shows assays of three ownces of gold and 191 ounces in silver. The strike was made by Palmer and Bendixen near Grassy Springs which is close to the old mining camp of Delamar. Considerable money has been spent by Judge Palmer in opening up a number of promising silver bearing veins which traverse the claims.

News of the discovery has attracted a number of mining men to the ground and several claims have been staked along the apparent trend of the mineralized area.

L. B. Amant of Caliente, must pay $500 and costs of the proceedings. He was charged with possession of liquor and still.

Joseph Columbo of Caliente, was fined $350 and costs on a sales charge.

MILITARY FUNERAL FOR REV BRYSON HELD FRIDAY

Lorrene Bryson who died at his home in this city on Wednesday Dec 27 of pneumonia induced by Delamar dust contracted while working in the mill at Delamar Nevada some years ago was a son of Mrs Olivia Bryson of this city and the late Hyrum S Bryson he was born at Pine Valley Utah August 30 1873 He was engaged in mining most of his mature life having aided much in the development of Goldstrike (Bull Valley) property where he held extensive interests at the time of his death He volunteered for military service during the Spanish American war and served under the colors at San Francisco but did not get into active service He never married but lived with his mother and was a kind loving son He was of a genial kindly disposition and was generally liked by his associates for his generous disposition

Funeral services were held in the Stake tabernacle Friday afternoon under the auspices of Lester Keate Post of American Legion The funeral expenses were all paid by the Odd Fellows lodge of Storrs Utah, he being a member of that order

The remains were escorted from the Bryson home to the tabernacle by the American Legion The band led playing a slow march, followed by the American flag with a guard of U S Marines in uniform Then followed the ex service men in uniform under command of Lieut Dean A Clark Then came the hearse carrying the remains of Ren Bryson six ex service men in uniform acting as pall bearers The hearse was followed by autos carrying the mother, relatives and friends

The funeral services were conducted by Bishop James McArthur The casket was draped with a national flag and there was an abundance of beautiful floral offerings

The services opened by the choir singing I Have Heard of a Land Prayer was offered by Elder R A Morris Song Shall We Meet Beyond the River"

Elder John E Pace spoke of deceased as a good citizen a good neighbor, and good to his mother.

Solo by Mrs Nellie Brooks

Elder Geo W Worthen said deceased was desirous of living the commandments of God that he was generous and cheerful His mother was a woman of faith and intelligence who had done all that was possible for her son

Mrs Hannah Pike sang When the Mists Have Rolled Away

Elder Albert E Miller spoke of his appreciation for what the American Legion had done for the departed and in lessering the grief of the mother and relatives

Solos were sung by Mrs Nemmie Pearce and by Mrs Nellie Brooks

Bishop McArthur made closing remarks and the choir sang Nearer My God To Thee "

The closing prayer was offered by Elder Geo F Whitehead

The grave was dedicated by Elder William Brooks The deceased was laid to rest beside three brothers and a brother-in law all of whose deaths was caused by Delamar dust

At the conclusion of the services the flag which had draped the body was presented to the mother by the American Legion post

Besides his mother the deceased is survived by one sister Mrs Flora Davis of Cleveland Utah, and two brothers, Samuel of Storrs Utah and John of Wattis Utah

The brothers endeavered to be here but got snowbound in Salina canyon and had to turn back

Beaver County News (Utah)
January 12, 1923

SOCIETY VISITS CALIENTE

The ladies of B. of L. F. E. went to Caliente Wednesday, where three new members were initiated. A banquet was served to the visiting members by the members of the Caliente lodge.

The members are Mrs. Mae Marquis, Mrs. Jennie Bumgard, Mrs. Inez Dula, Mrs. Carmen Cook. Mrs. Mary Woodworth. T

The ladies returned Wednesday night on No. 4.

Beaver County News (Utah)
January 26, 1923

Clyde Casterline, a former resident of Milford, but now of Caliente, Nevada, passed through Milford Monday en route to Salt Lake, where he will undergo an operation for appendicitis.

Mr and Mrs. Nolan of Caliente, have moved to Milford to make their home. Mr. Nolan is employed as fireman on the Union Pacific railroad.

Beaver County News (Utah)
February 2, 1923

Mr. and Mrs. J. Frank Calloway of Caliente, Nevada, spent last Thursday in Milford visiting with friends.

Iron County Record (Utah)
February 23, 1923

SAHARA

Mr. and Mrs. Athol Griffin spent Sunday with Hall Griffin.

Beaver County News (Utah)
February 9, 1923

F. E. Casterline, now of Caliente, was here this past week. He is gradually recovering from his serious railroad accident.

Beaver County News (Utah)
February 16, 1923

Clyde Casterline has fully recovered from his operation and can be seen at 780 South 13th East roasting his shins and doing the honors of "Rocky by Baby, Daddy is Near." Mr and Mrs. Casterline and son expect to return to Caliente soon, where he is employed by the railroad company

Iron County Record (Utah)
February 16, 1923

Geo. Center of Salt Lake City, state agent for the Studebaker cars, left here yesttrday for Caliente where he went to deliver two cars, sold through the Don Coppin agency.

Beaver County News (Utah)
February 23, 1923

BUNDLE SHOWER

Wednesday afternoon, at her home Mrs. John Hanlon entertained at a shower complimentary to Mrs. Sam Reveal. Cards was the main feature of the afternoon, and first prize was won by Mrs. Sam Reveal. Mrs. Dave Tanner received consolation.

Luncheon was served at small tables to the following guests:

Mrs. Dave Tanner, Mrs. William Dawson, Mrs. Charles Himstreet, Mrs. Tom Himstreet, Mrs. Langenbacker, Mrs. Chas. Husbands, Mrs. C. A. Bailey, Mrs. Geo. Ransom, Mrs Walter Ernst, Mrs. John Killam, Mrs E. A. Olson and Mrs. A. H. Millsap, of Caliente.

The honored guest was the recipient of many beautiful gifts.

Beaver County News (Utah)
March 9, 1923

Paul Evans is home form Pioche on a week's layoff. Paul says that if the business men of Milford had the kick in them that the Pioche men have, this town would be as big as Caliente—maybe so.

Beaver County News (Utah)
March 23, 1923

Mrs. R. W. Castle of Salt Lake, has come to Milford to reside permanently. Mr Castle has been here for some time.

Iron County News (Utah)
April 13, 1923

From Nada News

Alvin Couch returned Sunday night from Caliente for a three months stay at home.

Beaver County News (Utah)
April 20, 1923

Mr. and Mrs. Babe Waddingham, of Caliente, former residents of Milford, are moving back to the city.

Beaver County News (Utah)
May 4, 1923

Mrs. E. O. Puffer, Mrs. Bert Stoney and Mrs. Walter Tolton were the guests of friends Saturday night en route to their home in Beaver, after a weeks visit with their sister, Mrs. W. B. Langford, of Caliente, Nevada.

Iron County News (Utah)
May 23, 1923

From the Nada Section

J. W. Dinnwiddie returned to his work near Caliente after a week's stay at home.

Beaver County News (Utah)
June 8, 1923

Mr. and Mrs. E. A. Olson entertained on Sunday for Mr. and Mrs. J. F. Calloway, of Caliente Mr. and Mrs. C. I. Himstreet and Mrs. Ella Ernst.

The Misses Norma and Romain Cody have been guests since Friday of Mr. and Mrs. W. F. Cottrell. The family is moving to Caliente, where Mr. Cody has been assigned as agent for the Union Pacific.

Iron County Records (Utah)
August 10, 1923

From the Nada Section

Aug. 4, 1923.
J. W. Dinwiddie took unto himself a new ford a few days ago.

·—OO—·

Beaver County News (Utah)
August 17, 1923

Among the people who came to Milford from Caliente on last Sunday, were, Mr. and Mrs. Sam Barton, Mr. and Mrs. Francis . O. F. Crane, C. W. Moore, J. Dinwoody, Hans Olsen and T. H. Denton.

Beaver County News (Utah)
August 24, 1923

Mr. and Mrs. Foster Dewey, formerly of Caliente, have bought the Myron Lewis home and will reside permanently in Milford.

Iron County Record (Utah)
September 30, 1923

E. C. D. Marriage, editor of the Caliente News, was a caller in the Record office oday. The gentleman came over, accompanied by his wife. Mrs. Marriage came especially to enter the maternity department of the county hospital.

Beaver County News (Utah)
October 5, 1923

WRECK AT CALIENTE

A near-disastrous head-on collision, between two freight trains occurred Tuesday, October 2, at 1 p. m. in the Caliente yards.

Engineer Curry and fireman T. W Hoke were aboard one engine and H. J Conway, engineer, and Bill Ashworth, fireman aboard the other.

Conway was the only one who suffered injuries. He was rushed to Salt Lake immediately after the accident.

Beaver County News (Utah)
November 23, 1923

Iron County Record (Utah)
November 23, 1923

Beaver County News (Utah)
November 30, 1923

Iron County Record (Utah)
November 30, 1923

Beaver County News (Utah)
December 14, 1923

Box Elder News (Utah)
January 29, 1924

Iron County Record (Utah)
February 1, 1924

From the Nada Section

Las Vegas Age
February 2, 1924

Beaver County News (Utah)
February 29, 1924

Beaver County News (Utah)
March 28, 1924

Iron County Record (Utah)
May 9, 1924

Beaver County News (Utah)
June 20, 1924

CALIENTE FIRE

Fire broke out in Caliente Wednesday afternoon, and before the flames could be extinguished, fifteen buildings had been destroyed in the very center of the town.

The loss is estimated at $150,000 with but little insurance.

Las Vegas Age
June 28, 1924

DESTRUCTIVE FIRE DOES DAMAGE AT CALIENTE

The business district of Caliente was visited by a disastrous fire Wednesday afternoon and twelve buildings went up in smoke. The fire started in the Caliente Hotel, supposedly from a pile of smoldering ashes at the rear of the building. Willing workers toiled untiringly in the hope of checking the flames and finally concentrated their efforts on the big cement structure known as the Riding building. This was saved, though badly damaged. The valiant efforts of the fire fighters, with the excellent water supply, checked the flames at the Clair Norris residence by dragging out the Norris garage. The total loss, as near as can be estimated, is placed at $60,000, only partially covered by insurance.

The following buildings were destroyed: The Caliente Hotel and adjoining buildings owned by Charles Culverwell; the Hans Olson store and residence; the pool hall and restaurant owned by George Jeffs and the rooming house owned by A. L. Norris.

Beaver County News (Utah)
July 11, 1924

Mrs. H. T. Hanks, Mrs. J. C. Love of Caliente; Mrs. J. Wardenburg of Salt Lake and Jane Hanks and Peggy Peterson, spent Sunday evening at the Roosevelt Hot Springs, returning to Milford Monday morning.

Iron County Record (Utah)
July 11, 1924

SEE IRON SPRINGS
Mrs. A. H. Millsap has returned to her home in Caliente after a three month trip during which time almost every place of interest in the United States was visited. Mrs. Millsap kept a diary of the trip which is most interesting reading.—Caliente News.

Richfield Reaper (Utah)
July 17, 1924

* * *

Mrs. Sid Pace with daughter of Alamo, Nevada, is visiting her parents, Mr. and Mrs. E. P. Erickson

and expects to remain here for about a month. Last week Mr. and Mrs. Erickson with their guests, Mr. and Mrs. T. F. Young and Bishop and Mrs. Ray Utley of Cove spent at Fishlake where Mr. Erickson beat all records in fishing this year, catching six big mackinaw trout, one weighing ten, one eight, one seven and three six pounds each.

Iron County Record (Utah)
July 18, 1924

Mr. Marriage, editor of the Caliente News, was operated no at the county hospital Monday for removal of the appendix. The gentleman is resting nicely and gaining strength as rapidly as could be expected. He expects to be able to return home within a week.

Richfield Reaper (Utah)
July 24, 1924

Mrs. A. B. Devine entertained at dinner Wednesday, the 16th, in honor of Mrs. Sid Pace of Alamo, Nevada, and Mrs. Nickel of Salt Lake City. Covers were laid for ten. Centerpieces were of sweet peas.

Iron County Record (Utah)
August 1, 1924

—oo—
Mr. E. C. D. Marriage, Editor of the Caliente News will soon be well enough to leave the hospital for his home.
—oo—

Beaver County News (Utah)
August 22, 1924

CHAS. BAILEY IN CALIENTE

Chas. Bailey, chief clerk to master mechanic of Milford, came in on No. 25 Tuesday evening, accompanied 'v Sam Hickman on a trip of inspecti at the railroad offices at this point. Having been a former resident of Caliente, his many friends are always pleased to see him in town. He reports conditions at Milford rapidly improving.—Caliente News.

Iron County Record (Utah)
August 22, 1924

Home Cooking In Smokehouse
H. McBride of Salt Lake City has purchased Scotty's well known restaurant in Caliente and will make every effort to please the public, the restaurant is located in the rear of the Smokehouse and is famed for its real home cooking.—Caliente News.

Beaver County News (Utah)
September 12, 1924

ENTERTAINS

Mrs. Carl Levi entertained Tuesday afternoon in honor of her two daughters, Mrs. Miles White of Caliente, and Mrs. Owen Tanner of Cedar city.

A delightful afternoon was spent in playing "500", high score being won by Mrs. May Chilton. Consolation was given to Miss Louise Levi.

Dainty refreshments were served to the following:

Mrs. Fred Levi and daughter, Louise, Mrs. May Chilton, Mrs. Roy White, Mrs. Ross Lang, Mrs. Harry Coon, Mrs. Warren Atkin, Miss Letha Schow and guests of honor, Mrs. Miles White and Mrs. Owen Tanner.

Mrs. Miles White of Caliente and little daughter, have spent the past week here visiting with her parents, Mr. and Mrs. Carl Levi.

Beaver County News (Utah)
September 19, 1924

Mrs. George Lunt of Caliente, was the guest of friends here during the week.

Iron County Record (Utah)
September 19, 1924

NADA
—oo—
Oscar Stephenson has been called back on the road as fireman, going out from Caliente.

Beaver County News (Utah)
October 24, 1924

Mr. and Mrs. Miles White of Caliente, were visitors here during the past week.

Mrs. Oscar Stephenson of Caliente, was with us today. Mr. Stephenson has gone to Ohio to bring his father on a visit to his sons here in Utah.

Beaver County News (Utah)
November 21, 1924

A farewell party was given for Mr and Mrs. Maurice Johnson, Wednesday evening at their home, by six of their friends. The young couple will soon depart for Caliente, where Mr. Johnson has accepted employment.

Las Vegas Age
November 22, 1924

ASSOCIATION OF CLERICAL EMPLOYES ELECTS OFFICERS

Las Vegas Lodge No. 3, Clerical Employes Association, L. A. & S. L. R. R. Unit of the Union Pacific, held its annual election at the regular meeting at American Legion Hall on Thursday evening, November 20. The following officers were elected.

President—Arthur S. Riggins, city ticket agent.

Vice-President—Earl M. Smith, assistant timekeeper, mechanical department.

Treasurer—Miss A. Pennie, clerk to shop superintendent.

Secretary—Ernest G. Adams, chief clerk to storekeeper.

Trustees—Jack Tomlinson, chief timekeeper, mechanical department; A. K. Smith, yard clerk; and R. B. Williams, freight house foreman.

Conductor—Don Bremner, round house clerk.

This lodge was organized less than one year ago and now numbers about 70 members, 55 of whom are clerks of the Union Pacific employed at Las Vegas, the balance of the membership being the clerks employed at Caliente and Kelso.

Through the efforts of Unit Chairman N. E. Davis of Los Angeles and the unit committee there has been organized at each division point and in each assigned combination of departments as directed by the general manager an "office council" consisting of the supervising heads of all departments and clerical employes' association representatives from each department to the end that the employes may receive the full benefit of co-operation with the company. At these office councils matters that concern working conditions, healthful surroundings and comfort of employes, and in a general way and question which may result in the mutual advantage of both employes and company are discussed.

Many benefits have come to the clerks through the association and from testimony of heads of departments and officials the clerical force has improved in efficiency, industry and effectiveness and, while the idea of co-operation and close affiliation between the railroad supervisors and their clerical forces is a new one, it holds forth bright prospects for all concerned.

VEGAS HELPS CALIENTE TO THREE NEW CITIZENS

Las Vegas assisted very materially in the growth of Caliente with the arrival at the Las Vegas Hospital of three lusty youngsters.

Saturday there was born to Mr. and Mrs. John Knox, a son, who will answer to the name of Robert William.

Saturday, November 15, witnessed the arrival of twins, born to Mr. and Mrs. John Joseph Eyraud. One is a girl who is to be called Joan Lorraine, while the other is a boy who will be known as Lloyd Raymond.

The happy parents are receiving the congratulations o ftheir friends.

Beaver County News (Utah)
November 28, 1924

Mr. and Mrs. Miles White and little daughter, of Caliente, spent Thanksgiving here.

Ray J. Casterline, now of Caliente, was visiting old friends in Milford this week.

Las Vegas Age
December 6, 1924

DISTRICT NURSE HELD MEETING IN CALIENTE

District Nurse Sadie Lee held a well attended meeting at the school house during the week at which arrangements were discussd which would enable Pioche mothers having children under school age to take proper advantage of the provisions of the Shepard-Towner act.

Lincoln county mothers would be fortunate if a qualified nurse would be at all times available for help and advice in the county and if the requisite financial aid can be arranged a nurse will be hired in the narer future, naturally only serving such of the communities in the county as desire the service. Epidemics of scarlet fever, measles and other infectious diseases which have visited the county in the past will be less feared with competent assistance available at a normal per capita cost.—Pioche Record.

CALIENTE COUPLE WED HERE

Mr. Reuben Acklin and Miss Alice Margaret Kelly of Caliente were unittd in marriage at the Methodist parsonage at noon Tuesday, December 2, by Rev. W. H. Stockton.

Made in the USA
Charleston, SC
07 August 2015